Getting to know Ian Hamilton over the years has been a great delight. Ian is widely regarded as a 'warm-hearted Presbyterian,' and I can say from experience that this is true. Anyone who spends even a brief time with him immediately recognizes his gracious, affectionate demeanor, genuine piety, and deep love for all the saints. These qualities shine so brightly in our dear brother that I have lovingly dubbed him my paedobaptist grandfather—a title of no small significance, especially coming from a Reformed Baptist! With all that could be said about Ian, I am thrilled to see this volume written in his honor by his friends. The essays within are both edifying and engaging, reflecting the rich legacy of this excellent servant of Christ. May the Lord, in His grace, be pleased to use this work far and wide for His glory alone.

Rob Ventura
Pastor, Grace Community Baptist Church
North Providence, Rhode Island

Anyone who has ministered in Reformed circles in Britain knows (or should!) who Ian Hamilton is. His shadow touches so many of us, even who have met him only briefly and learned the lessons he would teach indirectly from others who have been more closely mentored by him. This volume nobly sets out some of the core convictions in which we should all hope to emulate Ian Hamilton: Reformed confessional fidelity, catholic spirit, and pastoral heart. Many of these essays are uniquely informative and soul stirring as snapshots into a model of magnificent ministry.

Harrison Perkins
Pastor, Oakland Hills Community Church (OPC)
Farmington Hills, Michigan

Ian Hamilton is an international treasure. Our lives have intertwined in one way or another for the last half century. We have spoken at conferences together and over the years his towering strength and sense of purpose have become something from which to learn the shape of godliness and how Calvinism, viewed winsomely, can really shape an individual into something glorious and wonderful. These chapters written in his honor will only accentuate our love and admiration for him. Multi-authored books don't always work, but this one has a sense of unity and cohesion to it. Ian is a preacher, theologian, author, international conference speaker, and much more. These chapters are a very fine attempt to address all aspects of his ministry. As one recently retired, I watch with considerable esteem the way he continues to help the church be the bride of Christ. This book is a triumph in every respect.

Derek W. H. Thomas
Chancellors Professor, Reformed Theological Seminary;
Teaching Fellow, Ligonier Ministries

Catholic Calvinism is such an appropriate title for this collection of essays in honour of Ian Hamilton, since he is the catholic Calvinist par excellence, embodying all that is best in this tradition. If you want to understand principially what catholic Calvinism is all about, this excellent and thoughtful book will tell you; but the life and example of Ian Hamilton will show you.

Warren Peel
Pastor, Covenant Christian Fellowship
Galway, Republic of Ireland

It is a privilege to commend this volume of warm and thoughtful essays in thanks to the Lord for a dear friend whose desire has been to echo John the Baptist: 'Christ must increase, I must decrease.'

William VanDoodewaard
Professor of Church History
Greenville Presbyterian Theological Seminary
Taylors, South Carolina

It is a great joy to commend a book which reflects the character of Ian Hamilton himself: theologically rigorous and historically confessional, pastorally orientated, warm-hearted and above all breathing a spirit of true piety, of love and faith directed towards the Triune God. Ian has, for many years, been a father and a friend to so many, whose love for Christ and for the church of Christ shines through his whole life and ministry.

Paul Yeulett
Pastor, Grove Chapel
Camberwell, London

There are believing repenting sinners whose lives have a certain fragrance, humility, and love for the truth that is Christ, and enflesh powerfully and unmistakably in their own lives His holy blessed life, as Ian, so unconsciously, does to our enormous delight and doxology.

Geoff Thomas
Conference Speaker and Author

Ian is a gift to the local church whose desire is to see the glory of God take root in our hearts. I have benefited greatly from his ministry and friendship, his warmth and love for the Lord have been a constant example. These essays in honour of Ian will not only hold forth biblical truths that he treasures, but Lord willing cause you to treasure them too.

Gerald White
Pastor, Hope Church Bingham (20Schemes)
Edinburgh

Catholic Calvinism

A Vision for Ministry

Essays in Honour of
IAN HAMILTON

Edited by Peter Sanlon

Unless otherwise noted, Scripture quotations are from *The Holy Bible, English Standard Version*, copyright © 2001 by Crossway Bibles, a publishing ministry of Good News Publishers. Used by permission. All rights reserved. ESV Text Edition: 2011.

Scripture quotations marked "LSB" are taken from the Legacy Standard Bible®, Copyright © 2021 by The Lockman Foundation. Used by permission. All rights reserved. Managed in partnership with Three Sixteen Publishing Inc. LSBible.org and 316publishing.com.

Scripture quotations from the King James Version are marked with KJV.

Scripture quotations marked "NKJV" are taken from the New King James Version. Copyright © 1982 by Thomas Nelson, Inc. Used by permission. All rights reserved.

Scripture quotations marked "NASB" are taken from the New American Standard Bible®, Copyright © 1960, 1962, 1963, 1968, 1971, 1972, 1973, 1975, 1977, 1995 by The Lockman Foundation Used by Permission. (www.Lockman.org)

Westminster icon on cover by Rafiico Creative Studio from IconScout.com, modified. Licensed under CC BY 4.0: https://creativecommons.org/licenses/by/4.0/

Copyright © Peter Sanlon 2025
Each contributor retains copyright for their chapter

paperback ISBN 978-1-5271-1190-5
ebook ISBN 978-1-5271-1264-3

10 9 8 7 6 5 4 3 2 1

Published in 2025
in the
Mentor Imprint
by
Christian Focus Publications Ltd,
Geanies House, Fearn, Ross-shire,
IV20 1TW, Scotland.

www.christianfocus.com

Cover design by Daniel van Straaten

Printed and bound by Bell & Bain, Glasgow

All rights reserved. No part of this publication may be reproduced, stored in a retrieval system, or transmitted, in any form, by any means, electronic, mechanical, photocopying, recording or otherwise without the prior permission of the publisher or a licence permitting restricted copying. In the U.K. such licences are issued by the Copyright Licensing Agency, 4 Battlebridge Lane, London, SE1 2HX. www.cla.co.uk

Contents

Introduction
Donald John MacLean 9

Ian Hamilton
A Personal Appreciation
Sinclair B. Ferguson 13

Part 1
Orientation to Catholic Calvinism

1. Calvinism:
The Glory of the Triune God
Mark Johnston 27

2. Catholicity:
Christ Has Only One Bride
Peter Naylor 39

Part 2
Catholic Calvinist Convictions Lived Out

3. Lessons Learned for Ministry:
Four Men Trained by Ian Hamilton
David Pfeiffer, Andy Young, Dan Peters & Douglas McCallum ... 49

4. Preaching:
How Shall They Hear Without a Preacher?
John MacArthur 61

5. Doctrine
Jonathan Master 77

6. Cultivating Catholic Calvinism through Religious Affections
Joel R. Beeke 89

8. 'The Weight of the Paradigm':
Infant Baptism and the Covenant of Grace
Jonathan Gibson 105

9. The Zurich Consensus:
The Lord's Supper and Unity in an Age of Discord
Jon D. Payne 145

10. Training and Forming Ministers
in the Catholic Calvinist Vision
Joseph A. Pipa Jr 163

11. A Confessionally Catholic Calvinism?
Chad van Dixhoorn 175

Part 3
Historic Role Models

12. Augustine:
The Original Catholic Calvinist
Peter Sanlon 191

13. John Calvin and Catholicity
W. Robert Godfrey 203

14. John Owen:
Catholic Calvinist
Benedict Bird 217

15. A Surprising Catholicity?:
The Church in Scottish Theology
Donald John MacLean 237

Contributors...255

Introduction

Donald John MacLean

It is my pleasure to introduce this *Festschrift* for Ian Hamilton, which explores the theme of *'Catholic Calvinism'*. It is fair to say the idea of a generous spirited, outward looking and confessionally robust theology is central to Ian's ministry and to Westminster Seminary (UK), which Ian has faithfully led for the past few years. As such, as well as honouring a significant milestone in Ian's life, it is hoped this volume will also serve as something of a window into the pulse beat of the Seminary.

Westminster Seminary (UK)—'Catholic Calvinism'

All that Westminster does is from a spirit of rigorous *ex animo* commitment to the Westminster Confession. We are unashamed in our commitment to 'Calvinism', understood as the doctrine, worship and practice taught in the Westminster Standards. Precisely because of this, our desire is to serve the broader evangelical church. Our doctrinal standards, in faithfulness to Scripture, remind us that 'All saints, that are united to Jesus Christ their Head by His Spirit and by faith … being united to one another in love, they have communion in each other's gifts and graces, and are obliged to the performance of such duties, public and private, as do conduce to their mutual good, both in the inward and outward man' (Westminster Confession 26:1). We therefore exist to promote the 'mutual good' of the church, not simply one corner of it. This is part of our 'catholic' spirit.

We are also committed to equipping the church with the riches of the past to enable her to serve in the present. Our theology at Westminster Seminary (UK) is not idiosyncratic, majoring on the emphases of any one particular stream of reformed theology—it is 'catholic'. Nor is it obscurantist, as if we were preparing for ministry in a bygone age. Rather we aim to prepare men for ministry *today*, by equipping them with the wisdom of the 'catholic' church through the ages.

In both these areas Westminster (UK) reflects core commitments of Ian's life, ministry and thought.

Ian Hamilton as President of Westminster Seminary (UK)

As well as a 'catholic Calvinism' two further emphases are embedded in Westminster Seminary (UK) through Ian's time as President. The centrality of what might be called a personal piety, and of Christ-centred preaching. Regarding the former, Ian has often quoted the powerful words of James W. Alexander,

> At judgment I heartily believe that some heresies of heart and temper will be charged as worse than heavy doctrinal errors. To you I may say this, because you understand me as holding, not merely that the tenets of our church are true, but that they are very important. But I see how easy it is to 'hold the truth' in rancour, and hate, which is the grand error of depraved human nature; yea, and of diabolism itself.[1]

The men Ian, and our seminary, seek to train, are those who heed Alexander's warning; men who truly love the truth, and therefore are 'kind to everyone, able to teach, patiently enduring evil, correcting his opponents with gentleness' (2 Tim. 2:24-25). Men whose lives bring credit to their profession.

There is also a 'tincture' that runs through Ian's preaching and lecturing—the exaltation of the Lord Jesus Christ. What the Synod of Bern said in 1532 could be true of Westminster Seminary (UK) under Ian (and I trust will always be true): 'We are faithfully to exhort one another, that as the servants of Christ

---

1. James W. Alexander, *Forty Years' Familiar Letters of James W. Alexander* (ed. John Hall; New York: C. Scribner, 1860), 227.

we should preach only Him, our Lord, on whom rests the whole counsel of God.'[2]

Catholic Calvinism—The Festschrift

Many of these themes recur throughout this volume: Doctrinal rigour; generosity of spirit; equipping for ministry today via the riches of the past, piety and Christ-centredness. As the chapters span doctrine, practice and history, friends and colleagues of Ian unite around these themes, themes that Westminster Seminary UK stands for as it seeks to 'prepare leaders to plant churches in every nation and proclaim Christ to the ends of the earth.'

My prayer is that this volume will be used to encourage a commitment to the *'Catholic Calvinism'* that characterises Ian and the Seminary he has faithfully served as President.

Donald John MacLean
Westminster Seminary (UK)
June 2024

---

2. James T. Dennison, ed., *Reformed Confessions of the 16th and 17th Centuries in English Translation, Volume 1: 1523-1552* (Grand Rapids, MI: Reformation Heritage Books, 2008), 237.

Ian Hamilton

A Personal Appreciation

Sinclair B. Ferguson

We do not always recall first encounters with those who are destined to become long-time friends, but my own earliest meeting with Ian Hamilton—in the early summer of 1971—is etched in my memory. It has been a privilege therefore to have observed, sometimes at close hand, at other times at a distance, the formation and growth of a life committed to Christ, devoted to the people of God and the ministry of the gospel, and marked by grace, faithfulness, and fruitfulness. No doubt the graph of that growth is not one of simple straight-line ascent; the Christian life never is. But about Ian I think we can say with confidence, 'whose faith follow' (Heb. 13:7 av).

A Glasgow Boy

Ian Hamilton was born on 29 March 1950. A glance at the early twentieth-century edition of the mammoth *Dictionary of National Biography* underlines the fact that 'Hamilton' is one of the greatest names among the families of Scotland—with somewhere in the region of one hundred pages of entries. Doubtless for Ian the greatest of these would be the brave young Scotsman Patrick Hamilton, whose martyrdom in 1528 John Knox regarded as the real beginning of the Scottish Reformation.

But the young man who would now bear the same surname and confess the same gospel was not born into a palatial Hamilton mansion, but into the urban depression of the Glasgow of the early 1950s. It was the alcohol capital of Scotland (and perhaps all Europe), and known for its areas of deprivation, its gangs, and its heavy industry. It was the most religiously divided city in Europe. The country's two leading soccer teams, Rangers (who at that time had never been known to sign a Roman Catholic player) and Celtic (originally founded by Roman Catholic priests), were the secularised sacraments of a deep religious hostility.

Against that background Ian was born into the only kind of 'mixed marriage' Glaswegians then knew: his father, John, a fireman, was a nominal protestant while his mother, Barbara, had been raised Roman Catholic. Given his father's occupation there is perhaps an appropriateness in thinking of Ian Hamilton as 'a brand plucked from the fire' (Zech. 3:2).

In mid-twentieth century Scotland it was still commonplace for parents who themselves never attended church to send their children to a local Sunday School. Ian briefly attended—until the clear logical thinking that would later mark his ministry led him to inform his parents that since they never went to church it was not necessary for him to attend Sunday School. His only religious connections until his later teens were several devout and kindly Roman Catholic relatives on his mother's side. Those on his father's side Ian has described as 'rascals'!

The Hamilton family lived in Easterhouse, one of the 'housing schemes' established in the 1950s in the East End of Glasgow. Here, in the providence of God, a primary school teacher had an interest in teaching his eleven-year-old charges a smattering of foreign languages, including Scottish Gaelic (then, as now, a 'foreign' language to most Scots). This opened the possibility of attending a select Gaelic-teaching school in the West End—a considerable journey across the city. It proved to be not only a better environment to stimulate the obvious intellectual gifts of the young schoolboy, but a stepping stone towards Christ.

Coming to Faith

Life for Ian then was—as for many youngsters his age—school, soccer, and discos. He was generally unaware of Christians apart from one boy he knew at school who was 'different' (he would later become a minister and a moderator). Through a 'chance' encounter with him one Saturday, Ian accepted an invitation to go to his Bible Class the next day (after all, perhaps there might be some attractive girls?). It was the first time he heard the words of John 3:16, and the experience led to his coming to a living faith in Christ, and to the subsequent transformation and redirection of his whole life. From that point on Paul's personal testimony—'to me to live is Christ' (Phil. 1:21)—has been written over Ian's life. That Sunday afternoon the seeds of both new life and his calling to serve Christ were planted deeply in him. It may bring a wry smile to those who have known him only in his adulthood to learn that under the influence of his Bible Class teacher his early Christian life was accompanied by a dispensationalist chart on his wall!

Higher Education

Strathclyde University soon followed. Today that would be expected of perhaps fifty per cent or more of Scottish school leavers. Not in the late 1960s when about only five per cent advanced to university education. Ian was an exception in his family circle. University meant not only the nurturing of his superior intellectual ability but also introduced him to other Christians in the Inter-Varsity Fellowship. There he was to encounter biblical teaching and preaching that would further shape his thinking and his personal aspirations. At the same time his theological interests were taking shape. Looking back, it is perhaps no surprise to learn that he managed to persuade his professor to allow him to write the mandatory graduating thesis in Economic History on *'John Calvin and the Struggle for Reformed Orthodoxy in Geneva with Special Attention to the Doctrines of the Church in Predestination, 1541-1545.'* It was the beginning of a friendship with the Genevan Reformer that has lasted until the present day. For all Ian's wide reading, probably no theologian would have more influence on the ministry that lay ahead.

Ian graduated from Strathclyde University in 1972, and with the encouragement of the minister and elders of his congregation in Glasgow matriculated for a B.D. degree at New College in the University of Edinburgh. Here, with rare exceptions, the most conservative members of the faculty were Barthians.

One feature of Ian's character that often strikes people was already beginning to manifest itself: the ability to disagree (which as a student he sometimes did boldly and directly) while maintaining an appreciation of God's common grace in the lives of those with whom he disagreed. What was true at this personal level would also become increasingly true as he reflected on the theologians of the Christian Church. Not all who seemed to be only halfway up the hill of biblical orthodoxy, were hurtling down disastrously to the foot of the mountain. Some were still climbing with few mountain guides as companions to help them.

Graduating with a high-quality honours degree, this time in Ecclesiastical History, Ian proceeded to Aberdeen to serve his mandatory year's assistantship in Northfield Parish Church.

Influences and New Friends

Here we should press the pause button on the narrative to note some of the influences—apart from the beginnings of his lifelong commitment to reading great theological works—that were now shaping his understanding of the work of the ministry in general and preaching in particular.

The 1960s had brought something of a resurgence in Scotland of younger evangelical men sensing a call to the ministry. No doubt an element in this was the growing influence of Inter-Varsity, often introducing them to quality biblical preaching.

More significantly for Ian Hamilton was the example of ministries with which he was now becoming familiar, including his own minister George Philip, in Sandyford-Henderson Memorial Church in Glasgow and his older brother James Philip whose ministry at Holyrood Abbey Church in Edinburgh

Ian would attend as a divinity student. In due season he would come to know (and later succeed) Eric Alexander, minister at Loudon East Church in Newmilns, Ayrshire, and William Still, minister of Gilcomston South Church in Aberdeen, the father-figure of what became known as 'The Crieff Fellowship' (an invited gathering whose list of invitations extended into the hundreds). These men spearheaded a vision for congregational ministry focussed on the consecutive exposition of Scripture, prayer, fellowship, and relatively simple church structures. They were also remarkably diverse in both personality and preaching style—this was doubtless helpful to Ian as he would progressively develop into 'his own man' as a minister and preacher. From this womb was born the expository and pastoral ministry that has made him so widely appreciated internationally.

Narrative Resumed
The year Ian spent as an assistant minister in Aberdeen was to have long-lasting consequences in the friendships he made, not least with older Christians. It was one of the mothers-in-Israel at Gilcomston South Church, Vi Robb, who would later enquire (doubtless graciously scheming!), had he met Joan Ross? Joan, from Edinburgh, had come to study Geography at the University of Aberdeen and had been involved in the Christian Union. Happily, they met (I believe at a missionary farewell gathering) and courtship and love would lead to marriage in 1980, and the following year to the birth of their firstborn son, David. Thereafter Jonathan, Rebecca and Sarah joined him. Now the family circle is extended by the addition of six grandchildren.

Once again we have run ahead of the story. Ian received a scholarship to pursue graduate work in the Ecclesiastical History department at Edinburgh University. The fruit of his labours was a dissertation on confessional decline in Scotland, later to be published as *The Erosion of Calvinist Orthodoxy: Drifting from the Truth in Confessional Scottish Churches* (1990). But while he enjoyed academic study, the academy was not his immediate calling. It would be much later in his ministry that he would devote time to teaching theological students.

Minister of the Gospel—Newmilns

The year 1979 marked an ending and a new beginning. Ian graduated with his third degree—an M.Phil, again from Edinburgh University (a fourth would follow in 2012 when he was honoured with a Doctor of Divinity degree by Greenville Presbyterian Theological Seminary in South Carolina). He was called to succeed Eric Alexander in Newmilns, Ayrshire.

Newmilns is a small town in what was once, but no longer, covenanting country. In addition to inheriting members of a well-taught congregation however, Ian found himself sole minister of a church union with 1100 members. The Kirk Session had 42 elders (more than half Moses' number!) by no means all of whom were familiar with the New Testament. It would be an understatement to say there was little or no spiritual superglue to bond the people together. But with 'complete patience and teaching' (2 Tim. 4:2) Ian exercised a careful preaching and pastoral ministry appropriately measured to the capacity of the people. (Jesus himself told his disciples that after three years he still had much to teach them that they were not yet able to bear [John 16:12])

In addition Ian engaged in a strenuous pattern of pastoral visitation and personal care. A young minister in a church today would find it almost inconceivable if he were to be told that in the next two decades he would conduct over seven hundred (yes, 700) funerals, with the attendant burden-bearing and personal visiting of so many families. But this was the pastoral calling for the minister of Newmilns.

Careful teaching, great patience, and much love meant that by the end of the first decade of his ministry the character of the congregation had changed (the eldership was eventually a group of twelve); the gospel was firmly established. In the decade that followed the fruit of Ian and Joan's ploughing and planting, welcoming and loving was apparent—not only in terms of the quality of the eldership and people, but also in the family atmosphere of congregational life, and in the sense of God being among his people in worship.

Cambridge Presbyterian Church

The year 1999 brought about another sea change. Ian was called from a church founded in the fifteenth century to be minister of the Cambridge Presbyterian Church, a small congregation of The Evangelical Presbyterian Church in England and Wales (EPCEW) founded in the early 1990s. It was no easy thing for the Hamilton family to leave the people they loved and who loved them in return. The bonds would last.

From Newmilns, Cambridge must have seemed truly a foreign place. Now life in an old mill town in Scotland gave way to the very different world of one of the greatest (some would say the greatest) university cities in the world. But here—albeit now in Athens rather than Jerusalem, in a multi-ethnic rather than a mono-ethnic context—the same central features of Ian's biblical ministry would continue and prove their own power and relevance. The measure of Ian's capacity (and adaptability) is evidenced by the fact that he loved ministry in both Newmilns *and* Cambridge.

No doubt Ian discovered that intellectual ability in Cambridge students was by no means the same thing as biblical understanding, spiritual maturity, or even theological reading capability. But for the next seventeen years he and Joan devoted themselves to the same task of welcoming, nurturing and nourishing the church family, teaching, caring for and spiritually strengthening students and others who would go on to serve the Lord in many parts of the world. And during these years they would also see their children spread their wings and grow to maturity, as the family scattered across both England and Scotland.

Ian's ministry, already fully developed, now began to stretch well beyond the confines of Cambridge. For some twenty-five years he served as a vital member of the Board of the Banner of Truth Trust Publishers and played a significant role in organising and speaking at conferences in the United Kingdom, the United States and beyond. He served on the Board of Greenville Presbyterian Seminary in South Carolina. He travelled internationally to preach and lecture. And on his retirement from Cambridge in 2016, he devoted himself increasingly to training the next generation of ministers—teaching for Edinburgh Theological Seminary as well as for Greenville Seminary, and guest lecturing elsewhere. In 2021 he became President of the fledgling Westminster Theological Seminary in Newcastle. At the same time he served as Associate Minister in Smithton Free Church, Inverness.

Such then is a bird's-eye view of a life committed to Christ over six decades. Later in these pages, men who have grown into their own ministries with Ian's help reflect 'from the inside' on aspects of his ministry. What follows are a few reflections (necessarily limited) 'from the outside' as a friend and fellow-traveller.

A Model to Imitate

It would suffice to say that for four decades Ian Hamilton has been a model (yes, 'warts and all') of what a minister should be. The contents of any reliable book on the ministry would serve as an outline of what he has modelled for us. But conscious of the themes that others will handle in the chapters that follow, four features stand out to me.

Friendship

Scripture in general sets high store on friendship, and this is particularly evident in the life of our Lord Jesus. In the Upper Room, he told his disciples that they had become his friends. He was willing to lay down his life for them and bring them into his confidence; they would be bound in faithfulness to him (John 15:13-15). Anyone who has known Ian Hamilton for any length of time will have been struck by his range of friends and his ongoing contact with them. (I have always imagined mobile phone plans with unlimited calls were providentially created to enable his friendship-ministry to continue without bankrupting the Hamilton family!) As someone who has been blessed by that friendship I am often fascinated to encounter people he has befriended and to whom he exercises an ongoing ministry of encouragement.

In addition, listen carefully to an occasional comment Ian may make about someone whose name you may know but whose personal theological convictions are different from his and you may be surprised to discover that he has managed to maintain friendly relations. Again, listen to a casual remark he may make about regular pastoral visitation in his first congregation; what is a chore for evangelical ministers who prefer the study was a delight to Ian—who is a better, more learned and more careful student and scholar than most of us! And that pastoral visitation was done by a man with little or no staff to help who all the while was preparing several new messages each week. There is much for us to learn here.

I hazard a guess that the roots of this feature of Ian's ministry are threefold. First, his humble interest in people and their spiritual welfare. Second, the fact that he has seen pastoral visitation as an essential element in the 'apostolic tradition', emulating Paul's ministry 'from house to house' (Acts 20:20). He has always wanted to expound and apply the Word of God to the people in his charge, not to an amorphous group of unknown believers. Thirdly, perhaps more subliminally, Ian's friendship in this context has been undergirded by the strength of two elements in his theological framework: that we are all created in the image of God (Gen. 1:26-27) and remain so even in the wake of the Fall; and in addition the way our understanding of 'common grace'—that our God is generous to all men, not only to believers—stimulates his children to be like him. This is at least one element in what it means to be 'perfect as your heavenly Father is perfect' (Matt. 5:48). Such friendship is an attractive—and sometimes disarming—grace.

Ministry

If the personal dimension of Ian's ministry has been a blessing to those who have known him more intimately as pastor and friend, undoubtedly the best-known feature of his service of Christ has been his ministry of the Word. While following Calvin and others in a *lectio continua* style of preaching through the Scriptures,

Ian has also intuitively followed in their footsteps by valuing additional forms of that ministry.

In addition to preaching the Word and ministering it 'from house to house' he has also ministered the same Word in writing. Ian himself would say that he has never thought of himself primarily as a writer. But it is obvious that he possesses writing gifts, and that these have had a significant place in his ministry, especially to those who have neither met him nor heard him preach.

The evidence of this is found of course in the books he has published, representing his ability in biblical exposition [*Let's Study the Letters of John* (2008); *Ephesians* (2017)]; historical theology [(1990)] and the relation between biblical doctrine and practical Christian living [*The Faith-Shaped Life* (2013); *What Is Experiential Calvinism?* (2015); *The Gospel Shaped Life* (2017); *Salvation: Full and Free in Christ* (2018); *Words from the Cross* (2022)].

In addition, however, are the many occasions he has written exclusively for the congregations he has served. Here he has addressed personal needs, theological issues, questions of conscience and much else. He has helped many people to see the immediate, the wider, and even the historical context of their lives through the lenses of Scripture and encouraged them to reflect the characteristics of the men of Issachar in King David's day 'who had understanding of the times to know what Israel ought to do' (1 Chron. 12:32).

It would leave a hiatus in these brief reflections if we overlooked Ian's interest in, concern for, and labour-intensive investment not only in other ministers but also in those who are preparing for future ministry. This is a characteristic of model ministers in every age. It is represented by his willingness to take on the role of President of Westminster Presbyterian Seminary in Newcastle; but perhaps more significantly, if less publicly, in the quantum increase in the number of lectures he has given and seminars he has led for theological students since 'retirement' (not a word Ian favours!). This is a limited audience which is time-consuming, and not widely seen. But it is a massive investment in ministries that will serve our children and grandchildren. It is a work for which the Lord has supplied both the gifts and the energy. And all the while Ian continues to preach in Smithton Free Church and other congregations in the north of Scotland as well as elsewhere. Many roles are discharged by Ian and they are all a valued investment in the Church catholic.

Central to all these aspects of his ministry of the Word has been Ian's patient study of Scripture, and his love for the whole church, both in the present and throughout the corridors of church history and theology, from the Fathers to modern times. It has been both his task and his joy to harvest the fruits of this for himself and then to share them with the congregations and conferences he has served.

Preaching

We lack today what was more commonplace in yesteryear—descriptions of what it was like to sit under a notable minister's preaching of the Word. Here there is space to make only a few personal observations on some of the characteristics of Ian's preaching:

Firstly, faithfulness to the teaching of the text—the *sine qua non* of authentic preaching—in the recognition that it is God's Word and voice and therefore (as Calvin underlined) should be honoured as God himself is honoured.

Secondly, a disarming combination of clarity, simplicity and warmth that draws the hearer into the Word. Ian preaches to a congregation as though speaking to an individual. It would be easy—but erroneous—to think this comes easily as though Ian had inherited Alexander Maclaren's 'golden hammer'—tap the text and a sermon falls naturally into place, headings and all! Not at all—behind these features lie hours of hard study and prayer.

Thirdly, his preaching is marked by gentle but where necessary pointed, application, Ian ministers without attacking the congregation! This is possible because of a potent combination of exegesis and theology—mining Scripture's inbuilt connections and depth-logic—with love. Ian's ministry is more than exegesis;

it is exposition. This combination of exposition, Biblical theology, spiritual logic, careful doctrinal formulation, and loving application means that his preaching leads ultimately to doxology. Different in style from Jonathan Edwards, there is the same conviction that— 'Our people don't so much need to have their heads stored, as to have their hearts touched; and they stand in the greatest need of that sort of preaching that has the greatest tendency to do this'.[1] With Edwards, Ian's preaching has sought to lift his hearers' affections as high as possible into the presence and praise of God. And therefore, those who have sat under his ministry have been both well-instructed and well nourished.

Family

Last, but no means least in importance, a few words should be said in commendation of the Hamilton family life. No one has been a closer witness to these features of Ian's life and ministry than his beloved and honoured wife Joan. He has never made any secret of the fact that he believes he found the modern equivalent of the 'excellent wife' of Prov. 31:10-31. His love for and proper pride in her and in each of his children and grandchildren is evident in his life (and is reciprocated). He has sought to model the loving wisdom of the Heavenly Father in his devotion to them.

More could be said. But perhaps more does not really need to be said by way of testimony to Ian's faithfulness in private as well as in public. In expressing personal gratitude to God for the privilege of his friendship over five decades, I (with a multitude of others throughout the world) am thankful also to the whole Hamilton family for their willingness to share him with us.

---

1. *The Works of Jonathan Edwards*, vol. 4, *Some Thoughts Concerning the Revival in New England*. Ed. C.C. Goen (New Haven and London: Yale University Press, 1972), 388.

PART ONE

Orientation to Catholic Calvinism

CHAPTER ONE

Calvinism

The Glory of the Triune God

Mark Johnston

It is both a great privilege and a pleasure to be asked to contribute to this volume of essays in appreciation of my dear friend, Ian Hamilton. We first met when I was living in London and had been asked to give Ian a lift to Heathrow Airport; but, when we arrived at the check-in desk, he was told he was unable to fly. When he insisted that I just put him on a train, I replied, 'I'm happy to drive you home.' And so began a car journey of eight hours and a friendship that has lasted and deepened ever since. The more I have come to know him the more I have come to realise in all kinds of ways he is a living paradigm of the kind of Calvinism that not only 'glorifies God,' but truly 'enjoys him forever'—notably as one God in three Persons, the blessed Trinity.

The doctrine of the Holy Trinity is the distinguishing doctrine of the Christian faith. It sets it apart from every other religion or concept of God the world has ever known, and it confronts us with mystery and majesty of the highest order. Little wonder then, that this doctrine dominated the landscape of theological reflection for the first seven centuries of church history and, indeed, has done ever since. It should also come as no surprise that the system of doctrine that has been labelled 'Calvinism' is trinitarian in its very essence. In his *Institutes of the Christian Religion,* which follows the contours of the Apostles' Creed, John Calvin considers the doctrine of the Trinity in depth and, more than this, he ties it into the fact that all doctrine has a trinitarian flavour.

As Calvin articulates and explains the great mystery bound up with the doctrine of God, he shows that the only appropriate response to this greatest of all divine realities is doxology. That is, in the language of the apostle Paul in his letter to the Ephesians, not only should the outworking of God's redemptive decree 'be to the praise of his glorious grace' (Eph. 1:6), but also that its fruit will be displayed in the life the Lord's people in such a way that they themselves 'might be to the praise of his glory' (Eph. 1:12). Believers individually and together should mirror God's majesty in a way that reflects his multifaceted wisdom and beauty. The apostle began his letter to the church in Ephesus with a trinitarian greeting. He refers to the Father and the Son directly, but includes the Holy Spirit implicitly with the words, 'who has blessed us in the heavenly realms with every spiritual blessing in Christ' (Eph. 1:3, NIV). In so doing he reminds us that the glory and significance of the very nature of the God is mirrored in the warp and weft of even seemingly trivial details of life.

Such is the depth and wonder of this axiomatic truth that eternity will not exhaust our grasp of what it entails and where it leads. It is bound up with the very essence of the God who is infinite and eternal. Not even the angels of heaven, nor perfected saints in the glory of the age to come will ever fully comprehend or do justice to the One who is ultimately incomprehensible. So too, eternity in all its vastness will never exhaust the depth and freshness of the praise this elicits from angels and redeemed humanity.

The danger that has never been far from this pivotal doctrine in the history of Christian thought is that it can be reduced to a theological conundrum that stretches the minds of great academics but leaves us spiritually and emotionally cold. It can become detached from its actual locus, which is the being and beauty of God and what it means to relate to him. The Bible is never dispassionate in the way it presents the divine self-revelation and, indeed, it often explodes into spontaneous praise and wonder at the very thought of who and what God is. The apostle Paul demonstrates this again and again in his epistles; but, especially in Romans after his lengthy excursus on God's dealings with his ancient people, Israel, he cries out in spontaneous praise and wonder:

> Oh, the depth of the riches and wisdom and knowledge of God! How unsearchable are his judgments and how inscrutable his ways!
> "For who has known the mind of the Lord, or who has been his counsellor?"
> "Or who has given a gift to him that he might be repaid?"
> For from him and through him and to him are all things. To him be glory forever, Amen (Rom. 11:33-36).

Theology in all its aspects must always lead to doxology. If we are handling and reflecting on the life-giving words of the living God in a way that truly engages with his self-disclosure, then we cannot but be affected by it because he himself is engaging with us by his Spirit. The very fact God is incomprehensible means we will always be wonderfully 'out of our depth' as we grow in our knowledge and love of him.

It is, in macrocosm, the equivalent of the thrill we experienced as little children in microcosm as we were growing up and growing into an ever richer, deeper knowledge and appreciation of our earthly parents. There were moments when our appreciation of the mother and the father who brought us into the world and had cared for us took a quantum leap forward. So too, it was often only much later in life we began to appreciate there was far more to them than we had ever imagined. How much more, then, in our appreciation of our God and heavenly Father and all he has been to us, every step along the way. This natural wonder ought to be replicated spiritually as we grow from infancy in the Faith towards maturity in Christ in our shared life as the church. This will be taken to an altogether different plane in the glory of the age to come and will never be exhausted because God's infinite beauty and greatness are inexhaustible.

In the most basic sense, this is what happens as we grow in our knowledge of God simply as God. The very concept of 'God' as the only infinite and eternal divine being, by definition, takes us into realms that are far above all human thought or understanding. But it is only when we begin to grasp and appreciate God's trinitarian nature that we are taken to infinitely greater depths and heights. We are inexorably drawn beyond the realm of the apprehension of God—however limited and inadequate that may be—into measureless depths of praise, adoration; but, supremely, enjoyment.

It is the fact that this knowledge always leads to worship that stands out again and again in the biblical record. Just as God in himself is infinite in the glory of his being, his beauty, and his attributes, so too our knowledge of him—along with the reciprocal response of praise that it generates—can ultimately have no limits.

It would be tempting to think that the revelation of God's trinitarian nature is restricted to the New Testament where this doctrine is set forth explicitly in the classic texts that point to the triunity of God in the three Persons; but this would be a mistake. Since the God of the New Testament is the self-same God we meet in the Old Testament it stands to reason that we should expect to find clues to his trinitarian nature there as well. When we look closely, this is indeed apparent, even from the very opening chapter of Genesis.

In fact, the opening chapter of the first book of the Bible would have given its original Hebrew readers pause for thought in several places where the plural noun *Elohim* [God] is used with a singular verb *bara* [created] in the same sentence. The God they daily confessed as 'The LORD our God, the LORD is one' (Deut. 6:4) was the self-same God who in some sense exists in plurality. Even though the full significance of this lay 'over the horizon' in the timeline of divine revelation, it was a marker, laid down by God himself in his self-disclosure—that would reverberate throughout the Old Testament and come into sharper focus in the New.

This detail in the early glimpses we are given of God in Genesis becomes even more apparent in the account of God's creation of man:

> Then God said, "Let us make man in our image, after our likeness. And let them have dominion over the fish of the sea and over the birds of the heavens and over the livestock and over all the earth and over every creeping thing that creeps on the earth." So God created man in his own image, in the image of God he created him; male and female he created them (Gen. 1:26-27).

Although this has often been explained as 'the plural of majesty'—the 'royal "we"'—there is good reason to see it as pointing to something infinitely more profound in terms of the progress of the divine self-revelation. Given that the Scriptures were not given in an instant; but, rather, progressively over many centuries from the days of Moses to the visions of John in Revelation, the God who makes himself known in them is always God in all his fulness. But he chose to make himself known incrementally and by increasing degrees as his written revelation was expanded. So, what we have in the opening chapter of his Word is but a glimpse of the fulness of what was to come over the rest of his self-disclosure, and even this is but a part of his immeasurable greatness that will only be revealed at the Parousia.

Robert Letham highlights this helpfully in his *Systematic Theology* when he says:

> We must distinguish between the doctrine of the Trinity and the Trinity itself. God always is, and he always is triune. From eternity he is the Father, the Son, and the Holy Spirit, one indivisible being, three irreducible persons…The Trinity is revealed in the Old Testament in latent form and in the New Testament implicitly but pervasively. However, the fully fledged *doctrine* awaited prolonged reflection on the biblical record.'[1]

---

1. Robert Letham, *Systematic Theology* (Wheaton IL: Crossway, 2019) 67

Letham also points helpfully to the way in which the trinitarian nature of God is reflected in all that he has made. There is a 'unity within diversity [in] his creation.'[2] He traces this out in the Bible's teaching on the nature of our humanity—both at an individual level; but, also in its corporate expression in humanity as a whole. Indeed, he takes this further, following Herman Bavinck, into the 'unity-in-diversity' manifest everywhere in the intricacy and complexity of creation. In support of this and pointing to where it ultimately leads, he cites Bavinck's statement, 'The Christian mind remains unsatisfied until all existence is referred back to the triune God.'[3]

Not surprisingly, therefore, the doctrine of the Trinity is more pervasive and far-reaching than we often assume. When we begin to appreciate how it is not only woven through God's self-revelation, but also imprinted upon every atom of creation, it serves only to enhance his glory and elicit ever more fulsome praise. When we appreciate the fact this pivotal element in the divine self-disclosure is not confined to the classic trinitarian proof-texts, it makes us look more closely at this particular doctrine as it is woven through the unfolding history of redemption in the Scriptures of the Old as much as of the New Testaments. When we do so, it becomes apparent that the glory of the Trinity is not simply latent in its pages, but is also acknowledged and leads to adoration.

We have already noted the details in the creation account in Genesis that hint at plurality within the unity of God and how the essential nature of the Creator is quite understandably reflected in the works of his hands. Just as the oneness within the created order is enhanced by its breathtaking diversity; so too it points to the unity within diversity of its Maker. From its macrocosm in the vastness of the cosmos, down to the complexity of the tiniest particles of matter; creation in its totality points to

---

2. Ibid. 217
3. Ibid. 283 citing Herman Bavinck, *Reformed Dogmatics* Vol. 2 (Grand Rapids MI: Baker Academic) 330

the wonder of the God who brought it into existence and daily sustains it by his Word. As has sometimes been suggested, we live in a sacramental universe. That is, as Paul avers, through the testimony of creation itself:

> The wrath of God is revealed from heaven against all ungodliness and unrighteousness of men, who by their unrighteousness suppress the truth. For what can be known about God is plain to them, because God has shown it to them. For his invisible attributes, namely, his eternal power and divine nature, have been clearly perceived, ever since the creation of the world, in the things that have been made. So they are without excuse. For although they knew God, they did not honour him as God or give thanks to him, but they became futile in their thinking, and their foolish hearts were darkened. Claiming to be wise, they became fools, and exchanged the glory of the immortal God for images resembling mortal man and birds and animals and creeping things (Rom. 1.18-23).

The created order bears witness not just to the existence of its Creator, but also to the splendour of his nature and attributes. This is borne out by several references in the Old Testament which provide subtle, but unmistakeable hints to plurality within the oneness of God. We have already noted the distinctive wording in the account of God's creation of man, but other references in the Old Testament sound similar notes.

When we look back at the opening verses of Genesis and the language used to describe the creation of Adam and Eve, we cannot help but notice further hints that there is more to God than meets the eye. After the summary statement of God's work of creation in its totality (Gen. 1:1), we are immediately told, 'The earth was without form and void, and darkness was over the face of the deep. And the Spirit of God was hovering over the face of the waters.' (Gen. 1:2). Despite the ambiguity bound up with this reference to the 'Spirit of God'—God is by definition 'spirit' (John 4:24)—it nevertheless adds a little detail to how God wants to be understood that makes us pause and take note.

Add to this the fact we then hear a sequence of references to the voice of God (Gen. 1:3, 6, 9, 14, 20, 24) as the means by which he created the component parts of the world and universe, we sense this little detail too may have more bound up with it than we might at first assume. Millennia later, the apostle John, in the Prologue to the Gospel that bears his name, would open our eyes more fully to the significance of this in the Genesis record. The 'Word' by which the world and universe were brought into existence was none other than the eternal *Logos*—the preincarnate Son of God—by whom all things were made (John 1:1-4). The very thought of a spoken word implies a speaker and a speaker, likewise, a person and the Person in question is identified as God.

As we follow the progression of the divine self-revelation further into the Old Testament, we encounter further details regarding the divine ontology that point to his being more than just a monadic deity. Perhaps most noteworthy is Isaiah's encounter with God—either in a vision while he was in the Temple, or else through a theophanic revelation—during which he saw God in his heavenly dwelling, surrounded by angelic beings. He records the antiphonal anthem which is ever on their lips:

> Holy, holy, holy is the Lord Almighty; the whole earth is full of his glory (Isa. 6.3 NIV).

This trifold repetition declaring the pervasive holiness of God may simply be a device for emphasis; but, at the same time—especially in light of the fuller revelation of God in the New Testament—we cannot help but surmise that this is a glimpse of the Trinity. It is, however, only as the fulness of God's self-disclosure is given with the dawn of the New Covenant epoch, that what is foreshadowed in Old Testament begins to come into focus. The synoptic Gospels each contain distinct allusions to the involvement of the Trinity in the incarnation. In the Matthean account, an angel of the Lord tells Joseph in advance of Jesus' birth:

> Joseph son of David, do not be afraid to take Mary home as your wife, because what is conceived in her is from the Holy Spirit. She

will give birth to a son, and you are to give him the name Jesus, because he will save his people from their sins (Matt. 1:20-21 NIV).

The reference to the Holy Spirit's involvement and the command to give the child the name 'Yahweh Saves' are indicators of the dimensions of the divine involvement. This is seen not only in the miracle of the incarnation, but ultimately in the identity of the incarnate One and, supremely, in what he alone would achieve in redemption – because he alone was uniquely able to accomplish it. Likewise in the gloss that Matthew adds to his record of Joseph's encounter with the angel:

> All this took place to fulfil what the Lord had said through the prophet: "The virgin will be with child and will give birth to a son, and they will call him Immanuel"—which means, "God with us" (Matt. 1:22-23 NIV).

This miracle foretold through Isaiah (Isa. 7:14) was more than just a divinely enabled conception, as had been true of Sara and Hannah in the Old Testament; rather, it would be the result of the Holy Spirit's direct action in the womb of Mary while she was still a virgin. Likewise, the fact that the incarnate One would be acknowledged as 'Immanuel'—in a way that would take the 'with-ness' of God to a hitherto unimaginable intensity—pointed in advance to the utter uniqueness of Jesus as the Christ.

Not surprisingly, Matthew's Gospel—with its uniquely Jewish flavour—points to Jesus as the Messiah promised from of old to God's ancient people; but he also highlights the key moments during Christ's earthly ministry when God the Father publicly acknowledged him as his Son at his baptism (Matt. 3:17) and again at his transfiguration (Matt. 17:5). The Matthean record of the baptism contains overt indicators of the Trinity with the Father's voice being heard, the Spirit descending in the form of a dove and Jesus being acknowledged by the Father as 'my beloved Son.' It is, however, the ending of the Gospel according to Matthew where we hear the most striking declaration of God as Trinity in the baptismal formula which Christ commands for the church to use in its missionary endeavour. He uses the singular 'name' to embrace the plurality of persons:

> Go therefore and make disciples of all nations, baptising them in the name of the Father and of the Son and of the Holy Spirit, teaching them to observe all that I have commanded you. And behold, I am with you always, to the end of the age (Matt. 28:19-20).

The Gospel according to Mark opens with the bold declaration, 'The beginning of the gospel of Jesus Christ, the Son of God' (Mark 1:1)—a claim he goes on to substantiate in the chapters that follow. All of which leads to the pivotal moment at Caesarea Philippi where Jesus is confessed by Peter as 'the Christ' (Mark 8:29).

It is, however, only when we move from the record of the Synoptics to that of John that we encounter the most overt trinitarian teaching found anywhere in the Gospels. Its opening in the Prologue to the Gospel takes us into eternity past with the declaration:

> In the beginning was the Word, and the Word was with God, and the Word was God. He was in the beginning with God. All things were made through him, and without him was not anything made that was made. In him was life, and the life was the light of men. The light shines in the darkness, and the darkness has not overcome it (John 1:1-5).

The enigma surrounding the identity of 'the Word [Logos]' in verse one is resolved a few verses later when John states:

> And the Word became flesh and dwelt among us, and we have seen his glory, glory as of the only Son from the Father, full of grace and truth (John 1:14).

Jesus of Nazareth, announced and proclaimed by John the Baptist, is none other than the eternal Son of God who was made man for us and for our salvation. The 'Upper Room Discourse'—the section that dominates John's Gospel in terms of space—records the clearest clues to the trinitarian nature of God found anywhere thus far in his unfolding self-revelation in Scripture. It was there, around the table spread for the celebration of the Last Supper, that Jesus chose to give his disciples the most breathtaking glimpse thus far of the nature of God. In response to Phillip's request, 'Lord, show us the Father,' Jesus says:

> Have I been with you so long, and you still do not know me, Philip? Whoever has seen me has seen the Father. How can you say, 'Show us the Father'? Do you not believe that I am in the Father and the Father is in me? The words that I say to you I do not speak on my own authority, but the Father who dwells in me does his works. Believe me that I am in the Father and the Father is in me, or else believe on account of the works themselves. (John 14:9-11).

This reference to *perichoresis*—the mutual indwelling of the Persons of the Trinity—is arguably the most glorious glimpse we are given anywhere in Scripture of the depth and intimacy bound up with the intra-trinitarian bond. It is a glimpse of God echoed by John decades later with his declaration, 'God is love' (1 John 4:16). Love, in all its fulness, is not some abstract concept; but the perfection of relationship rooted in God as Father, Son and Holy Spirit—the eternal Trinity. The depth and wonder of this glorious truth take us beyond the limits of human understanding; but Jesus does not leave it there. Three chapters later, in what has come to be known as his 'Great High Priestly Prayer', Jesus leaves us gasping in even greater wonder as he teases out the ultimate outworking of this glorious truth. Praying that all his people would truly experience the full depth of his saving and life-transforming grace, Jesus prays:

> That they may all be one, just as you, Father, are in me, and I in you, that they also may be in us, so that the world may believe that you have sent me. The glory that you have given me I have given to them, that they may be one even as we are one, I in them and you in me, that they may become perfectly one, so that the world may know that you sent me and loved them even as you loved me (John 17:21-23).

Given that these words were spoken in the aftermath of the argument over 'who would be the greatest' among the disciples resurfacing, it seemed as though the very notion of being 'perfectly one' was impossible. Yet it was precisely against this stark reality that Christ's words—filled with redemptive promise—were spoken. And the very next day those words would be sealed with Jesus' cry of triumph on the cross, 'It is finished!' (John 19:30). It is in the outworking of our Lord's answered prayer that the glory of the Trinity is displayed as God had always intended: through its reflection in the unity-within-diversity of our humanity.

CHAPTER TWO

Catholicity

Christ has only one Bride

Peter Naylor

It is a privilege to contribute something to a volume that gratefully acknowledges the goodness of God in giving us our dear brother and friend, Ian Hamilton, and that recognises the grace of God in him, our beloved fellow worker for the kingdom of our Lord and Saviour Jesus Christ. It is wholly fitting that this volume should include something under the title 'Christ has only one Bride,' for Ian has often spoken of 'warm-hearted Calvinism,' and reminded us of the importance of having a 'catholic spirit,' by which he means recognising that there is one universal church, whose boundaries are far larger than any particular denomination.

Ian's warm and generous spirit does not equate to a flabby indifference to truth. At times, our brother has contended for the faith, and reasoned against positions that he considered to be in error, as for example when he wrote against Amyraldianism, defending the full Calvinistic doctrine set forth in the Canons of Dort and the Westminster Confession of Faith.

This chapter will attend to biblical, historical, and practical aspects of the truth that Christ has only one Bride, one Church.

In the Scriptures

The New Testament wonderfully compares the marriage of a man and his wife to that of Christ and his church. 'Husbands, love your wives, just as Christ also loved the church and gave himself for her, that he might sanctify and cleanse her with the washing of water by the word, that he might present her to himself a glorious church, not having spot or wrinkle or any such thing, but that she should be holy and without blemish' (Eph. 5:25-27). In the same epistle, Paul declares, 'There is one body and one Spirit ... one Lord, one faith, one baptism, one God and Father of all, who is above all, and through all, and in you all' (Eph. 4:4-6 KJV). Paul applies the same marriage metaphor to his own preaching of the gospel when he writes to the Corinthians, 'I have betrothed you to one husband, that I may present you as a chaste virgin to Christ' (2 Cor. 11:2 NKJV).

In these places, we contemplate the deep and eternal love of Christ for his church, and the sweet way in which he has wooed us through the gospel, so that we may one day come to the marriage supper of the Lamb. 'Blessed are those who are called to the marriage supper of the Lamb' (Rev. 19:9 NKJV). The Revelation to John on Patmos divides the world into two parts, one 'the great harlot' and two 'the bride, the Lamb's wife' (Rev. 17:1; 21:9 NKJV). And the Spirit and the bride yearn for Christ to come (Rev. 22:17).

This New Testament view of the church as the one Bride of Christ has its roots in the Old Testament where we find one covenant people. When God called Abraham, he separated him from the land of his birth unto himself. Later, he brought Israel out of Egypt. He chose the seed of Abraham, the nation of Israel, and passed over the rest of the nations (Deut. 32:7-9; Isa. 43:3-5). In numerous places, the covenant bond is spoken of as a marriage (e.g., Ezek. 16). When the ten tribes were torn from Solomon's son, Rehoboam, and the division between Israel and Judah took place, it was a divine judgment, a dreadful tragedy, and a great wound, but one that would eventually be healed. Ezekiel was commanded to take two sticks and write on one 'For Judah…' and on the other

'For Joseph ... ' and then to join the two sticks together, because, the Lord promised, 'They will be one in my hand' (Ezek. 37:15-28). They would be united under David (that is, under his greater Son, our Lord Jesus Christ, *the* Servant of the Lord), and they would never be divided again. This is the work of God to sanctify his people and to dwell among them, that the world may know that he is the LORD. This thought permeates our Lord's prayer, recorded in John 17, that 'they all may be one, as you, Father, are in me, and I in you; that they may be one in us, that the world may believe that you sent me' (John 17:21). When the church is united, and full of the love of Christ, God is glorified in her (Eph. 3:14-21). The Psalmist rejoiced in the sight of Jerusalem 'compactly built together' and loved it. 'Behold, how good and how pleasant it is for brothers to dwell together' (Psalm 133). There is one God: three persons yet one God (Deut. 6:4; John 10:30) and one Mediator (1 Tim. 3:5). Therefore, the church cannot but be one. From one perspective, we may say that the church *is* one—it is a fact, a work of God. But from another perspective we see it as a goal to strive for.

In our history

When we turn from Scripture to church history, we do not discover 'one church.' The Reformers confessed, 'We believe and profess one catholic or universal church, which is a holy congregation and assembly of the true Christian believers, who expect their entire salvation in Jesus Christ, are washed by his blood, and are sanctified and sealed by the Holy Spirit ... that has existed from the beginning of the world and will be to the end ... spread and dispersed throughout the entire world ... joined and united with heart and will.'[1] And yet, they continue, 'we ought to discern diligently and very carefully from the Word of God what is the true church ... which must be distinguished from all sects that call themselves the church.'[2] Although the Belgic Confession says that these two churches (the true and the false) are 'easily recognised

---

1. *The Belgic Confession*, 1563, Article 27.
2. *The Belgic Confession*, Article 29.

and distinguished from each other', the Westminster Confession, written afterwards, carefully says that the true catholic church 'hath been sometimes more, sometimes less visible.'[3]

In his book, '*Christianity and Liberalism,*' J. Gresham Machen, weighs up the differences of opinion and the divisions we face in the church: 'It is perfectly possible for Christian fellowship to be maintained despite differences of opinion.'[4] So, for example, there are differences of opinion over the order of events in connection with our Lord's return. Machen says that we may not be indifferent about this matter, and we may see error arising from false methods of interpretation, but, he says, it is 'not deadly error.'[5] Similarly, differences over the mode of efficacy of the sacraments exist. Luther and Zwingli did not agree. Machen says, 'Luther was wrong about the Supper, but not nearly so wrong as he would have been' if he had regarded it as a trifle, a matter of indifference. Machen deplores indifferentism. 'Such indifferentism would have been far more deadly than all the divisions between the branches of the Church.'[6] Anglican episcopal principles differ from Presbyterian polity; Calvinists disagree with Arminians. 'Far more serious still is the division between the Church of Rome and evangelical Protestantism in all its forms,' and we may wish to deny that Rome is a true church of Jesus Christ; and yet, Machen notes, there remains a common heritage, although 'the gulf is profound'. All that said, 'naturalistic liberalism is not Christianity at all.'[7] Machen weighs these things and strikes a balance. It is of ultimate importance not to overlook a principle which Machen insisted upon: 'in the modern vituperation of "doctrine," it is not merely the great theologians or the great creeds that are

---

3. *Westminster Confession of Faith,* 1647, 25.4.

4. J. Gresham Machen, *Christianity and Liberalism,* (Wm. B Eerdmans: Michigan, 1923), 48.

5. J. Gresham Machen, *Christianity and Liberalism,* (Wm. B Eerdmans: Michigan, 1923), 49.

6. J. Gresham Machen, *Christianity and Liberalism,* (Wm. B Eerdmans: Michigan, 1923), 50.

7. J. Gresham Machen, *Christianity and Liberalism,* (Wm. B Eerdmans: Michigan, 1923), 52.

being attacked, but the New Testament and our Lord himself. In rejecting doctrine, the liberal preacher is rejecting the simple words of Paul, "Who loved me and gave Himself for me," just as much as the *homoousion* of the Nicene Creed... The liberal preacher is really rejecting the whole basis of Christianity.'[8]

The ecumenical movement, in its quest for church unity, has adopted such a fundamentally flawed approach. It deprecates doctrine: only bad things can proceed from doctrine; division and schism are its fruits. And so we hear slogans such as 'No confession of faith but deeds of faith' and 'Doctrine divides, service unites.'[9] More than once, during the course of my ministry, a professing Christian has said to me, 'Doctrine does not matter.' That is dangerous folly. In every case the path chosen by that individual has led off the straight and narrow way of Christ into byways and dead ends. Those who are indifferent to doctrine build on sand, not on the rock.

So then, on the ground we find many divisions, differences of opinion, numerous denominations, hardly 'one church.' Presented with the actual situation that we have inherited from two thousand years of history, what must we do?

In practice

Some godly men in the past have set us good examples. Outstanding among the Reformers was Pierre Viret (1511-71), a colleague of John Calvin (1509-64). Farel testified of Viret:

> I know him better than I know myself, and I can say that never have I found in him anything but a sincere affection for Christ and His Gospel, a character devoid of all harshness, a truly Christian soul, walking in love and seeking peace If he beheld not a multitude rushing to their ruin, nor felt compelled by the command of God, he would never enter into dispute with anyone. And when he is

---

8. J. Gresham Machen, *Christianity and Liberalism*, (Wm. B Eerdmans: Michigan, 1923), 47.

9. K. Deddens and M. K. Drost, *Balance of Ecumenism. The Ecumenical Movement viewed in the Light of the Bible*, (Premier Publishing: Winnipeg, 1989), contains a useful survey of the ecumenical movement.

thus forced, he proceeds with such moderation that his adversaries themselves are obliged—whether they like it or not—to confess that he at least possesses the character of a man worthy of perfect respect.[10]

This godly man, on the one hand, contended stoutly against the claims of the civil magistrate, for the right of the church to govern its own affairs, and, at the same time he was a peacemaker who loved his enemies. Sheats describes how on one occasion he intervened to rescue his enemy, the Jesuit Edmond Auger, from execution. When his request for clemency was refused, Viret leapt upon the scaffold and declared that if Auger were to die, he would die with him. Interposing his own life, he rescued his enemy.[11]

Valiant for truth, and yet large-hearted, moved by the love of Christ, Viret stands among a precious band of like-minded men. George Whitefield (Calvinist) highly esteemed John Wesley (Arminian). C. H. Spurgeon (Calvinist) invited D. L. Moody (Arminian), when he was visiting England, to preach in his 'Tabernacle'. J. C. Ryle held firmly to infant baptism while graciously acknowledging his Baptist brothers:

> The subject of infant baptism is undoubtedly a delicate and difficult one. Holy and praying men are unable to see alike upon it… The great majority of Christians hold that infant baptism is scriptural and right. A comparatively small section of the Protestant church, but one containing many eminent saints among its members regard infant baptism as unscriptural and wrong… But the difference now referred to must not make members of the Church of England shrink from holding decided opinions on the subject.[12]

It is to Ryle's credit that he remained firm in his convictions while honouring believers who did not accept his position. What should we do, but emulate such examples, seeking to cultivate strong convictions combined with love? Reformed preachers, we must

---

10. These words of William Farel are taken from R. A. Sheats, *Pierre Viret: The Angel of the Reformation,* (Psalm 78 Ministries: Monticello, 2012), 127-8.

11. Sheats, 179.

12. J. C. Ryle, *Expository Thoughts on Mark*, (Banner of Truth: Edinburgh, 2012, [1857]), 161, on Mark 10:13-16.

be 'valiant for truth'. Christ's ministers must stand before the congregation and faithfully read the Scriptures, and preach the Word, taking pains over the interpretation and the doctrine. True, they may well divide people with the sword of the Spirit, and at the same time unite those who hear the Word. The truth proclaimed plainly and boldly will divide and it will unite. Visualize the scene: in every church the people hear the same Word of God week by week, hearing 'the Holy Spirit speaking in the Scripture.'[13] This serves to promote an agreement of mind, as we each hear the same passages week by week. We must never fall into the trap of indifferentism. Doctrine matters. It is Christ's doctrine, not ours. Yet we need to be clothed with humility, learning meekness from Christ, gentle, kind, and full of love, 'speaking the truth in love' (Eph. 4:15). We must embody the words of Paul:

> A servant of the Lord must not quarrel, but be gentle to all, able to teach, patient, in humility correcting those who are in opposition, if God perhaps will grant them repentance, so that they may know the truth, and that they may come to their senses, and escape the snare of the devil, having been taken captive by him to do his will (2 Tim. 2:24-26 NKJV).

If we are ever so orthodox but lack a gracious spirit and brotherly love, we are empty vessels; we are nothing (1 Cor. 13:1-3). If we tithe mint and cummin but neglect justice, mercy, faith, kindness and love, what are we? (Matt. 23:23). How grotesque it would be to have a perfect form of government and precise canons and rules, but then apply those rules without love to beat the brethren rather than heal and forgive (Matt. 24:49)? And if we do not forgive, and forgive, and forgive—seventy times seven—we are lost (Matt. 18:21-35). Charity (love) will endure, when faith has turned to sight. We must never forget that we are sinners rescued from an eternity in hell by a merciful God. 'Amazing grace, how sweet the sound that saved a wretch like me' (John Newton). What grace God shows when he makes a man a living

---

13. Westminster Confession of Faith, 1.10.

member of the body of Christ, grafting him into the Bride, and calling him to the marriage supper of the Lamb. All undeserved: grace, abounding grace! By grace he calls us to strive for the unity of the church. May the Bride of the Lamb become a beautiful bride, with no schism, no wound, no blemish—that they all may be one. May she be a glory to her glorious Bridegroom. Pray for the peace of Jerusalem. Behold, the Bridegroom comes! Yes, come, Lord Jesus. Amen.

PART TWO

Catholic Calvinist Convictions Lived Out

CHAPTER THREE

Lessons Learned for Ministry

Four Men Trained by Ian Hamilton

David Pfeiffer, Andy Young, Dan Peters, Douglas McCallum

David Pfeiffer
I have known Ian Hamilton since 2003. For the subsequent nine years, I worshipped at Cambridge Presbyterian Church where Ian served as minister. For the last four years of my time there, I served as a deacon in the church, and the last three years of that period coincided with me training for ministry under the guidance of the Cambridge session. Ian preached at my wedding as well as my ordination to the Christian ministry. He has kept in contact with me and my family over the years. I now serve with him in a teaching capacity at Westminster Seminary, UK.

I write all of this to highlight something of the context of his influence on my life and ministry. I have learnt from Ian not only in the pulpit, but also in his home, in his car, through his pastoral visits, in session meetings, over coffee and through merely observing his interactions with others from a distance. Much of what I have learnt has been by osmosis rather than direct instruction.

This highlights a key element to the training of Christian ministers: seminaries, while extremely valuable, cannot teach everything needed for ministry. A man must learn about the

Christian ministry in the context of the church, both local and catholic, and under the influence of godly Christian ministers.

In the rest of this short reflection, I want to highlight four foundational elements that have pervaded Ian's ministry, and four significant lessons I have learnt from his ministry.

The first foundational element is Ian's absolute commitment to God's Word. Ian's commitment to God's Word is absolute because his commitment to God is absolute. This is seen not only in his persistent (though not exclusively) consecutive expository preaching but also in his attention to the detail of Scripture. Every word of Scripture matters. There are Greek words seared into my mind through Ian's preaching and conversations!

Second, and of course, intimately related to this, is a commitment to the doctrinal articulations of the Christian church throughout the centuries. Ian exemplifies what it means to learn together "with all the saints", past and present, "what is the breadth and length and height and depth" of the love of Christ (Eph. 3:18-19). We do not learn God's truth apart from God's people. We humbly listen to our forebears as the wisdom of the Spirit was given in the ecumenical creeds and confessions of the church, as well as through eminent teachers of the past. To fail to do this is individualistic hubris and folly.

Third, a true commitment to God's Word and truth is always married to a transformed life of piety. A man's ministry without a sacred weight of character is hollow. We may be the most gifted preacher the world has known, but if we do not love God, his people and the lost, we are just a "clanging cymbal" (1 Cor. 13:1).

Finally, and above all, the glory of God is the ultimate goal and vision for authentic Christian ministry. Man's chief end is to glorify God; the same is true of the chief end of ministry. Christian ministry is motivated by the goal of seeing the knowledge of the glory of the Lord cover the earth as the waters cover the sea. Its present high point is each Lord's Day as we sit at Christ's feet beholding that glory.

In the context of these foundational aspects, here are four key lessons I have learnt from Ian that have profoundly shaped my outlook on ministry: firstly, the church is bigger than the local church. The main bulk of Ian's ministry has been done in the context of the local church. In his first ministry alone in Newmilns, Ayrshire, Ian conducted 701 funerals! However, this unwearied commitment to the local church has been matched by a love and concern for the wider church. Several times I remember Ian quoting John Calvin's letter to Archbishop Cranmer in April 1552, which discusses divisions in the church throughout Europe:

> Thus it is that the members of the Church being severed, the body lies bleeding. So much does this concern me, that, could I be of service, I would not grudge to cross even ten seas, if need were, on account of it.[1]

Calvin is not speaking of the local church here, but the visible church of Christ in Europe. This echo is found in Ian's heart.

Secondly, one must apply God's Word pastorally in the context of a complicated fallen world. Ian is a staunch defender of the truth. He has written a defence of men only being eligible for the office of elder and against Amyraldianism. He is committed head to toe to the Westminster Standards as the finest confessional expression of Christian truth available to us.

But that does not make him a hard, clinical, cold man. God's truth needs to be applied pastorally. People's lives can be messy and complex. Pastoral ministry means hours of listening to the struggles of others, hours of wrestling in prayer over them and hours of discussions within session meetings. The teaching of God's Word is to be done with great patience (2 Tim. 4:2).

Thirdly, Christian ministry is profoundly idiosyncratic. There are certain characteristics that should exemplify every Christian minister, four of which I have highlighted above. Nevertheless, all Christian ministers are different. They all have their unique backgrounds, temperaments, strengths and weaknesses. Ian is his own man. He does not try to be someone he is not, and neither should we.

---

1. John Calvin, *Tracts and Letters*, Volume 5 (Banner of Truth, Edinburgh), 348.

Fourthly, preaching is to be married with pastoral visitation if it is to have a lasting impact on God's people. All true Christian ministers have Paul's final instructions to Timothy ringing in their own ears: "Preach the Word!" But this preaching of the Word does not come to God's people at a distance. Ministers are to be as gentle "nursing mothers" and "exhorting fathers" among God's people (1 Thess. 2:7-12). Ministers share not only the gospel to their people, but also themselves.

These are some of the things I have learnt from Ian and for which I give thanks to God.

Andy Young

The phrase 'warm-hearted Presbyterianism' is so closely associated with Ian Hamilton, and so often used by him, he probably owns the copyright to the expression. It sums up much of who Ian is and what he is like. A man who blends orthodoxy with catholicity, he embodies that rare mix of Reformed convictions and formidable intellect, with a genuine heart for others and ability to keep the gospel of Christ the main thing.

To say that Ian has had a significant influence on my life is an understatement. Not only did he preach and officiate at my wedding, and baptise my first two daughters, he was frequently in our home and reliably at our side during several stays in hospital. I served alongside him as a student minister, a Deacon, and Church treasurer. He mentored me through my seminary career and hosted a bespoke 'pastoralia' course for those preparing for ministry. More recently we served together as fellow Presbyters, and I had the privilege of attending his final Banner of Truth Trustees meeting. There is no doubt that my own preaching and pastoring would be so much worse if it was not for Ian. Many of my theological convictions, doctrinal emphases, and even homiletical vocabulary, trace their origins to him. Everyone I know that have served alongside or been mentored by him, whilst very different in their personalities and gifting, share a common warm-heartedness which we must thank Ian for.

Warm-hearted Personal Life

Ian's warm-heartedness is 'home grown'. He is ever-conscious that at best he is a sinner saved by grace. One of his oft-used quips is 'we are sheep before we are shepherds'. He is palpably aware that before a gospel minister he is a hell deserving sinner. This personal reality is the seedbed of his gospel warmth as the wonder of Christ for him and in him, exudes from him. Ian is also married to Joan, who is his never-failing support. Her love and care for him and their children, as well as everyone in the church, was vital to his ministry. As he would often tell anyone who was with him, coming home was the best part of his day. Joan's warmth radiated to all, and I have no doubt his warm-heartedness grew from the soil of a very happy and warm-hearted homelife.

Warm-hearted Theology

The nineteenth-century Scottish Minister, Rabbi Duncan, once said, "I'm first a Christian, next a catholic, then a Calvinist, fourth a paedobaptist, and fifth a Presbyterian. I cannot reverse this order." Ian embodies this maxim. If you were to cut him, he would bleed Reformed orthodoxy. He knows the history, debates, exegesis, and doctrinal minutiae of Patristics, the Reformation, Post-Reformation thought, and modern theological developments. He can articulate and defend the theology of the Westminster Confessions as well as anyone. However, these convictions are always infused with capaciousness. They never caused him to lose sight of the centrality of Christ or the gospel. On the contrary, he would often say that emphasising the love of God in Jesus Christ is pristine Reformation theology. Gospel warmth is not an optional extra to his theology, but essential to it.

Warm-hearted Preaching

Ian follows no set or predictable homiletical method. He is as enigmatic in the pulpit as he is powerful, and as idiosyncratic as he is pastoral. His sermons are sometimes straightforward—an introduction, a handful of main points, and a conclusion with pastoral applications. Yet often his introductions will last more than twenty minutes followed by several rapid-fire truths and exhortations, all ending in a eulogy on the greatness of God's grace in Jesus Christ. The congregation would know things were drawing to a climax when Ian would take his watch off the pulpit and put it back on his wrist. At that moment you knew the best was about to come and it seemed all were on the edge of their seats in anticipation. We would be enthralled with an extended paean on the glory of God or the grace of Christ, and many would bow in the final prayer with our hearts overflowing at the sheer wonder of the gospel.

Striking evidence of the warm-heartedness of Ian's preaching is found in the men he trained. Many of the contributors to this volume have sat for extended time under Ian's ministry and cut their preaching teeth under his mentorship. Despite his significant influence on us all, each of our style and 'voice' in preaching is as varied as the men he helped equip for ministry. This is testimony to Ian's gospel breadth. As brilliant a preacher as he is, he hasn't produced clones of himself. On the contrary, the men who owe so much to him for their spiritual formation are their own men. Ian always encouraged us to be the best men we could be, and not mimics of others, least of all himself. This is surely a product of his gospel warmth which positively encourages a spectrum of gifting for the blessing of the wider church.

When I grow up, I want to be more like Ian Hamilton. I would love his encyclopaedic knowledge of church history. I hope to have a modicum of his theological insight. And I can only dream of preaching as consistently well as he does. But much more than these, I aspire to his warmth, catholicity, and relentless capaciousness. His warm-hearted Presbyterianism is infectious, and we should all desire to live it out as transparently as he does. Not because of Ian per se, but because as much as you see that warm-hearted Presbyterianism in him, you see it more in Jesus Christ. Ian is himself but an echo of his Saviour, and so to aspire to be like Ian, is to aspire to be like Christ.

Dan Peters

I first met Ian Hamilton outside the Great Hall at Aberystwyth University. It was the summer of 2003, and I was there attending the annual Evangelical Movement of Wales Conference. He was there as one of its speakers, and he had just preached a sermon on Ezekiel 33:1-11.

It was a breathtaking sermon. Entitled 'A Pleading God,' it portrayed vividly a Father who implores sinners to turn to him. In Ian's presentation that night, the gospel was warm and inviting. To be sure, he did not gloss over the vileness of sin and the horrors of hell. But his aim was not to terrify his hearers into a response. He sought instead to captivate hearts with the vision of a beautiful God who prefers to save rather than condemn.

When, exactly a year later, I began a very blessed thirteen months under Ian's mentorship, I soon realised his Aberystwyth sermon had not been uncharacteristic. Ian does not have a warm 'mode' that he can switch into when preaching a certain kind of message. Rather, his entire Christianity exudes warmth: it flows from his view of God, through his understanding of the gospel, and then out into many other areas.

One of those areas is his ecclesiology. While some who bear the name 'reformed' equate faithfulness with a sectarian spirit, Ian has a warmly expansive conception of the Christian church. He appreciates its catholicity. He is unwilling to write off sections of the church just because they are unlike his own. But whereas, often, that kind of generous outlook goes hand-in-hand with an indifference towards theological detail, with Ian it is not so. To know him at all is to know a man who thrives on the intricacies of Christian doctrine. Here, then, we have the rare convergence of theological precision and ecclesiological breadth. If pressed on this, Ian, I suspect, would be unapologetic. He would insist it is because of (not in spite of) his theology that he so readily embraces the whole family of God.

It is often in low-key ways that Ian manifests this generous spirit. When, however, it is your privileged role to shadow him for a sustained period, those low-key manifestations gain a cumulative weight. I think of conversations we would have in the car on the way to meetings or visits. A particular theologian or preacher might be mentioned who doctrinally, or stylistically at least, is different from Ian. Ian would proceed to express his reservations plainly and often convincingly—but never gracelessly. You could almost guarantee that sooner or later he would add a qualifying remark envying the other man's godliness or zeal.

I think, too, of an event we attended together. It was organised by the local hospital chaplaincy and attracted a broad spectrum of church leaders. If my first experience of Ian was in the robustly conservative context of the Aberystwyth Conference, on this day I observed him in a rather different setting! These church leaders were from every conceivable denominational background, male and female, sedate and outlandish. Many of us would have become stiff and defensive in such circumstances. Ian, however, comported himself with courtesy and unfaltering respect. He smiled; he initiated conversations; he shook hands; he expressed his pleasure at meeting people. He was not the surly Calvinist in the corner casting a cynical eye over the room. Something has stayed with me from that day: the sight of a man who refuses to shrink God's church to the dimensions of his own reformed comfort zone.

The experience of shadowing Ian revealed another thing that may not be unrelated: his composure amidst the many challenges facing Christianity in the western world of the twenty-first century. He likes to cite the NIV's colloquial rendering of Paul's charge to Timothy: 'Keep your head in all situations' (2 Tim. 4:5). And he practises the apostle's advice. He is stable and unflappable, cheerfully doing the work of ministry, week after week, year after year. What is the secret of this ability to keep his head in an era of decline and discouragement?

Largely, I believe, it is his confidence in the sovereignty and promises of Jesus Christ. He believes that Christ is 'head over everything for the church' (Eph. 1:22 NIV), and that he will, inexorably, build his church (Matt. 16:18). But I think Ian's catholicity may be another factor aiding his general stability. A catholic spirit preserves him from Elijah's skewed outlook: 'I am the only one left' (1 Kings 19:10 NIV). It prevents him retreating into a siege mentality. His keen sense that his own affiliations do not exhaust the church of Christ encourages Ian. It suppresses the despairing 'Ichabod!' which many of us can too hastily cry.

As I reflect on these things, I only wish I might emulate better what I saw in Ian during my time with him. I wish I might combine as well as he does the ability to uphold our reformed distinctives, understanding their finer details, with the ability to see over them and past them to a blood-bought church that utterly dwarfs our little tribe within it. While I do not attain that standard which Ian set, I am abidingly thankful for my exposure to it. And as he continues to be active in the training of prospective ministers, I pray that many more young men, sitting at his feet, will be inspired by a Christianity that from beginning to end is warm: warm in its understanding of the God who is love; warm in its construal of the grace of the gospel; and warm in its appreciation of the one, catholic church of Jesus Christ.

May the triune God richly bless you, Ian, as you pass this milestone! May your service bring glory to his name as long as he gives you life and breath.

Douglas McCallum

I first got to know Ian Hamilton when I was a student in the early 2000s and worshipped in the church of which he was the minister. During that time, Ian became a father in the faith to me and has, since then, been a very dear friend. I had the privilege of working alongside Ian as his ministry trainee for a year in 2013-14 before becoming, towards the end of 2017, the minister of Cambridge Presbyterian Church, the church where Ian served so faithfully for seventeen years. Through the warmth and grace of both his ministry and his character, Ian has exercised a profound influence upon me, shaping me to serve in the wider church and instilling in me a deep appreciation of catholic Calvinism.

I had rarely, if ever, heard anyone speak so glowingly of Calvin until I sat under the preaching of Ian as a student for three years. Until that time, I had always associated Calvinism with a certain narrowness and coldness of spirit, and viewed Calvin himself as a harsh and unforgiving figure. I soon came to realise what a gross caricature that was. Far from being an oppressive and inhumane system of truth, I began to appreciate, thanks to Ian's ministry, the beauty and breadth of Calvinism and how, when rightly understood, the doctrines of grace inculcated a spirit of generous humility rather than ugly pride.

It is important to say, however, that I came to relish the rich truths and large-hearted catholicity of Calvinism, not because Ian was forever 'banging on' about Calvin, but because he preached the Bible and proclaimed Christ faithfully, powerfully and pastorally. The hallmark of Calvinism is an unwavering stress upon the glory of God—glory that is native to his triune being as Father, Son and Holy Spirit, and glory that is manifested in his sovereign, saving grace to hell-bound sinners through Jesus Christ. And it was this—the glory of God and the glory of his gospel grace—that rang forth from Ian's preaching every week and vastly delighted me.

I remember, in particular, a series he preached in my final year as a student on John 13-17. Here, as Jesus prepares his disciples for his impending departure, our Lord seeks to comfort their troubled hearts by directing their gaze heavenwards and impressing upon them the grace and sufficiency of the holy Trinity. It is probably the most moving and theologically rich portion in the whole Bible. And every Sunday, as Ian walked us through these chapters, my heart was warmed and my soul enlarged as my gaze was directed away from myself and towards the grace of my Saviour, the love of my Father, and the fellowship of my Comforter. I came away from those sermons—and this was invariably the case with Ian's preaching—feeling as though I had tasted and seen more of the goodness of the Lord. It was an exhilarating experience.

In saturating his public ministry with a wonderful emphasis on the glory of Christ and the grace of the gospel, Ian instilled in me a desire to serve the wider church body and to promote a spirit of warm-hearted catholicity. But perhaps even more than the richness of his preaching and public prayers, it is Ian's own personal warmth and unfeigned generosity that has left a lasting mark on me.

In his first letter to the church in Thessalonica, Paul says that he and his companions were gentle among them, 'like a nursing mother taking care of her own children' and that, having a deep affection and desire for the Thessalonians and their spiritual good, 'we were ready to share with you not only the gospel of God but also our own selves, because you had become very dear to us' (1 Thess. 2:7-8).

Whenever I read these words of the apostle Paul, I am reminded of Ian and of the way he has cared for me over the years. I think, in particular, of my time as an undergraduate, when I endured some dark providences and sore trials. There were days when I felt unable to cope and I wished, like the psalmist, that I had the wings of a dove so that I could fly away and be at rest (Ps. 55:6). But God, in his goodness, gave me a pastor who loved me.

Ian was always kind to me. Like a nursing mother, he took care of me and, like a wise father, he listened to me patiently and exhorted me gently. He did not indulge me if I was wallowing in self-pity or had sin I needed to repent of—he could be firm when necessary. But such firmness was never hard or harsh; it always came couched in a spirit of affectionate desire and tenderness. I knew that I was very dear to Ian.

Among other things, he would meet up with me, pray with me, give me godly counsel, read the Bible (and Calvin's *Institutes*) with me, welcome me into his home, show me hospitality, and just spend time with me. In all these ways (and many more besides), Ian shared with me, not only the gospel of God, but his own self and, in doing so, helped me greatly.

Always quick to commend and praise others, I vividly remember one occasion when a visiting minister had been invited to preach at Cambridge Presbyterian Church and, before the service, Ian took me to one side and said of this particular individual: 'This man is the best preacher you will ever hear. But he is a better man than he is a preacher.' I often think about those words. It is good to be a fine preacher. But it is even better to be a fine and godly man. To paraphrase Paul a little, we could preach the most powerful and eloquent sermons the world has ever heard, but if we do not have love, we would be but noisy gongs or clanging cymbals.

Ian Hamilton is the best preacher I have ever heard. But he is a better man than he is a preacher. He persuaded me of the truth and beauty of warm-hearted, catholic Calvinism because he preached it, but, even more so, because he lived—and still lives—it.

CHAPTER FOUR

Preaching

How Shall They Hear Without a Preacher?

John MacArthur

Ian Hamilton has faithfully served for many years as a pastor, seminary president, author, and church historian. He has been a strong prophetic voice of warning against the dangers of doctrinal drift and spiritual decline. He and I share many common interests, activities, and outlooks. The love of Christ compels him and a mutual love for Christ binds our hearts together. Although we have spent most of our respective ministries on opposite sides of the Atlantic and in different denominational circles, we follow the same Lord; we preach the same gospel; and we both affirm the absolute authority and inerrancy of Scripture. We also share an unshakable conviction that the preaching of God's Word ought to be the centrepiece and focus on the Lord's Day, when the church comes together for worship. This chapter will examine some of the biblical convictions that undergird faithful preaching.

Heartfelt commitment to the primacy of preaching in the church's corporate gatherings is disconcertingly rare nowadays. Across the broad landscape of popular evangelicalism, music is typically regarded as the highest form of worship, and the sermon is seen as almost an intrusion on worship. The chief musician is commonly called 'the worship leader,' even if there is nothing truly worshipful in the way he leads the service. Such a person might imagine his primary duty is to stir the emotions of the congregation and keep them entertained. Indeed, most churchgoers have been taught and conditioned to think worship has not really occurred unless they have been made to feel a rush of well-being and exhilaration.

Meanwhile, sermons are often short and shallow and devoid of deep biblical instruction. In the typical twenty-first-century megachurch, what the pastor gives in place of biblical exposition is more like a TED talk, a motivational speech, or a comedy routine. Real preaching has fallen on hard times, because storytellers, pop psychologists, and stand-up comics have little use for doctrine, reproof, correction, and instruction in righteousness. The time *has* come, as the apostle foretold, when people simply 'will not endure sound doctrine; but after their own lusts ... they heap to themselves teachers, having itching ears and ... turn away their ears from the truth ... unto fables' (2 Tim. 4:3-4 KJV).

For the past half-century or more, raw pragmatism has dominated books and seminary courses on pastoral ministry, indoctrinating multiple generations of pastors with the bizarre notion that one of the greatest hindrances to effective ministry is a sermon with too much biblical content. The most widely-read book on church ministry in the past hundred years cautions pastors not to start their sermons with a biblical text. 'You cannot start with a text expecting the unchurched to be fascinated by it,'[1] that bestselling author intones. That claim flatly contradicts the thoroughly biblical philosophy that was so well described by D. Martyn Lloyd-Jones, arguably the twentieth century's finest biblical expositor. He wrote, 'A sermon should not start with the subject as such; it should start with the Scripture which has in it a doctrine or a theme.'[2] Lloyd-Jones continued:

---

1. Rick Warren, *The Purpose Driven Church* (Grand Rapids: Zondervan, 1995), 295.
2. David Martyn Lloyd-Jones, *Preaching and Preachers* (Grand Rapids: Zondervan, 1971), 72.

> You must begin with the exposition of your passage or single verse. This is essential, this is vital; as I have said, all preaching must be expository. You do not start with a thought, even though it be a right thought, a good thought; you do not start with that, and then work out an address on that ... It should be clear to people that what we are saying is something that comes out of the Bible. We are presenting the Bible and its message. That is why I am one of those who like to have a pulpit Bible. It should always be there and it should always be open, to emphasise the fact that the preacher is preaching out of it.[3]

Instead, the philosophy that dominates popular religion today spurns those principles and purposely caters to the interests and desires of unconverted people. The new strategy is clearly and succinctly stated in the same book that tells pastors the Bible should not be their starting point. Here is the type of thinking that shapes the liturgy of Sunday morning church gatherings throughout the mainstream of large-movement evangelicalism today:

> Create a service that is intentionally designed for your members to bring their friends to. And make the service so attractive, appealing, and relevant to the unchurched that your members are eager to share it with lost people they care about.[4]

Thus the corporate gatherings of the visible church today are purposely ordered to suit the tastes and indulge the feelings of unconverted people. The result, of course, is not worship at all. It is not a sacrifice of praise offered to God; it is entertainment used as a tool of manipulation. It may leave congregants high-spirited and intoxicated with feelings of enjoyment and satisfaction, but good feelings *per se* are not proof that real worship has taken place. True worship points to the majesty and holiness of God. It results in joy, exultation, deep gratitude, and effusive praise, but those feelings (if genuine) are always undergirded by a deep, penitent humility. Such a response can be wrought only by the work of God's Word in the heart of the worshiper.

---

3. Ibid., 75.
4. Warren, 253.

Therefore, the pinnacle and primary feature of our corporate gatherings should be the declaration and exposition of God's Word. Biblical preaching is not something distinct from worship; it is a true and essential expression of worship. Those who preach, as well as those who hear with ears of faith, are all engaged in an act of worship, extolling and exalting the glory of God—and responding with glad submission to his Word. That is the pure essence of genuine worship. Scripture not only makes clear that the preaching of God's Word is the primary duty of a pastor; it also emphatically warns against catering to the whims and wishes of people who have no tolerance for biblical instruction. Here are the apostle Paul's final instructions on pastoral ministry, written to his best-known protégé in the last epistle he wrote before giving his life for Christ's sake. He underscores the priority of biblical preaching:

> I solemnly charge you in the presence of God and of Christ Jesus, who is to judge the living and the dead, and by His appearing and His kingdom: preach the word; be ready in season and out of season; reprove, rebuke, exhort, with great patience and teaching. For the time will come when they will not endure sound doctrine, but wanting to have their ears tickled, they will accumulate for themselves teachers in accordance to their own desires, and will turn away their ears from the truth and will turn aside to myths. But you, be sober in all things, endure hardship, do the work of an evangelist, fulfil your ministry (2 Tim. 4:1-5, LSB).

Notice the strategy Paul commends to Timothy has nothing to do with seeking more inventive or entertaining means of trying to reach a new generation. In fact, while acknowledging the difficult challenges of ministry in a generation where people simply have no taste for Scripture and sound doctrine, Paul's answer was a straightforward and unequivocal reaffirmation of the primacy and centrality of the preached Word. Rather than pandering to the feelings and felt needs of the audience, the wise preacher will cultivate in his people a healthy appetite for the spiritual nourishment the flock truly needs.

Scripture is, after all, the Word of God, and it is essential for spiritual growth. Christians ought to crave it the way infants demand to be fed—urgently, frequently, zealously (1 Pet. 2:2). In Jesus' words, 'Man shall not live by bread alone, but by every word that proceedeth out of the mouth of God.' God's Word is therefore to be proclaimed fearlessly and faithfully—regardless of how the winds of fashion seem to be blowing. The priority for pastors is clear: 'Preach the word . . . in season and out of season' (v. 2).

It is significant that those familiar words come in the verse immediately preceding Paul's prophetic warning about seasons of apathy and indifference. A time was coming when people's interest in God's Word would be so severely diminished that they would simply not tolerate doctrinal instruction. But before he even mentions that fact, Paul instructs Timothy how to respond. He knows (and he wants Timothy to be reminded) that Scripture is the only source of the spiritual nourishment people are starving for.

Paul then lays out a complete philosophy of ministry for the preacher in nine simple imperatives.

Remember to Whom You Are Accountable

Bear in mind that this is the final chapter in the final inspired epistle from the pen of the apostle. He was looking forward to a time not far hence when he would stand before God to give an account, and his own anticipation of that judgment no doubt filled his heart and mind. So, he reminded Timothy that the young pastor would likewise one day be called to give account before God. He prefaces his instructions to Timothy with this solemn invocation: 'I charge thee therefore before God, and the Lord Jesus Christ, who shall judge the quick and the dead at his appearing and his kingdom' (v. 1 KJV). He was urging Timothy to live and work in light of the impending judgment. Timothy needed to fear God more than he feared the opinions of people.

'We shall all stand before the judgment seat of Christ ... So then every one of us shall give account of himself to God' (Rom. 14:10, 12 KJV). The faithful preacher who remains steadfastly conscious of his ultimate accountability to God will not be susceptible to the paralysing fear of human opinion. 'Do I seek to please men? For if I yet pleased men, I should not be the servant of Christ' (Gal. 1:10 KJV).

Preach the Word

Paul begins to close his last epistle by summing up his advice to Timothy in the fewest words possible. He has penned two inspired epistles to Timothy, full of counsel that all points (in one way or another) to Timothy's chief duty, which Paul now states in three simple words: 'Preach the word' (v. 2). Nothing should ever dissuade or distract a pastor from that task. No approach to pastoral ministry is sound and faithful if it diminishes or downplays the preeminent place of biblical preaching.

The word pastor means 'shepherd.' And it is true that properly shepherding the flock of God entails a host of duties, including things like visiting the sick, showing hospitality, and otherwise serving people's multifaceted needs—from seeking those who stray, to mourning with those who mourn (and countless similar tasks whereby the shepherd tends the flock). It is a calling that requires a true servant's heart.

But the chief duty of any minister is to be a faithful shepherd—one who leads and feeds the flock. In a church, those two aspects of shepherding emanate primarily from the pulpit, through the preaching ministry. Again: God's Word is the ultimate and only infallible source for both the nourishment and the guidance the flock requires. That is why preaching is primary. Careful, accurate biblical exposition requires hard work, so the pulpit is no place for a lazy man. Furthermore, no preacher who is true to the text can expect constant acclaim. 'Yea, and all that will live godly in Christ Jesus shall suffer persecution' (3:12 KJV). It is, therefore, easy to succumb to pressure or fear. In the pulpit, timidity finds no rightful place. After all, the message we are called to proclaim is (without apology) an offense to some and foolishness to others (1 Cor. 1:23; Gal. 5:11). Christ himself is a stone of stumbling and a rock of offense (Rom. 9:33; 1 Pet. 2:8). Multitudes will reject the message, heap scorn upon the messenger, or turn away in anger.

Everyone to some degree, naturally craves affirmation. Obviously, then, preaching is not a task for weak men who cannot master the impulse to seek adulation.

Timothy may have been naturally a somewhat timid soul. Paul therefore reminded him, 'God hath not given us the spirit of fear; but of power, and of love, and of a sound mind' (2 Tim. 1:7 KJV). He implored the younger man not to be 'ashamed of the testimony of our Lord, nor of me his prisoner: but be thou partaker of the afflictions of the gospel according to the power of God' (v. 8 KJV). Thus he pointed Timothy to a strength that lay outside himself. He urged him to rely on the power of God, which is the only source any preacher of the Word should ever look to for the energy, toughness, and courage we need in the face of worldly opposition. Those who are merely self-reliant will invariably default to the ear-tickling approach Paul condemns in this passage.

Timothy was an eyewitness to Paul's suffering, probably over an extended period of time. The apostle's trials were fierce and extraordinary (2 Cor. 11:23-28). The peril had now reached its apex; Paul was literally on the brink of being put to death for the gospel's sake. The danger was so great that everyone except Luke in Paul's own missionary team had forsaken him (2 Tim. 4:11). Timothy's close association with Paul was well known, and that fact probably meant Timothy was also in imminent danger. Preaching the gospel in Ephesus certainly would have incurred opposition from civic officials and Jews who were hostile to Christ. Paul's preaching had once sparked a riot there (Acts 19:21-32).

Timothy therefore knew he faced the very real prospect that he might be called upon to suffer or die for the gospel's sake. It is perhaps not surprising that he was somewhat apprehensive about preaching. When Paul exhorted him to proclaim God's Word boldly, he was, in essence, encouraging the young pastor to overcome every innate human inclination and inhibition that would hinder him.

Paul stressed the singularity of what Timothy was to preach: "The word"—Scripture. Paul had just reminded Timothy that God's Word is the supreme authority and the only profitable and legitimate source of material for any preacher's sermons. 'All Scripture is given by inspiration of God, and is profitable for doctrine, for reproof, for correction, for instruction in righteousness' (2 Tim. 3:16 KJV). At the beginning of this epistle, Paul had given a similar charge: 'Hold fast the form of sound words, which thou hast heard of me' (1:13 KJV). He spoke of Scripture as a treasure that had been entrusted to Timothy (v. 14, cf. 1 Tim. 6:20).

Paul's exhortation was clear: Timothy should immerse himself in the study of the Word, diligently handling it with precision (2:15). He must preach the Word boldly despite his natural apprehension. Virtually all the counsel Paul has given Timothy he now condenses and summarizes in those three words: 'Preach the word.' Faithfully preaching the Word is undeniably the top priority in pastoral ministry according to Scripture.

The apostle frequently made clear that he himself saw preaching as his first and most important duty. In Colossians 1:25, he wrote, 'I was made a minister according to the stewardship from God given to me for you, so that I might fully carry out the preaching of the word of God' (LSB). It wasn't oratory or eloquence that he commended, but a clear proclamation of the truth. And he was not interested in polishing the truth, sanding off its sharp edges, or omitting any of the features that people find offensive. He wrote to the church at Corinth: 'For after that in the wisdom of God the world by wisdom knew not God, it pleased God by the foolishness of preaching to save them that believe' (1 Cor. 1:21 KJV). The phrase can be rendered this way: 'God was well-pleased, through the foolishness of the message preached, to save those who believe' (LSB). No matter what people think of it, or how they respond to it, the message is not to be modified.

Thus, the apostle identifies what he considered to be his own supreme priority, both as a pastor and as an evangelist. It is the noble task of preaching. Nothing—not fear of persecution, nor the weight of public opinion, nor someone's stylish, pragmatic approach to ministry—should ever motivate a minister to muzzle the preaching of God's Word. Any man who yields an inch under pressure to tone down the pulpit has abdicated his high calling.

Be Faithful In and Out of Season

Preaching is the heart and soul of church ministry. This non-negotiable fact does not change whenever there is a shift in public opinion. Paul's instructions to Timothy were clear. He was to preach the Word whether preaching was popular or not—'in season and out of season' (4:2). We are obviously living in an era when preaching the Word is 'out of season' and totally out of style. A faithful pastor will not flinch in the face of such trends; he will continue preaching the Word—earnestly, powerfully, faithfully, and with unwavering resolve—because he not only believes this is God's Word; he also is personally submissive to its commands. Paul wants to see that kind of steely commitment in Timothy. He wants him to 'be instant in season, out of season.' That way of employing the word 'instant' is now archaic. In the early seventeenth century, when the Authorized Version was translated, the word included the sense of readiness, preparedness, availability, and eagerness. It translates a Greek term: *ephistemi*. That was a military term meaning 'to stand beside,' and it described the attitude of a guard, always at his post, on the watch, prepared. Timothy was supposed to be always fully equipped, eager to preach, ready to preach—even when people did not seem particularly ready to hear.

Reprove, Rebuke, and Exhort

The apostle Paul proceeded to delineate the essential elements of a well-rounded sermon. Effective preaching, he emphasised, encompasses three essential components: reproof, rebuke, and exhortation. It is striking that two of these components bear a negative connotation, involving the correction of error or misguided behaviour. Exhortation, however, is the encouraging aspect of preaching—a warm-hearted entreaty and incitement to positive action.

Proclaiming the whole counsel of God requires the preacher to maintain a balance. Scripture is full of both positives and negatives. This is a definitional aspect of the whole counsel of God: 'All Scripture is given by inspiration of God, and is profitable for doctrine, for reproof, for correction, for instruction in righteousness.' (2 Tim. 3:16 KJV) Always, there is a proper balance of correction (the negative) and exhortation (the positive).

So, the faithful preacher will not shy away from rebuke and correction. Nevertheless, his ultimate aims are edification and encouragement. And he pursues the task patiently and diligently—'with all longsuffering and doctrine.' (4:2 KJV) As Timothy's mentor and living example, Paul had modelled that balance, exhorting and comforting and beseeching people 'as a father doth his children' (1 Thess. 2:11 KJV).

Don't Compromise in Difficult Times

For a timid soul such as Timothy seems to have been, the outlook from a human perspective was bleak. Not only was the apostle about to be put to death; the whole church was facing even more difficult times in the days to come. And one of the greatest difficulties would be apathy and even hostility toward preaching—this antagonistic attitude coming from within the church itself:

> For the time will come when they will not endure sound doctrine; but after their own lusts shall they heap to themselves teachers, having itching ears; and they shall turn away their ears from the truth, and shall be turned unto fables (2 Tim. 4:3-4 KJV).

Timothy had heard similar warnings from Paul before. In 1 Tim. 4:1 (KJV), the apostle wrote, 'Now the Spirit speaketh expressly, that in the latter times some shall depart from the faith, giving heed to seducing spirits, and doctrines of devils.' He repeated the warning:

> This know also, that in the last days perilous times shall come. For men shall be lovers of their own selves, covetous, boasters, proud, blasphemers, disobedient to parents, unthankful, unholy, without natural affection, trucebreakers, false accusers, incontinent, fierce, despisers of those that are good, traitors, heady, highminded, lovers of pleasures more than lovers of God; having a form of godliness, but denying the power thereof (2 Tim. 3:1-5 KJV).

We live in an age that fits that description perfectly. In such times, faithful, fearless preaching is only more vital. When there is an epidemic of hostility toward the truth and people have no taste for listening to the preaching of God's Word, the need for clear, compelling, potent preaching is greater, not less. If preachers tone down their message to accommodate the spirit of the age, they are merely advancing the success of the enemy's strategy.

Ear-tickling preaching is the exact opposite of what Paul wanted Timothy to be known for. He therefore warned Timothy to stay at the task of preaching God's Word in all its dynamic truth—even if people found preaching distasteful. Don't give into those with 'itching ears [who] turn away their ears from the truth' (2 Tim. 4:3 KJV). Don't cater to popular tastes. Don't pander to people's felt needs. Don't think you can be more relevant than Scripture already is. Don't fall for the lie that 'too much Bible' will alienate the people you want to reach. Don't permit opinion polls to dictate the content of your sermons.

There is an irony here. When biblical instruction is out of season, the problem that ensues is not a shortage of teachers and teaching. Just the opposite. It opens the door to a glut of ear-tickling teachers who promote fables and falsehoods. Marvin Vincent, a Presbyterian scholar from the late nineteenth century, saw this same trend in his era:

> In periods of unsettled faith, scepticism, and mere curious speculation in matters of religion, teachers of all kinds swarm like the flies in Egypt. The demand creates the supply. The hearers invite and shape their own preachers. If the people desire a calf to worship, a ministerial calf-maker is readily found.[5]

Feeding the appetites that spring from people's felt needs leads inevitably to spiritual catastrophe. People who heap to themselves teachers who will scratch their itching ears soon 'turn away their ears from the truth ... unto fables' (2 Tim. 4:3-4 KJV). Their own deliberate refusal to hear the truth predictably drives them into error.

---

5. Marvin R. Vincent, *Word Studies in the New Testament*, 4 vols. (New York: Scribner's, 1900), 4:321.

This whole passage chronicles precisely the course of the evangelical movement over the past century and a half, with the problem accelerating. What the apostle Paul predicted has unfolded before our eyes. Multitudes of evangelicals have lost their tolerance for careful, didactic, biblical preaching, and they demand instead to be entertained. Pastors have acquiesced to public opinion. Now it is rare to find a church where either pastors or people are willing to distinguish truth from falsehood. Having turned aside from the truth, they became susceptible to all kinds of fables, fabrications, and false worldviews.

When a preacher caters to public opinion or fears the world's contempt or opposition, his inclination will be to soften the biblical message, try to hide or eliminate the scandal of the cross, and give people a message that suits their tastes. Scripture condemns all such man-pleasing motives.

Be Sober in All Things

One powerful (and essential) deterrent to that man-pleasing impulse is a godly, sober-minded watchfulness. Paul tells Timothy, 'But watch thou in all things' (v. 5 KJV). He employs a Greek term that speaks of sobriety, and that is how the verse is translated in most modern Bible versions: 'Be sober in all things' (LSB). Paul was not here warning Timothy against drunkenness. Nor was he suggesting that Timothy should assume a sombre, sullen, doleful disposition. Paul was calling him to vigilance, steadfastness and self-control—watchful, consistent, mature stability. Paul was urging Timothy to grow spiritually into full Christlike manhood—to be steady and serious-minded, to bring his passions (especially, perhaps, his fear of opposition) under complete control. This kind of sobriety is the polar opposite of the flaky, whimsical, superficial, celebrity-type televangelists who colour the public perception of preachers today. He wanted Timothy to be well rooted and grounded, steadfast, rock-solid—and always on guard against any effort to dissuade him from his work. It is an echo of Paul's admonition in 1 Corinthians, applied to the preacher: 'Be steadfast, immovable, always abounding in the work of the Lord, knowing that your toil is not in vain in the Lord' (1 Cor. 15:58 NASB).

Endure Hardship

As we have already noted, a yearning for earthly applause underlies much of the nervous compromise that has paralysed modern pulpits. Too many preachers have an unhealthy fixation with earthly standards of success. They are actually sabotaged by a craving for worldly acclaim. How can their preaching bear genuine spiritual fruit if their driving motive is to avoid the hardship that follows when people are offended at the message? Hardship is an inevitable by-product of all faithful ministry. 'Yea, and all that will live godly in Christ Jesus shall suffer persecution' (2 Tim. 3:12 KJV).

The church I pastor has trained and sent numerous young men into pastoral ministry. Every now and then, one of these young men tells me he hopes to find a church without significant problems—a ministry where he can preach and minister without opposition. The desire is understandable, but there is no such place for the faithful preacher of the Word. Ministry cannot be both effective and painless. Those who preach the Word faithfully must expect to encounter hardship, and they have to be willing to endure such trials, or they will be seized by fear and unable to minister effectively. Hardship, an inevitable part of every faithful preacher's life, must be embraced along with every other aspect of our calling.

It is likely that Timothy was on the verge of severe hardship when Paul wrote this epistle. One of the last verses in the book of Hebrews says, 'Know ye that our brother Timothy is set at liberty; with whom, if he come shortly, I will see you' (13:23 KJV). Evidently, at the very time Hebrews was written, Timothy was being released from imprisonment somewhere. So apparently he did suffer great hardship for his faithfulness in the ministry. Perhaps the apostle Paul knew a trial like that—or perhaps an even greater one—was coming to Timothy when he wrote this epistle.

Whatever the historical circumstances, Timothy's fear of hardship becomes a running theme in 2 Timothy. Paul wrote: 'Be not thou therefore ashamed of the testimony of our Lord, nor of me his prisoner: but be thou partaker of the afflictions of the gospel according to the power of God ...' (2 Tim. 1:8 KJV) 'Endure hardness, as a good soldier of Jesus Christ' (2:3 KJV). He reminded Timothy of the eternal value of suffering for Christ and for the gospel: 'Therefore I endure all things for the elect's sakes, that they may also obtain the salvation which is in Christ Jesus with eternal glory' (2:10 KJV). And he testified that God's grace had sustained him through his own sufferings: 'Persecutions, afflictions, which came unto me at Antioch, at Iconium, at Lystra; what persecutions I endured: but out of them all the Lord delivered me' (3:11 KJV). 'At my first answer no man stood with me, but all men forsook me: I pray God that it may not be laid to their charge. Notwithstanding the Lord stood with me, and strengthened me; that by me the preaching might be fully known, and that all the Gentiles might hear: and I was delivered out of the mouth of the lion' (4:16-17 KJV).

Paul had faced incredible hardship for many years without any relief. But the Lord strengthened him, sustained him, and at times pulled him from the very jaws of his tormenters. So, Paul learned to remain faithful and to lean on the Lord for strength, regardless of his circumstances (cf. Phil. 4:11-13). Paul did not want his young disciple to be paralysed by fear of hardship, and thus miss the blessing Paul had enjoyed. Timothy just needed to trust the Lord in all his trials.

Do the Work of an Evangelist

Timothy's fears of opposition, popular opinion, and the hostility and ridicule aimed at gospel preachers may have been causing him to seek a comfort zone, by avoiding outreach to people who were not always sympathetic to his ministry. So, Paul adds this command: 'Do the work of an evangelist' (v. 5). I do not believe Paul meant that Timothy was supposed to fill the office of an itinerant evangelist rather than that of a pastor-teacher (cf. Eph. 4:11). Paul was teaching that evangelism is part of the work of a pastor, too.

This fits perfectly with the themes of Paul's message to Timothy: He was to declare the truth boldly. He had to set aside his fears. He needed to step outside the comfort-zone of his own flock. He needed to take his ministry to the front lines, face his opposition courageously, and preach without fear.

Fulfil Your Ministry

Paul concludes his charge to Timothy with this final imperative: 'make full proof of thy ministry' (v. 5 KJV). The Greek word translated 'make full proof' is *plerophoreō*—meaning 'carry it out fully; perform all of it thoroughly.' He employs the same word later, in verse 17: 'The Lord stood with me, and strengthened me; that by me the preaching might be fully known [*plerophoreō*], and that all the Gentiles might hear' (KJV). He was urging Timothy to cultivate the same steadfast courage. He was imploring him not to cave in to half-heartedness and craven fear, but to carry out his ministry with all his might.

Still, the heart of Paul's charge to Timothy is that three-word phrase at the start of v. 2: κηρυξον τον λογον: 'Preach the word.' All the imperatives that follow explain precisely how Timothy was to preach. Thus, this passage defines what faithful biblical preaching is to be like: There is no place for timidity. There is no time for delay. There is no latitude to adjust the message to suit the spirit of the age. The preacher of the Word must be bold, thorough, unrelenting, persevering in the face of hardship and opposition—and above all, fearless.

Anything less is unworthy of a true minister of Christ.

CHAPTER FIVE

Doctrine

Jonathan Master

"Sound doctrine does not enter into a hard and disobedient heart."
Justin Martyr

The health of the church is dependent on sound doctrine. The church stands as, 'a pillar and buttress of the truth' (1 Tim. 3:15), and sound doctrine is her heartbeat. So Paul wrote to Titus, 'But as for you, teach what accords with sound doctrine' (Titus 2:1), which is the positive command corresponding to Jesus's negative warning: 'In vain do they worship me, teaching as doctrines the commandments of men' (Matt. 15:9; Mark 7:7). Sound doctrine—*didaskalia*—is vital to the worship, teaching, and mission of the church. If it is removed or distorted, the church ceases to exist or function as ordained by God and governed by Jesus Christ.

It is not merely that God expects the church to preserve, teach, and worship according to the truths of sound doctrine, it is also that sound doctrine is inextricably linked with right behaviour. Most of the places in the Scripture which address sound doctrine do so by explicitly connecting it to a certain kind of action. Orthodoxy leads to orthopraxy. In fact, often the Scriptures commend sound doctrine on precisely those grounds. It is vital as the only way of preserving the kind of life suited to a Christian.

This stream between doctrine and practice flows in both directions. Understanding doctrine clearly and well—really comprehending it—is essential to Christian piety; but, in a similar way, a life of genuine Christian piety is itself the only proper posture for engaging in doctrinal study. This is especially true when engaging in doctrinal correction or debate. It would be a contradiction of the principles of sound doctrine to consider it in isolation from a consideration of practice. A life united to Jesus Christ, committed to serving God in the power of the Holy Spirit is both the outcome of sound doctrine and the only suitable condition of anyone presuming to teach it.

This raises an important question about the origin and organisation of sound doctrine. What is the source for the church's doctrine? How is it to be derived and structured? These are matters of critical significance. How can the church act as a pillar and buttress of a truth that is undefined? How can doctrine be clearly taught if its order and structure—its inner logic—is not well established?

To answer these questions we must examine: Firstly, the foundation of Christian doctrine, which lies in God's revelation; Secondly, we must understand the logic of doctrine, which is outlined for us in the Scriptures; Thirdly, we must give attention to the reality that sound doctrine is never divorced from life—rightly understood, it is inseparably connected to practices which are in keeping with the glorious gospel of Jesus Christ.

The Foundation of Doctrine: God Has Spoken

John Calvin, in his justly famous introductory sentence of the *Institutes*, wrote, 'Nearly all the wisdom we possess, that is to say, true and sound wisdom, consists of two parts: the knowledge of God and of ourselves.'[1] This true knowledge of God and of

---

1. John Calvin, *Institutes of the Christian Religion*, I:1.

ourselves is the substance of sound doctrine, and it must rest on revelation. Herman Bavinck summarises this:

> All knowledge of God rests on revelation. Though we can never know God in the full richness of his being, he is known to all people through his revelation in creation, the theatre of his glory. The world is never godless. In the end, there are no atheists; there is only argument about the nature of God. The recognition is universal of a power greater than human beings themselves, to whom they owe piety.[2]

When we examine this statement about revelation closely, we see that it is grounded upon three premises: Firstly, Bavinck assumes that human beings are contingent beings, dependent even when it comes to their knowledge of their Creator; Secondly, that the Creator has given, through both general and special revelation, a knowledge of himself to his creatures; Thirdly, that human beings are fallen creatures, searching for ways to offer worship and piety in a malformed fashion. These premises are axiomatic in the Bible. The creation account in the first chapters of Genesis reinforces both the special nature of humanity, but also the fundamental human status as a creature, contingent upon God for his being:

> Then God said, "Let us make man in our image, after our likeness. And let them have dominion over the fish of the sea and over the birds of the heavens and over the livestock and over all the earth and over every creeping thing that creeps on the earth." So God created man in his own image, in the image of God he created him; male and female he created them (Gen 1:26-27).

In one of his most famous sermons, recorded in Acts 17, Paul the apostle shows that this truth—man is a contingent creature—is both the starting place for his gospel proclamation and common ground shared with Athenian philosophers:

> So Paul, standing in the midst of the Areopagus, said: "Men of Athens, I perceive that in every way you are very religious. For as

---

2. Herman Bavinck, *Reformed Dogmatics: God and Creation*, vol 2 (Grand Rapids: Baker, 2004 trans) 53.

I passed along and observed the objects of your worship, I found also an altar with this inscription: 'To the unknown god.' What therefore you worship as unknown, this I proclaim to you. The God who made the world and everything in it, being Lord of heaven and earth, does not live in temples made by man, nor is he served by human hands, as though he needed anything, since he himself gives to all mankind life and breath and everything" (Acts 17:22-25).

Just as man's nature as a contingent creature provides a foundation for the Christian faith, so too do Bavinck's second and third premises about the revelation of God and the sinfulness of man. Clement of Alexandria, writing in the 2nd century, taught that through contemplation of creation, God is known as creator, 'by nature and apart from any instruction.'[3] He is echoed by Calvin, who writes,

> There is within the human mind, and indeed by natural instinct, an awareness of his divinity. This we take to be beyond controversy. To prevent anyone from taking refuge in the pretence of ignorance, God himself has implanted in all men a certain understanding of divine majesty. Ever renewing its memory, he repeatedly sheds fresh drops.[4]

As Bavinck points out, 'All the Reformed symbols and theologians say the same.'[5] In this, they are merely reflecting the teaching of the psalmist and of the apostle Paul. Psalm 19 is worth quoting from:

> The heavens declare the glory of God,
>   and the sky above proclaims his handiwork.
> Day to day pours out speech,
>   and night to night reveals knowledge.
> There is no speech, nor are there words,
>   whose voice is not heard.
> Their voice goes out through all the earth,
>   and their words to the end of the world (Psalm 19:1-4a).

---

3. Clement of Alexandria, *Stromata*, V, 13, 14.
4. Calvin, *Institutes*, III:1, 43-44.
5. Bavinck, *Reformed Dogmatics* vol II, 67.

The apostle Paul confirms this, combining it with a devastating indictment of humanity's fallen sinfulness:

> For what can be known about God is plain to them, because God has shown it to them. For his invisible attributes, namely, his eternal power and divine nature, have been clearly perceived, ever since the creation of the world, in the things that have been made. So they are without excuse. For although they knew God, they did not honour him as God or give thanks to him, but they became futile in their thinking, and their foolish hearts were darkened. Claiming to be wise, they became fools, and exchanged the glory of the immortal God for images resembling mortal man and birds and animals and creeping things. Therefore God gave them up in the lusts of their hearts to impurity, to the dishonouring of their bodies among themselves, because they exchanged the truth about God for a lie and worshiped and served the creature rather than the Creator, who is blessed forever! Amen (Rom 1:19-25).

This assessment of the revelation of God in creation coupled with a bleak assessment of the fallen human condition offers clear biblical support of Bavinck's assertions. And Paul's expressed view of man's condition is nothing new. The account of the Fall of Adam, recorded in Genesis 3, is followed by the record of Adam's firstborn son committing murder in Genesis 4, and this is followed closely by the comprehensive statement of Genesis 6:5: 'The Lord saw that the wickedness of man was great in the earth, and that every intention of the thoughts of his heart was only evil continually.' The psalmist writes, 'The Lord looks down from heaven on the children of man, to see if there are any who understand, who seek after God. They have all turned aside; together they have become corrupt, there is none who does good, not even one' (Ps. 14:2-3).

Yet God's revelation did not cease with humanity's rejection of general revelation. The history of the people of God is, in large measure, the history of God's revelation to a people whom he has chosen. This culminates in the revelation of his Son, the Lord Jesus Christ, who, as God, is identified as the Creator: 'Long ago, at many times and in many ways, God spoke to our fathers by the prophets, but in these last days he has spoken to us by his Son, whom he appointed the heir of all things, through whom also he created the world' (Heb. 1:1-2). This revelation of the Son is confirmed and testified to by the Holy Spirit through apostles, 'It was declared at first by the Lord, and it was attested to us by those who heard, 4 while God also bore witness by signs and wonders and various miracles and by gifts of the Holy Spirit distributed according to his will' (Heb. 2:3b-4). Therefore, for the church today, the foundation of sound doctrine is the Word of God, written by the prophets and apostles, and centred on the Lord Jesus Christ.

This is why sound doctrine is always connected with the teaching of Scripture. In 2 Timothy 3:16, Paul writes, 'All Scripture is breathed out by God and profitable for teaching, for reproof, for correction, and for training in righteousness...' In using the term for doctrine (translated by the ESV as 'teaching') he lays down one of the clear markers of Christian doctrine: it is centred on the Bible. This doctrine, as it was re-affirmed in the context of the Protestant Reformation, has often been referred to as sola scriptura—the Bible alone. As Ian Hamilton often reminds his students, this is not the same as nuda scriptura, a view held in the past by radical anabaptists as well as by some sects today. Christians emphatically must and do appeal to sources beyond the Scriptures. We look to teachers of the past and to creation. But it is the Word of God that holds authority. It alone is the *norma normans*; it is the *principium theologiae*. Against all competing authorities, whether traditions, inner-feelings, or contemporary conclusions from other sources, God's Word must reign supreme.

All this is merely another way of saying that our method of doctrine must follow that of the Lord Jesus Christ. Jesus held the Bible in the highest possible esteem. In his most famous sermon, he said:

> Do not think that I have come to abolish the Law or the Prophets; I have not come to abolish them but to fulfil them. For truly, I say to you, until heaven and earth pass away, not an iota, not a dot, will pass from the Law until all is accomplished. Therefore whoever

relaxes one of the least of these commandments and teaches others to do the same will be called least in the kingdom of heaven, but whoever does them and teaches them will be called great in the kingdom of heaven (Matt 5:17-19).

Even after his death and resurrection, it was about this very point that he rebuked his closest followers:

> "O foolish ones, and slow of heart to believe all that the prophets have spoken" … And beginning with Moses and all the Prophets, he interpreted to them in all the Scriptures the things concerning himself (Luke 24:25-27).

To assert the authority of Scripture in doctrine, therefore, is to recognise God's work in revealing himself to sinful creatures. But at least as importantly, when we affirm the Bible's unique role in this matter, we are following the guidance and instruction of our saviour, Jesus Christ. Scripture alone must be the foundation of our doctrine if we are to be Christ-like.

The Logic of Doctrine: God's Word is Ordered

The Scriptures teach that 'God is not a God of confusion' (1 Cor. 14:33) and therefore all things must be done 'decently and in order' (1 Cor. 14:40). This principle of decency and order should extend to the church's formulation and presentation of doctrine. Petrus Van Mastricht saw this truth as governing our understanding of the nature of the Scripture and thus of our presentation of doctrine:

> Surely for this reason he conferred on rational creatures the principles of order and method, that he might show that he is the author of all order and method, and also that he might direct us to preserve order and method, certainly in general, but especially in matters of great importance. And without a doubt, theological matters are of this sort. To that end, he also inspired the writing of his Scriptures by amanuenses in an order according to his choice, and yet certain and logical.[6]

---

6. Petrus Van Mastricht, *Theoretical-Practical Theology: Prolegomena*, vol 1, Beeke & Rester, eds (Grand Rapids: RHB, 2018), 68.

As Mastricht points out, a logical, systematised doctrinal presentation is not in tension with God's revelation in Scripture. It is fully in concert with the nature of Scripture and the nature of God. Scripture itself demands a systematised summary of doctrine. While all Scripture is profitable for *didaskalion* (doctrinal teaching), there are specific points within biblical revelation in which the narrative gives way to more direct doctrinal instruction.

As an example, after the exodus from Egypt and the crossing of the Red Sea, God informs the Israelites precisely how to worship and what to teach about the salvation that they recently experienced:

> Every firstborn of a donkey you shall redeem with a lamb, or if you will not redeem it you shall break its neck. Every firstborn of man among your sons you shall redeem. And when in time to come your son asks you, 'What does this mean?' you shall say to him, 'By a strong hand the Lord brought us out of Egypt, from the house of slavery. For when Pharaoh stubbornly refused to let us go, the Lord killed all the firstborn in the land of Egypt, both the firstborn of man and the firstborn of animals. Therefore I sacrifice to the Lord all the males that first open the womb, but all the firstborn of my sons I redeem' (Ex. 13:13-15).

This is a striking passage, and it illustrates a pattern repeated throughout Scripture. It recounts the events of Israel's redemption, but it clarifies and organizes them in a logical fashion so that their significance for worship and behaviour can be systematically presented.

Perhaps better known is the *shema* introduced in Deut. 6:4-6: 'Hear, O Israel: The Lord our God, the Lord is one. You shall love the Lord your God with all your heart and with all your soul and with all your might. And these words that I command you today shall be on your heart.' This is perhaps the clearest example of a doctrinal statement embedded in the Old Testament; a short creed providing foundational summary of the knowledge of the true and living God. As J.V. Fesko puts it, 'God wanted Israel to profess their faith, and he wanted their profession to protect theological orthodoxy, to express love for God, and to ground catechesis. Israel's confession was a theological guardrail to keep them on the road of biblical monotheism.'[7]

In the New Testament, the apostles speak of 'The faith once delivered' (Jude 3; see also Gal 1:23). This appears to be a body of doctrinal teaching systematising and summarising the truths revealed in Christ. Adding to this biblical witness are the various 'trustworthy sayings' presented in the New Testament (1 Tim. 1:15; 3:1; 4:7-9; 2 Tim. 2:11-13; Titus 3:4-8). 1 Timothy 4:7-9 is a particularly notable instance of the phrase, 'trustworthy saying' because it directly follows Paul's assertion in the preceding verse: 'If you put these things before the brothers, you will be a good servant of Christ Jesus, being trained in the words of the faith and of the good doctrine that you have followed' (1 Tim. 4:6). The presence of the 'trustworthy sayings', along with their close connection with sound doctrine, reinforces the notion that, like the 'faith once delivered', these were intended to be summative expressions of Christian doctrine. Mastricht writes, 'The nature of this [scriptural] theology, which, since it embraces diverse dogmas scattered throughout the vast corpus of Scripture that are among themselves mutually consistent, ordered, and aiming at the same goal, certainly requires those dogmas to be collected and constructed in a manner mutually consonant with one another.'[8]

When we begin to think about the precise connections between these 'dogmas of Scripture,' it soon becomes apparent that the Triune God, his eternal decrees, his work in creation, the fall of man, and God's saving acts, revealed in his covenant and culminating in the work of his son, Jesus Christ must take centre stage. It is notable that all the great creedal statements have placed these doctrines at the centre.

What Jesus said in condemning the religious leaders of his day—who carefully studied the Scriptures—ought not be said of

---

7. J.V. Fesko, *The Need for Creeds Today: Confessional Faith in a Faithless Age* (Grand Rapids: Baker, 2020) 5.
8. Petrus Van Mastricht, vol 1, 68.

us: 'You search the Scriptures because you think that in them you have eternal life; and it is they that bear witness about me, yet you refuse to come to me that you may have life' (John 5:39). Christ's work in creation, redemption, and in sending his Spirit, must remain at the centre of any doctrine that claims to be biblical. And as that biblical doctrine shapes biblical preaching, the model must be that of Paul, whose instruction to 'preach the word; be ready in season and out of season; reprove, rebuke, and exhort, with complete patience and teaching [lit. doctrine]' (2 Tim. 4:2), was in keeping with his practice, which was 'we preach Christ crucified' (1 Cor. 1:23a). Because, as he wrote, 'I decided to know nothing among you except Jesus Christ and him crucified' (1 Cor. 2:2).

The Possession of Sound Doctrine: God's Truth Brings Life

One of the disturbing tendencies of modern systematic theological study is its separation of doctrine from practice. This can happen even at the categorical level, when certain branches of study are labelled, 'Practical Theology,' in distinction, it must be supposed, against doctrine that is thought of as holding little practical value. It is worth noting that many, including Ian Hamilton, have stood firmly against this. And this division between doctrine and practice, however nominal, is repugnant to the New Testament. In fact, one of the striking features of the Bible's teaching on sound doctrine is the way in which it connects seamlessly with right behaviour.

The New Testament makes this connection in at least two major ways. The first is by making the link explicit. As an example of this, we might consider Paul's logic in advising Timothy how to deal with false teachers:

> For everything created by God is good, and nothing is to be rejected if it is received with thanksgiving, for it is made holy by the word of God and prayer. If you put these things before the brothers, you will be a good servant of Christ Jesus, being trained in the words of the faith and of the good doctrine that you have followed (1 Tim. 4:4-6).

Here we see an explicit positive connection between thankful reception of God's good gifts and the doctrine that Timothy and other teachers had been trained to follow. Where there was sound doctrine, there was gratitude and holiness of life. Teaching sound doctrine was an essential component of faithful service to Jesus Christ.

Secondly, the connection is drawn by identifying the absence of sound doctrine with disobedience. So, for instance, in 1 Timothy 6:3-4a, this is linked with conceit, lack of understanding, and a craving for controversy: 'If anyone teaches a different doctrine and does not agree with the sound words of our Lord Jesus Christ and the teaching that accords with godliness, he is puffed up with conceit and understands nothing. He has an unhealthy craving for controversy.' Similarly, lack of sound doctrine leads to division: 'I appeal to you, brothers, to watch out for those who cause divisions and create obstacles contrary to the doctrine that you have been taught; avoid them' (Rom. 16:17). Paul instructs Timothy to, 'charge certain persons not to teach any different doctrine' (1 Tim. 1:3b). This apparently extends to vain discussions, speculations, and even disobedience, lying, slave trading, and sexual immorality. Paul ends by mentioning, 'the sexually immoral, men who practice homosexuality, enslavers, liars, perjurers, and whatever else is contrary to sound doctrine' (1 Tim. 1:10).

What cannot be denied is that sound doctrine is connected to right practice. Paul is equally comfortable assuming that he can detect unsound doctrine by sinful behaviour and that truly sound doctrine will lead to obedience to Jesus Christ. True knowledge of God—the kind of true knowledge of which Calvin writes—come from the fear of the Lord (Prov. 1:7; 9:10). A true knowledge of God is a saving knowledge through Jesus Christ, as Jesus himself testifies: 'And this is eternal life, that they know you, the only true God, and Jesus Christ whom you have sent' (John 17:3).

Conclusion

A true knowledge of the Lord Jesus Christ and a life devoted to him is the proper objective of sound doctrine. Our wills must be governed by his Word, our minds must be conformed to the order and structure of its teaching, and our hearts must be enraptured by the beauty of Jesus Christ and the hope of heaven. Calvin, speaking of such knowledge, aptly concludes, 'Knowledge of this sort, then, ought not only to arouse us to the worship of God, but also to awaken and encourage us to the hope of the future life.'[9]

---

9. John Calvin, *Institutes*, I:10, 62.

CHAPTER SIX

Cultivating Catholic Calvinism through Religious Affections

Joel R. Beeke

In a letter on Christian unity to Archbishop Thomas Cranmer in 1552, John Calvin wrote, 'The members of the Church being severed, the body lies bleeding. So much does this concern me, that, could I be of any service, I would not grudge to cross even ten seas, if need were, on account of it.'[1] Calvin's calls for unity in the church would probably not sit well with some modern-day Calvinists who condemn, reject, or even excommunicate believers over minor doctrinal differences. To make that point, Ian Hamilton once declared, 'I'm not sure if Calvin would be "kosher" enough today to be invited to a Reformed conference.'[2]

Catholic Calvinism is not an oxymoron. Calvinism normally embraces a warm catholicity and, if understood correctly, promotes experiential, irenic, and contagiously warm Christianity. As B. B. Warfield observed, the core of Calvinism is not simply

---

1. John Calvin to Archbishop Thomas Cranmer, 1552, in *Letters of John Calvin*, ed. Jules Bonnet (Philadelphia: Presbyterian Board of Publication, 1858), 2:348. I thank Fraser Jones for his assistance and research on this chapter.
2. Ian Hamilton, '*Godly Catholicity*,' lecture, Calvinism and the Christian Life series, Ligonier Ministries, https://www.ligonier.org/learn/series/calvinism-and-the-christian-life/godly-catholicity.

predestination; rather, it is the overwhelming sense of human nothingness upon encountering God's glory.[3] In believers, this magnificent realisation blossoms into a thriving garden of religious affections and Spirit-worked impressions, transforming the emotions and the will.

Religious affections and catholic Calvinism, then, are inseparable, which also exemplifies the character and godliness of my good friend Ian Hamilton. This makes the title of this chapter assigned to me so apropos for his festschrift. For as many years as I have known Ian, I have observed that he is a thinker but not a fighter. He chooses to see good in his fellow Christians as much as possible. And perhaps even more importantly, I have never been with him without being edified by his humble wisdom and godly demeanour. I thank him for modelling this and feel that he should be the one writing this chapter for me to learn from.

After defining what catholic Calvinism is, I aim in this chapter to expound the catholicity of Calvinism in five religious affections—love, humility, meekness, peace, and trust—and show how each of these promote what may be called "catholic Calvinism."

What Is Catholic Calvinism?

Catholic means universal, orthodox, and apostolic Christian unity in contrast to sectarianism, factionalism, and heresy; while *catholicity* is the cluster of religious affections that true believers share when they recognize their Spirit-based unity in Christ through the gospel. *Catholic Calvinism*, therefore, is Reformed theology that embraces such Christocentric unity. To be a catholic Calvinist is to promote, within a Reformed framework, the visible unity that Christ desires for his church (John 17:21), which flows out of genuine union with Christ, both among Reformed Christians and among gospel-believing Christians from other traditions.

Let me be clear about what catholicity is not. Catholicity has nothing to do with Roman Catholicism, which is by no means

---

3. See Ian Hamilton, *The Gospel-Shaped Life* (Edinburgh: Banner of Truth, 2017).

catholic in the sense of universal, orthodox, and apostolic. Neither is catholicity quasi-unity with heretical groups or unorthodox denominations through institutional cooperation and force-fitted mergers. We do not call for the nebulous and least-common-denominator ecumenism that marked the ecumenical and interfaith movements of the last century. Calvinists who embrace catholicity do not discard doctrinal convictions and passion, for they remain zealous in treasuring even the finest grains of truth. Catholic Calvinism, then, avoids the two pitfalls against which Anthony Burgess warned: rigid and external uniformity on the one hand (like Rome), and unprincipled toleration on the other (like many Protestant churches today).[4]

As Richard Baxter observed, ecclesiastical pluriformity is inevitable: varying backgrounds, temperaments, and cultures produce diversity in the universal church.[5] After all, the church is not a single-celled organism but a complex one. This very complexity, however, is evidence of a healthy, unified body (1 Cor. 12:12). Catholicity is not strict theological uniformity, for the unity of the cruciform community is rather expressed in Spirit-worked religious affections practiced in the inevitable milieu of pluriformity.

The Holy Spirit distributes gifts, including theological acumen, to different members within the body of Christ. Calvinists believe not only that God sovereignly elects and saves sinners but also that every ray of spiritual enlightenment among believers, including insights in Reformed theology, are gifts from the sovereign God, flowing out of personal and experiential union and communion with Christ, being worked by his Word and Spirit. Weakness among believers who lack theological rigour is not ground for mockery and censoriousness but impetus for godly interaction between the strong and the weak. Recognising their place as members of a larger body, catholic Calvinists view the riches of Reformed theology

---

4. Anthony Burgess, *Advancing Christian Unity*, ed. Matthew Vogan (Grand Rapids: Reformation Heritage Books, 2019), 66-8.

5. Richard Baxter, *The Practical Works of Richard Baxter* (Ligonier, Pa.: Soli Deo Gloria, 1990), 4:716-9.

across denominational lines as both a privilege and a pleasure, for it is part of the glorious mission of building up the body of Christ.

Without abandoning theological convictions, catholic Calvinists also consider how they can adjust, adapt, and expand their theological system even as they interact with true believers with whom they disagree on minor doctrines. Every true member of the Christian body contributes to the health and growth of the entire organism as it progresses toward the fullness of maturity in Christ (Eph. 4:7-16). Thus, catholic Calvinists do not consider believers in other gospel-centered denominations as enemies or partners but as brothers and sisters in Christ. Recognizing the objective catholicity—the common faith in God's Word and his Son, Jesus Christ—that believers share should promote lifestyles, attitudes, and interactions fuelled by religious affections such as love, humility, meekness, peace, and hope.

The five religious affections treated here are representative of the full spectrum of virtues necessary to cultivate catholicity, which includes spiritual fruits such as joy, wisdom, faithfulness, compassion, perseverance, and self-control. All are descriptions of the single phenomenon of Spirit-worked fruitfulness. The five affections considered here, however, have been selected because they most directly promote catholicity. The order is intentional: love and hope bookend the list because they are foundational to each religious affection, while humility, meekness, and peace form a causal chain.

Love and Catholic Calvinism

To love is to cherish. Love of the brethren is cherishing or valuing those who we know are brothers and sisters in Christ. As such, love is an essential part of self-sacrifice for the glory of God and the good of man.[6] In regeneration, the Holy Spirit unites believers to the God of love and to one another. When the Spirit implants love in believers' hearts, they are no longer bent inward but

---

6. According to 1 Corinthians 13:1-3, there can be witness, preaching of the Word, care for the poor, and self-sacrifice without love. So love must be a factor in its own right.

become outward-focused and blissfully self-forgetful. Love is an overflowing virtue. Unlike a parasite that sucks nutrients out of its host, love delights in giving rather than taking, drawing from the infinite fullness of God's love, and pouring out its *esse* for the *bene esse* of the other in costly oblations of time, money, and energy.

Tracing Paul's manifold description of love in 1 Corinthians 13, we see that love directs us to point other believers to the truth with a kind, humble, and gracious temperament. Love is patient when others are slow to learn new concepts (including doctrines like divine sovereignty in salvation). Love promotes godly catholicity because it is cool-spirited and stable, free from the burning fires of selfishness, envy, and strife. Godly catholicity also promotes candid, generous, and loving dialogue with gospel-believing Christians from other theological perspectives. Love promotes godly catholicity because it precludes envy and stimulates joy. It does not envy the ministerial advancements of faithful men and denominations but rejoices when they flourish. It even rejoices when Christ is preached by human instruments driven by envy and strife (Phil. 1:15-18).

How Does Love Promote Catholic Calvinism?

Christianity is a diverse and global movement. It fosters unity, moving Reformed Christians to lovingly embrace our millions-strong spiritual family around the world, represented in many faithful churches. How enriching, elevating, and enlarging it is to expand the horizons of our tangible unity to the ends of the earth. For example, when we share the gospel, we are not doing so as solo evangelists. Instead, we minister as part of the grand project of the Great Commission with other believers, majoring in the majors when we evangelise others. When we partake of the Lord's Supper, we are expressing our union with all believers in all times and places, as well as our union with Christ. When we pray in the first-person plural, 'Our Father in heaven,' we are praying with not only Jesus Christ, our Mediator, but with all true believers throughout the world in sacred unison. Let us avoid sectarianism manifested in exclusively thinking about, praying for, and associating with believers only in our own church, as though ours is the only true church.

Calvinists can promote catholicity by loving the worldwide family of believers through prayer. Do not limit your prayers to your local church or denomination but also pray for other congregations and denominations, both in your country and around the world. Stay informed about persecuted believers and developments in evangelistic endeavours overseas, both within and outside your denomination, so you can fervently pray for your brothers and sisters suffering and labouring for Christ (Heb. 13:3). As you pray, realise that you are part of a chorus of voices rising to God from Christ's sheep from every tribe, tongue, people, and nation like incense from earth to heaven (Rev. 5:8).

Love cultivates catholicity by motivating Christians to promote physical flourishing among other believers. Catholic Calvinists demonstrate their unity with true believers of many denominations by providing food, clothing, shelter, money, medicine, hospitality, companionship, and counsel where it is needed, both locally and globally. Consider showing hospitality—literally, "the love of strangers" (φιλοξενία)—by opening your home to fellow Christians in the community, even those who are not part of your congregation.

Love moves Reformed Christians to foster spiritual flourishing among other believers. As members of one body in Christ and partakers of one Spirit, we should share our gifts and graces to build up other believers into the fullness of maturity in Christ. We must strive to understand the full counsel of God and communicate that counsel to fellow believers (Acts 20:20, 27). If the Holy Spirit has provided us the capacity and opportunities to expand our knowledge, including gaining insights into the Reformed faith, we are debtors to use these gifts to build up the church. On the local level, joyfully participate in God-glorifying conferences that are gospel-centred. On the international level, consider stewarding your theological education by training pastors overseas. Join forces with other Christians in promoting evangelism and missions in love to the elect (3 John 5-8).

Humility and Catholic Calvinism

Humility is the disposition that acknowledges the nothingness of self in the glorious, majestic, and magnificent presence of God. Ironically, considering humility as lowering ourselves manifests our sinful pride, for it assumes we have something worth boasting of. Instead, genuine humility acknowledges that self is lowly and only descends from its carnal arrogance, not from reality. While love edifies (or builds up), pride is like a balloon that puffs up without substance (1 Cor. 8:1). If humility were a person, one might conclude that it would be a Calvinist, for it understands that everything it is and has, is from God. If a humble person has any knowledge or skill, he regards himself as having God's treasure in an empty vessel and is charged with the duty of channelling that treasure to others.

Tragically, it is true that the classic 'cage-stage Calvinist' is often a far cry from the humble carpenter from Nazareth. After all, is not anti-anti-intellectualism (double negative intended!) essential to Reformed Christianity? Theological excellence is indeed important to Calvinism, but a proud spirit is not; it is antithetical to Reformed theology itself. Calvinists should be the humblest men and women on the planet. Pride in our understanding of Reformed theology shows that we have not internalized the teaching we profess, which not only extols the sovereignty of God in giving gifts but also places the glory of God (not self) at the centre of its entire theological system—from theocentric hermeneutics (covenant theology) to theocentric soteriology (the doctrines of grace) to theocentric doxology (the regulative principle of worship). There is no space for pride among those who confess the august doctrines of divine sovereignty, predestination, and consistent theocentrism. In such proud moments, we are practical non-Calvinists.

How Does Humility Promote Catholic Calvinism?

Humility promotes catholic Calvinism by cultivating a sense of unity with all genuine believers, including those who, before regeneration, we considered beneath us intellectually or socioeconomically. We are one with our brothers and sisters in Christ from every truly gospel-believing church or denomination, no matter its ethnicity, nationality, or socioeconomic status, so we must not consider ourselves superior to them (Col. 3:11). On the contrary, Christ calls us to esteem them better than ourselves (Phil. 2:3).

Humility also promotes godly catholicity by encouraging us to think and speak well of other believers. Disparaging or mocking Christians who disagree with us on non-essential matters gives unbelievers the impression that we are at each other's throats. If the catholic Calvinist recognizes that he has a theological blind spot, his pride should not prevent him from acknowledging the truth. Humility also promotes catholicity by eschewing the lust for personal pre-eminence that often divides churches (3 John 9).

The catholic Calvinist does not incline toward conflict like a moth to the light, nor does he see theological interchange as an opportunity to parade his intellectual gifts. In humble love, he refuses to vaunt himself. He does not gravitate toward the debating podium to exhibit his rhetorical skills, historical theological awareness, systematic theological acumen, or grasp of the biblical languages. The discourse of the catholic Calvinist, then, is exclusively for edification, not self-promotion. As Ralph Venning exhorted, 'Discourse not to cavil, but to convince or to be convinced.'[7] Theological discussion and debate become efforts to achieve greater knowledge, mutual understanding, and unity in the faith.

A humble spirit promotes catholic Calvinism by encouraging healthy theological dialogue among gospel-believing Christians of different backgrounds. As Calvinist Christians, we are duty bound to promote Reformed theology, which we believe reflects Scripture faithfully. As catholic Calvinists, we should support constructive centres for dialogue, from conferences to colloquiums. Such platforms will help us disseminate the light

---

7. Ralph Venning, *Mysteries and Revelations*, 19.

God has given us. We can also increase our own understanding of the faith we profess. We should engage in charitable dialogue with thoughtful Christians from different denominations and cultures. Ours should be a Christianity that is investigative, viewing the theological task as a time-spanning, cross-cultural, and multicultural project that involves the body of Christ of all times and places. While tenaciously retaining our Reformed theological distinctives, we can read and benefit from the work of true gospel believers from other regions and evangelical traditions past and present.

Meekness and Catholic Calvinism

There is a natural progression from humility to meekness, for 'humility begets meekness.'[8] Meekness is a gentle character manifested in humility, flexibility, and self-restraint. While the translators of the King James Version rendered the New Testament Greek word πρᾶος as 'meek,' the New American Standard Bible and English Standard Version often read 'gentle' (Matt. 11:29). In the Old Testament, the Hebrew word for meek (עָנָו) refers to the poor, lowly, and afflicted. The pious needy will inherit the earth (Ps. 37:11), for they drink in the Messiah's proclamation of glad tidings out of a sense of their spiritual poverty (Isa. 61:1; Matt. 5:3-12).

The word πρᾶος suggests the temperament of a tamed wild animal.[9] Meekness, then, is like the restrained strength of a stallion brought under control. With his self-control and slowness to anger, the meek person is stronger than one who conquers a city because he has dominion over himself (Prov. 16:32). Meekness is not weakness. Meekness is not the practice of avoiding necessary discussions that are uncomfortable or pride killing; nor is meekness the habit of abandoning convictions when convenient. Instead, the meek man or woman is mild, gentle,

---

8. Wilhelmus à Brakel, *The Christian's Reasonable Service* (Grand Rapids: Reformation Heritage Books, 2012), 4:79.

9. Henry George Liddell and Robert Scott, *A Lexicon Abridged from Liddell and Scott's Greek-English Lexicon* (Oxford: Clarendon Press, 1953), 582.

and submissive—not sharp, cruel, or proud. Above all, we see meekness in the humble Servant King who rode into Jerusalem on a donkey (Matt. 21:5). The apostle Peter pairs meekness with quietness, or a tranquil and peaceful spirit (1 Peter 3:4).

In English, the word meek comes from the Old Norse word mjúkr, which means 'soft' or 'gentle.' Soft and gentle things are pliable, tender, and impressionable. The meek person, therefore, is mild-tempered and sympathetic, quickly moved to compassion at the pitiable plight of others in need. He grieves for those who fall into heresy and error. There is nothing warlike or quarrelsome about him. But beneath his calm gentleness there is strength under control – the most powerful expression of strength.

Meekness submits to God's will and is self-restrained and forbearing toward others.[10] Brakel describes the meek man as agreeable, good-natured, friendly, polite, courteous, and pleasant. He explains how the meek endure and forgive injustice, reward evil with good, speak gently and softly (Prov. 15:1), and pursue reconciliation with a passion (Matt. 5:23-24).[11] As Jeremiah Burroughs writes, 'Milk quenches wild fire ... Opposition will heat, will fire up men, when meekness and gentleness will still and quench all.'[12]

How Does Meekness Promote Catholic Calvinism?

Like humility, meekness promotes godly catholicity by encouraging gentleness amid doctrinal disagreement. The catholic Calvinist has two ears and one mouth: he is quick to hear and slow to speak; he doesn't recklessly dive into controversy with acidity or without hearing both sides. In theological discussions, he does not mock or bite with sarcasm but carries himself with dignity. He saturates his mind with edifying topics, avoiding extreme hair-splitting that is found wanting in the balances of edification.

---

10. Joel R. Beeke and Paul M. Smalley, *Reformed Systematic Theology* (Wheaton, Ill.: Crossway, 2021), 3:860-1.

11. Brakel, *Christian's Reasonable Service*, 4:81-4.

12. Jeremiah Burroughs, *Irenicum to the Lovers of Truth and Peace*, ed. Don Kistler (Morgan, Pa.: Soli Deo Gloria, 1997), 407.

Meekness also informs interaction with other believers over theological disagreements. We should not strive or quarrel, and we should be selective with how much time we invest in debate. In passionate discussions, the catholic Calvinist restrains himself from interrupting, attentively and courteously listening to genuinely understand his opponent's position. With a teachable spirit, he believes that God may be using another believer to expand his own understanding of theology, whether in doctrine or praxis, even if he sharply disagrees with that person in the main. We should not 'listen' only so our opponent will listen to us when it is our turn to speak; we should not just listen to find as many things to critique as possible; and we shouldn't tune out and think about the next thing we're going to say while our opponent is speaking. Indicate your attentiveness with your body language. Offer a profitable response and demonstrate that you understood their point. Straw men have no place in Christian discourse.

Peace and Catholic Calvinism

In the chiastic pattern of the Beatitudes, meekness mirrors peacemaking.[13] Brakel writes that love, humility, and meekness combine to produce peace.[14] Peace is a disposition longing for fellowship and harmony toward God and man for mutual thriving. The biblical words for peace refer to 'harmonious relationships that are according to justice and to the prosperity that such relationships bring to individuals and the community.'[15]

The root of the Hebrew word for peace (שָׁלוֹם) denotes wholeness, prosperity, health, friendship, happiness, and harmony. Peace, then, is the internal sense of well-being, calm, and tranquility that blossoms into harmonious relationships, precluding hostility and promoting mutual flourishing. The Greek word for peace (εἰρήνη) probably comes from a word meaning 'to join,' so it has a similar semantic range as the English words 'concord' and 'harmony,'

---

13. Beeke and Smalley, *Reformed Systematic Theology*, 3:814.
14. Brakel, *Christian's Reasonable Service*, 4:91.
15. Beeke and Smalley, *Reformed Systematic Theology*, 3:852.

both of which are rooted in the idea of consonance. Peace joins in unison and promotes beauty, tranquility, and thriving, just as a musical chord combines notes to create euphony. External peace depends on internal peace; we can enjoy peace with other believers only if we first enjoy peace with God.

In imitation of our heavenly Father, we pursue peace with others because God has pursued peace with us. Meanwhile, there is no peace for the wicked (Isa. 48:22) because without reconciliation with God, there is neither peace vertically (with God) nor horizontally (with others). Peace with other Christians begins with the internal sense of harmony rooted in a right relationship with God in salvation; it then exudes into a relationship of harmony and well-being with others, especially in the family of God. The peaceful Christian suffers from a rupture of internal peace if external peace is broken, for broken relationships trouble the peaceful heart.

How Does Peace Promote Catholic Calvinism?

As Brakel observed, peace implies fellowship, not isolation.[16] We can pursue godly catholicity by cultivating fellowship and communion with other believers—especially face-to-face contact (2 John 12). Although we should focus on the local church, we should not shun participation in parachurch ministries as well, collaborating in various God-honoring projects to promote evangelism, Bible translation, Christian education, overseas training missions, engagement in the public sphere, and the alleviation of human suffering.

In our theological discussions with other Christians, we should pursue both width and depth. So it is important to discuss topics like supralapsarianism versus infralapsarianism, apologetic approaches, and the merits and limitations of natural theology. But we must keep these debates in balance and perspective. Such discussions should certainly be part of our theological universe, but they are by no means the center or the substance of

---

16. Brakel, *Christian's Reasonable Service*, 4:93.

that universe. Something is out of order when these discussions displace our zeal for piety, worship, fellowship in core doctrines, evangelism, mentorship, and training men in the global south (many of whom have yet to learn about the early church councils and the doctrines of grace). These discussions should sharpen us, but they should not preclude or exclude the rest of our fellowship and dialogue, becoming parasites that suck our spiritual lifeblood or invasive plants that smother our spiritual fruitfulness.

We show peace when we are not warlike, consumed by a quarrelsome spirit and addicted to debate. We desire the well-being of others and strive for fellowship, harmony, and mutual prosperity with them. We pray with and for fellow believers. We cannot have peace or fellowship without communication, as it is the basis for dialogue, discussion, prayer, accountability, and transparency. We should therefore cultivate Christian friendships, or 'intimate relationship[s] of love, trust, and loyalty.'[17] Such friendships involve 'affection, unity, communication, knowledge, joy, and partnership in shared concerns.'[18] Nevertheless, let us beware of selling truth and godliness for a false peace.[19] Striking hands with the world, the flesh, or the devil is an act of war against God (James 4:4).

Hope and Catholic Calvinism

Hope is the settled expectation that God will do what he has promised. It is not the unfounded wish that something good will happen, but it is a secure expectation that rests on the unshakable promises and declarations of the God who cannot lie (Titus 1:2). The hopeful Christian rests on Christ's declarations of the unity of his body (1 Cor. 12:12; Eph. 4:4-6). He knows that the Father will not deny Christ's prayer for unity among his people. The Lord Jesus Christ is returning, and he is coming with a reward. Persevere in hope, for he does not forget your labour of love for

---

17. Michael A. G. Haykin, Brian Croft, and James B. Carroll, *Pastoral Friendship: The Forgotten Piece to a Persevering Ministry* (Fearn, U.K.: Christian Focus, 2022), 16.

18. Beeke and Smalley, *Reformed Systematic Theology*, 3:848.

19. Brakel, *Christian's Reasonable Service*, 4:94.

the saints; your service to them is service to him (Matt. 25:40). By faith, the hopeful Christian foresees the promised day when all believers will unite in praise to God (Rev. 7:9-10).

How Does Hope Promote Catholic Calvinism?

Spirit-fuelled hope should encourage catholicity by creating expectations for the present. We expectantly hope that God will enlighten us through the Holy Spirit as we engage in thoughtful discussion and dialogue with godly Christians from other cultures and contexts. We expect the Holy Spirit to sanctify us and use our interactions with other Christians to promote love, humility, meekness, and peace in our hearts and theirs. We trust the Holy Spirit to make us a blessing in the body of Christ to others and to share with them what God has shared with us. We are part of the sacred project of nourishing and building up the body of Christ to a full and perfect man (Eph. 4:7-16). We expectantly hope that God will use discussion to encourage us, to convict us, and to help us grow in knowledge and both spiritual and intellectual strength.

As believers, we share one hope and one goal—the joy of everlasting life with our triune God in paradise. Our Sunday worship should stir our hearts to thirst for the union we will enjoy with all believers and with our Lord and Savior in heaven. As Jeremiah Burroughs counselled, 'Transform zeal in division into zeal for the kingdom.'[20] Ask yourself, Am I expending all my energy on parochial pursuits, or am I serving God's global, spiritual kingdom, in hope?

Hope should encourage catholicity by forming expectations for the future. Pray that the breaches of the church would be healed. Imagine the pleasure and profit of greater interaction among true Christians. Consider the beauty of joint evangelism, edifying conferences, worship services, and even Communion seasons with other congregations in your area. Expectantly hope that as the church becomes more united in godliness that Satan's empire will fall and that Christ's kingdom will reign in the heavenly world of perfect love forever.

---

20. Burroughs, *Irenicum to the Lovers of Truth and Peace*, 423.

Conclusion

These five affections—love, humility, meekness, peace, and hope—should promote catholicity by creating expectations for eternity. Certainly, this was evident in John Calvin's life, in which he showed great love for the church and established close friendships with the saints, as Michael A. van den Berg has irrefutably shown in his enlightening *Friends of Calvin*.[21] It was also evident in the life of George Whitefield, who often called himself a catholic Calvinist. Many other notable examples could be mentioned here.

But let us conclude on an even higher note. Reflect on the day when we will be around Christ's throne with believers from every nation (Rev. 7:9-10). There will be no more divisions. The blind spots and sins we and other believers have now will be gone. We will then have a perfect and ever-expanding theological system combined with perfect brotherly love and union in the church. Octavius Winslow summarises all of this so well:

> How productive is this truth of Christian union and brotherly love in the Church of God! In cultivating home feelings, domestic affections, and sympathies, in our anticipation of heaven, we shall instinctively feel drawn by a bond of irresistible attraction towards all who evidence their relation to the family of God. We shall prove our filial relation to God by our fraternal affection for his people. 'Every one that loveth him that begat loveth him also that is begotten of him' (1 John 5:1). Have we not all one Father? Are we not all brethren? Do we not sit at one table? And are we not all journeying to the same home? Why should we then fall out by the way? Why allow differences of judgment, or denominational distinctions, or party heats, suspicion, envy, and jealousy—those wretched fruits of the flesh—to sunder and alienate us the one from the other? Must not a lack of love like this be grieving to the heart and dishonouring to the name of our one Father? Let us no longer speak of tolerating a child of God or deem it condescension to fraternise with one of the Lord's saints because he belongs to another branch of God's family. Away with such spurious Christianity. Rather let us, in the meek and loving

---

21. Michael A. van den Berg, *Friends of Calvin*, trans. Reinder Bruinsma (Grand Rapids: Eerdmans 2009).

spirit of our elder brother, feel ourselves honoured in ministering to him in the lowliest office of Christian service, everywhere and on all occasions recognising and loving such as a brother beloved of God, and thus recognise, love, and honour the Father in his child. Oh, for more Christ-like love in the family of God! This I consider to be the great, the chief need in the professing Church of Christ in the present day. I speak not of differences of judgment, or modes of worship, or of denominational branches; these have existed, do exist, and will exist until Christ comes to unite all his people in one body, and blend all in one worship, and behold the answer to his prayer and the consummation of his desire: 'That they all may be one' (John 17:21). I speak of a lamentable deficiency of that love which may and should exist despite ecclesiastical position, which derives not its inspiration, form, and tint from a denominational source or mould, but which proceeds pure and holy from God, and in its influence on the church binds and assimilates in oneness of spirit, in fellowship of heart, and in unity of service all who are the children of God by faith in Christ Jesus.[22]

In the meantime, let us pursue catholic Calvinism with a passion, without sacrificing truth and keep praying, 'Even so, come, Lord Jesus' (1 Cor. 16:22).

---

22. Octavius Winslow, *Help Heavenward: Guidance and Strength for the Christian's Life-Journey* (Edinburgh: Banner of Truth, 2000), 190-1.

CHAPTER EIGHT

'The Weight of the Paradigm'

Infant Baptism and the Covenant of Grace[1]

Jonathan Gibson

> *'Baptism ... is the jewel displayed on the engagement ring of God's covenant people.'*
> Sinclair B. Ferguson[2]

Waters that divide

Christian baptism is a divine ordinance of the gospel instituted by Jesus Christ and dispensed by the application of water. Jesus Christ employed the ordinance as an essential element of his Great Commission, a means to furthering his kingdom in the world (Matt. 20:19). To be a member of his church is to be a baptised Christian, united to other believers in Christ. As the Apostle Paul reminds us, in one Spirit we have been baptised into one body (1 Cor. 12:13). 'One Lord, one faith, one baptism' is the Church's

---

[1]. This chapter is an excerpt from Jonathan Gibson, *One Baptism: A Biblical-Theological Exposition* (working title; forthcoming) and is used here with permission.

[2]. Sinclair B. Ferguson, 'Infant Baptism View', in *Baptism: Three Views*, ed. David F. Wright (Downers Grove, IL: IVP Academic, 2009), 100.

creed (Eph. 4:5). And yet the waters of baptism have been troubled waters since our Lord instituted the ordinance over 2,000 years ago. Rather than being waters that unite, they have become waters that divide.[3] And the divide shows no sign of abatement. On the one side, Baptists contend strongly that 'the invention of man in baptizing infants has totally set aside the ordinance of God'[4]; indeed, it amounts to 'living in disobedience to Christ'.[5] On the other side, Presbyterians, among others, contend that not baptising infants 'is a piece of greater cruelty and folly than was perpetrated by Esau' when he forsook his birthright[6]; in this regard, 'Anabaptist churches are not apostolic churches.'[7] For Anglicans such as J. C. Ryle, it is 'a complete mistake not to baptise [infants]'.[8] Each side also believes strongly that the scriptural proof is in their favour. For Baptists, the evidence is obvious: '[I]nfant baptism has not in the word of God an inch of solid ground on which to stand.'[9] Indeed, '[e]very New Testament instruction or command regarding baptism, and every clear instance of baptism that we see in the New Testament, relates to the baptism of those who have repented of sin (John's baptism) and come to faith in Christ (baptisms from Pentecost forward).'[10] Baptists also claim church history is in their favour: '[T]he conclusions of recent scholarship are that believers'

---

3. Donald Bridge and David Phypers, *The Waters That Divide: Two Views on Baptism Explored* (Leicester: IVP, 1977).

4. Alexander Carson, *Baptism: Its Mode and Subjects* (Philadelphia: American Baptist Publication Society, 1845 [1844]), 237.

5. Bruce A. Ware, 'Believers' Baptism View', in *Baptism: Three Views*, 20.

6. Thomas Witherow, *Scriptural Baptism* in *I Will Build My Church: Select Writings on Polity, Baptism, and the Sabbath*, ed. Jonathan Gibson (Glenside: WSP, 2021), 190.

7. Witherow, *Scriptural Baptism* in *I Will Build My Church*, 202. Anabaptism is an older term for the same position as credobaptism (believers' baptism); its origins go back to the sixteenth century and refers to those who would rebaptise infants who had already been baptised (hence the term Anabaptist, 'one who baptises again'). Up to the nineteenth century, the term was employed to speak of those holding to believers' baptism.

8. J. C. Ryle, *Knots Untied: Being Plain Statements on Disputed Points in Religion from the Standpoint of an Evangelical Churchman* (Edinburgh: Banner of Truth, 2016 [1874]), 99.

9. Carson, *Baptism: Its Mode and Subjects*, 237.

10. Ware, 'Believers' Baptism View', 23.

baptism was the conviction and practice for the first four to six centuries of the church as it was of the New Testament church itself.'[11] For Presbyterians, the evidence is equally obvious for their position, both in Scripture and church history:

> The Word of God refuses to sustain the claims of dipping [immersion]. For, when Christ baptized with the Holy Spirit, He did so by making the Spirit come, fall, and rest upon the person baptized; and when we make the water of the ordinance come, fall, and rest upon the person, we baptize after Christ's example. When Anabaptism refuses to recognize, by baptism, the church membership of infants, it sets itself in opposition to an unrepealed principle of God's Word, to the established practice of two thousand years [in the Old Testament], to clear statements of the New Testament Scriptures, and to the practice of eighteen Christian centuries[12]; while at the same time, it can produce no case from the Scripture where the child of Christian parents was treated as they say all children should be treated.[13]

With statements like these, one wonders at times if each side is reading the same Bible. An impasse clearly exists. Yet it remains the High Priestly prayer of Jesus that his Church would be one as he and the Father are one (John 17:20-21).

Waters that unite

Christ's call for unity is exemplified in Paul's creedal-like affirmation that there is 'one body ... one Spirit ... one Lord, one faith, one baptism, one God and Father of all, who is over all and through all and in all' (Eph. 4:4-6). Indeed, the reason Christ in his ascension gave gifts to men—apostles, prophets, evangelists, shepherds, teachers—was 'for building up the body of Christ, until we all attain to the unity of the faith and of the knowledge of the Son of God' (Eph. 4:12-13). Attaining the unity of the faith surely involves unity around an ordinance of the gospel such as

---

11. David F. Wright, 'Recovering Baptism for a New Age of Mission', in *Doing Theology for the People of God: Studies in Honor of J. I. Packer*, ed. Donald Lewis and Alister McGrath (Downers Grove, IL: InterVarsity Press, 1996), 57.
12. Witherow was writing in the nineteenth century.
13. Witherow, *Scriptural Baptism* in *I Will Build My Church*, 212.

baptism; and given that a divide remains, there is still work to be done. Every Christian minister therefore has a responsibility to persuade his hearers/readers towards attaining the unity of the faith—even on a controversial subject such as baptism. Of course, baptism is not a salvation issue, but it does not follow that it is an unimportant issue. For Jesus, baptism was important enough to include as an essential part of his Great Commission (Matt. 28:19).

Change of mind

In the interests of full disclosure, then, this chapter is an ambitious attempt, though I hope a humble one, to change the minds of credobaptist readers and to (re)confirm the minds of paedobaptist readers on the ordinance of Christian baptism, so that together we might affirm *ex animo*: 'one Lord, one faith, one baptism'. Part of the reason for this is that I myself experienced such a change of mind. My family church background was credobaptist (mainly in the Christian Brethren), and for many years I was a strong advocate for the Baptist position, pestering my Presbyterian friends for 'a verse'. My biblicist zeal, however, began to wane during my time at Moore Theological College in Sydney. Taking church history classes and reading through Calvin's *Institutes of the Christian Religion* made me more respectful of the paedobaptist position. By the time I began doctoral studies at the University of Cambridge, my views were beginning to shift. One factor among others in my eventual 'conversion' was encountering the ministry of Ian Hamilton. In my first conversation with Ian, he mentioned a young man from a Baptist background who had recently been convinced of infant baptism: 'The weight of the paradigm overwhelmed him.' The comment intrigued me. On another occasion some years later, Ian mentioned in passing that the reason he was a 'covenant baptist', as he liked to call himself, was because 'God does not change'. My interest was piqued again. Soon after, I found myself increasingly uncomfortable with 'rebaptisms' in the Baptist church that my wife and I were attending. So I chose to take a deep dive into the subject to see if 'covenant baptism' really could be defended from the Scriptures. As part of my journey, Ian's address 'To You and to Your Children: Ten Points of Paedobaptism' (at a Baptist church, no less),[14] played a significant role in the shift in my thinking. At the same time, I had been attending Presbytery meetings of The International Presbyterian Church (UK), and soon after began to seek ordination there. As part of that process, Ian was kind enough to facilitate my appointment as associate minister at Cambridge Presbyterian Church. I remain grateful for his part in my journey towards ministerial ordination and service in the Presbyterian Church. His teaching and pastoral care were a model to me and have remained so. As I reflect with gratitude on his ministry, I consider Ian to be among that rare breed of Christian ministers who can straddle the world of biblical and theological exposition on the one hand, and gentle and loving pastoral care on the other. It is therefore a delight to contribute to this *Festschrift* and honour the Cambridge pastor-theologian who was used by God, along with others, to point me towards the Presbyterian Church in which I now gladly serve as a minister. I can testify that 'the weight of the paradigm' did indeed overwhelm me. Once I saw it, it was hard to unsee it. It was like I woke up one morning, and the world looked different—as did my Bible.

My aim in this essay, then, is to do for others what Ian did for me: to change or (re)confirm one's view on Christian baptism through the lens of covenant theology. My prayer is that I may do so in the same catholic spirit that Ian has exhibited throughout his ministry.

Divide over baptism

To view the divide over baptism merely as infant baptism versus believers' baptism is to misunderstand the divide. Presbyterians who hold to infant baptism also affirm believers' baptism for new converts from outside the Christian church. In this respect, we are all 'Baptists' (albeit differing on the mode of administration).

---

14. The address may be accessed online: https://www.cambridgepres.org.uk/resources/hot-topics

Scripture presents many cases of adult baptism following repentance and faith, none of which Presbyterians deny. The book of Acts records many conversion-baptisms: the Jews at Pentecost (Acts 2:38, 41), the Ethiopian Eunuch (Acts 8:34-38), Saul (Acts 9:18), Cornelius and his household (Acts 10:44-48), Lydia and her household (Acts 16:14-15), the Philippian jailor (Acts 16:29-33), Crispus and the Corinthians (Acts 18:8; 1 Cor. 1:13-17), and the disciples at Ephesus (Acts 19:1-5). In each case, the conversion-baptisms occur with adults from various ethnic, religious, and social backgrounds who are born outside the church (with no Christian parents) and who come into the church by repentance and faith. The order of entrance to the Christian church for each of them is repentance-faith-baptism. In the old dispensation, the order for Abraham was similar: repentance-faith-circumcision. In this respect, the book of Acts, when read in a redemptive-historical groove, simply contains the record of 'a bunch of Abraham's' being converted and welcomed into God's community by receiving the sign of the new covenant. This sign marked them as belonging to God, just as circumcision as a sign of the Abrahamic covenant marked God's people Israel as belonging to him. Circumcision and baptism, each in their respective dispensations, draw a distinction between the visible church and the world. Thus, Presbyterians can affirm with Baptists that for converts outside the church fold, baptism follows faith and repentance. It is not a sign for someone outside the visible church; it is only for those who repent of their sins, profess faith in Christ, and display an obedience to him (WSC Q&A 95). Thomas Witherow, a nineteenth-century Irish Presbyterian minister, states our position with characteristic clarity: 'We maintain that, when anyone born *beyond the membership* of the Christian church, whether a pagan, a Samaritan, or a Jew, would seek admission within its pale, he cannot be baptised until he believes.'[15] The point of debate is thus not over whether credobaptism is a biblical practice; it most certainly is for converts

---

15. Witherow, *Scriptural Baptism* in *I Will Build My Church*, 178 (emphasis original).

coming into the Christian church from the outside. The issue is how the gospel ordinance of baptism relates to the children of such converts or to the children of parents who have been Christian for many years. In short: *When should the children of Christian parents receive the ordinance of baptism: upon birth or upon repentance and faith?* This is the crux of the divide between credobaptists and paedobaptists, and nothing else.

The order of when Abraham's descendants received the sign of the covenant should at least give Baptists pause for thought here. While the order for Abraham was repentance-faith-circumcision, the order for Isaac and Jacob was circumcision-repentance-faith. The offspring of Abraham were born into the covenant that God had made with him and were given the sign of that covenant on their bodies *before* they were able to express repentance or faith. The observation reveals that for Abraham the requirement to receive circumcision was different to that of Isaac and Jacob. Witherow provides a helpful illustration: 'A foreigner, who means to settle in our islands, requires to take out letters of naturalization before he can claim the rights of a British subject; but it does not, therefore, follow that one who is British-born requires to do the same.'[16] In other words, the qualification to acquire naturalization for a parent is different to that of a child. Presbyterians argue that this is also true when it comes to membership in the Church, whether in the old dispensation or the new dispensation. What is required of an adult convert under either dispensation is not by necessity required of their children. Under both dispensations, the order for converted adults is repentance-faith-sign; for children of converted adults, it is sign-repentance-faith. What makes sense of this order is a Reformed view of covenant theology, and in particular, the covenant of grace.

Covenant of Grace

The covenant of grace and its continuity across old and new dispensations is one reason, among others, why Presbyterians

---

16. Witherow, *Scriptural Baptism* in *I Will Build My Church*, 178.

believe that children of believing parents are the legitimate recipients of Christian baptism. Working on the assumption that there is no union and communion with God for human creatures outside a covenant relationship (cf. WCF 7.1), Presbyterians understand the covenant of grace to be God's response to the breach of the covenant of works (WCF 7.3). The covenant of grace is first announced in Genesis 3:15. However, the 'mother promise', as Geerhardus Vos calls it,[17] is not a mere promise but the first administration of the covenant of grace in redemptive history, albeit in embryonic form. As the first iteration of the covenant of grace, it is not the last iteration. Rather, as the first iteration, it begins the organic development of the covenant of grace in the unfolding history of redemption, with each covenant thereafter a progressive revelation of its operation in history. That is, the covenant of restoration with Adam (Gen. 3:15), the covenant of preservation with Noah (Gen. 6:18; 9:8-17), the covenant of promise with Abraham (Gen. 12:1-3; 15:1-21; 17:1-14; 22:16-18), the covenant of law with Moses/Israel (Exod. 19-20, 24; Deut. 28-29), the covenant of peace with Aaron/Phinehas (Num. 18:6-8, 11, 19; 25:10-13), the covenant of the kingdom with David/Solomon (2 Sam. 7:12-16; 1 Kings 2:1-4; Ps. 89:3-4), and the new covenant of fulfilment with Jesus and his church (Matt. 26:26-29; Mark 14:22-25; Luke 22:18-20)—these are all different administrations of the one covenant of grace in various dispensations of redemptive history (see Diagram 1 on page 128).

Augustine was one of the first to articulate a form of covenant theology, memorably stating that 'the new covenant lies concealed in the old covenant, and the old stands revealed in the new'.[18] Covenant theology was further developed in the Reformation era, with Calvin explaining the connection between the Abrahamic covenant and new covenant as follows: 'The covenant made with all the patriarchs is so much like ours in substance and reality that the two are actually one and the same. Yet they differ in

---

17. Geerhardus Vos, *Reformed Dogmatics. Volume Two: Anthropology* (Bellingham, WA: Lexham Press, 2013), 124.

18. Augustine, *Seven Questions Concerning the Heptateuch*, 2.73, in *PL*, 34:623.

the mode of dispensation.'[19] The covenant formulations of Augustine and Calvin, among others, reached confessional status in the Westminster Confession.[20] Three articles encapsulate the Presbyterian view of the covenant of grace:

> 7.5: This covenant [of grace] was differently administered in the time of the law, and in the time of the gospel: under the law, it was administered by promises, prophecies, sacrifices, circumcision, the paschal lamb, and other types and ordinances delivered to the people of the Jews, all foresignifying Christ to come; which were, for that time, sufficient and efficacious, through the operation of the Spirit, to instruct and build up the elect in faith in the promised Messiah, by whom they had full remission of sins, and eternal salvation; and is called the old testament.
>
> 7.6: Under the gospel, when Christ, the substance, was exhibited, the ordinances in which this covenant is dispensed are the preaching of the Word, and the administration of the sacraments of baptism and the Lord's Supper: which, though fewer in number, and administered with more simplicity, and less outward glory, yet, in them, it is held forth in more fullness, evidence and spiritual efficacy, to all nations, both Jews and Gentiles; and is called the new testament. There are not therefore two covenants of grace, differing in substance, but one and the same, under various dispensations.
>
> 8.6: Although the work of redemption was not actually wrought by Christ till after his incarnation, yet the virtue, efficacy, and benefits thereof were communicated unto the elect, in all ages successively from the beginning of the world, in and by those promises, types, and sacrifices, wherein he was revealed, and signified to be the seed of the woman which should bruise the serpent's head; and the Lamb slain from the beginning of the world; being yesterday and today the same, and forever.

---

19. Calvin, *Institutes*, 2.10.2: Other Reformed theologians used different language to distinguish substance and administration of the covenant of grace: essentials/essence vs circumstantials/circumstances.

20. Probably most influential on the Westminster divines view of covenant theology was John Ball's work, published in 1644: *A Treatise of the Covenant of Grace: Wherein the Graduall Breakings Out of Gospel-Grace From Adam to Christ Are Clearly Discovered, the Differences Betwixt the Old and New Testament Are Laid Open, Divers Errours of Arminianism and Others Are Confuted.*

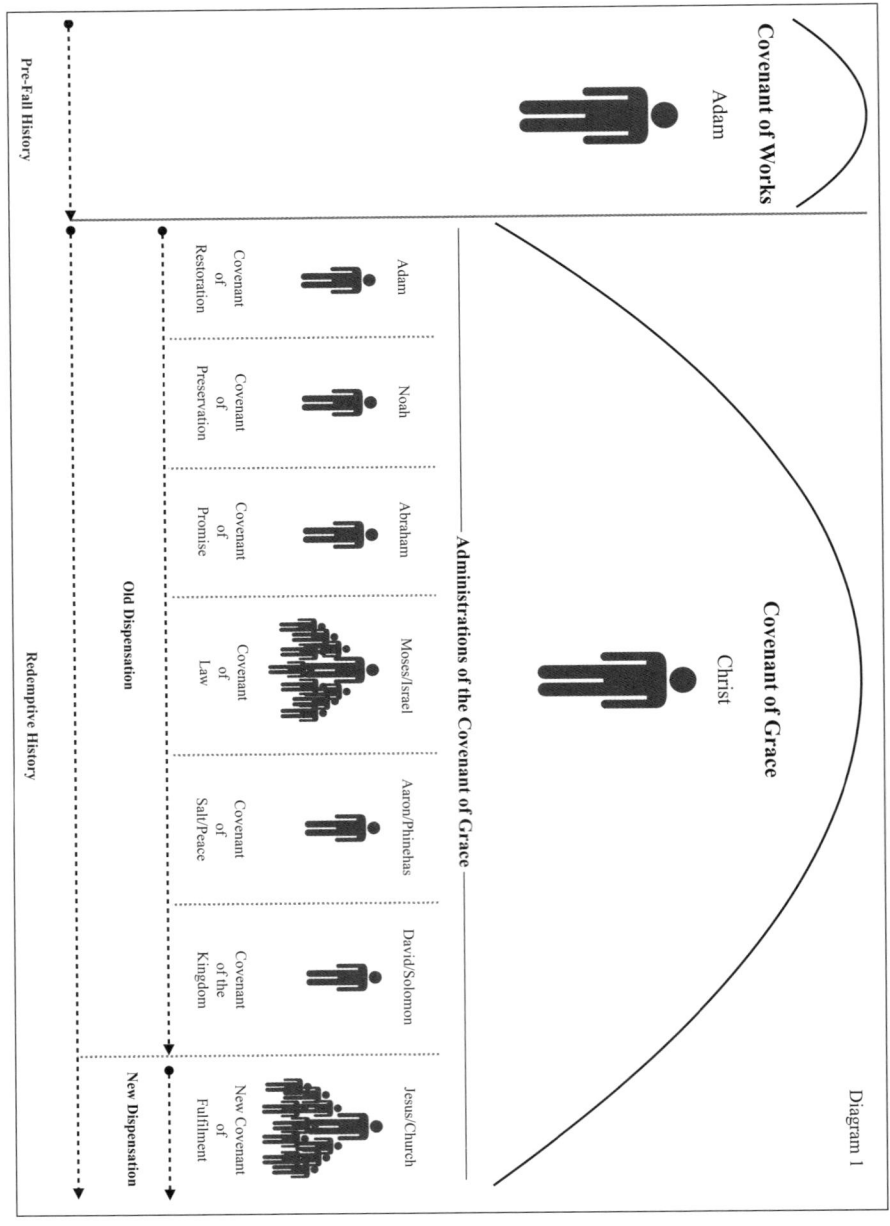

Diagram 1

Our aim, then, is to convince the reader that there is one covenant of grace in substance, structure, and signage across old and new dispensations, and having established this scriptural principle, to see its implication for baptism.

A. Substance of the covenant

That each redemptive covenant is of the same substance may be demonstrated from the common promissory elements that exist in each of them. Either the context in which the covenant is established or the words that accompany its establishment serve to prove the point. Five such elements are worth considering.

1. The promise of enmity

Common to most of the biblical covenants is the promise or presence of enmity. In the covenant of restoration with Adam (Gen. 3:15), God institutes a principle of enmity between two seeds, the offspring of the serpent and the offspring of the woman. This principle is later enacted in the covenant of preservation with Noah in the submission/dominance dynamic between Ham/Canaan, on the one hand, and his brothers Shem and Japheth, on the other (Gen. 9:25-27). The principle of enmity plays out again in the covenant of promise with Abraham, in which God predicts that his offspring will go into a foreign land and become slaves for a time before being delivered (Gen. 15:13-16); indeed, his offspring will possess the gates of their enemies (Gen. 22:17). In the patriarchal covenant, this is reiterated in Jacob's blessing on Judah when he promises that Judah's hand will be on the necks of his enemies (Gen. 49:8). Enmity becomes more prominent in the covenant of law with Israel when Moses sets before Israel the promise of covenant blessing and the threat of covenant curse upon the condition of their obedience or disobedience: if they obey, they will rule over opposing nations (Deut. 28:7, 10, 13); if they disobey, they will be oppressed by the opposing nations (Deut. 28:25-34, 43-44, 49-52, 68). The covenant of salt/peace with Aaron and his sons entails guarding the tent of meeting and ensuring that an 'outsider' does not come near (Num. 18:4, 7); the covenant of peace is confirmed with Phinehas in the context of him slaying the Midianite who had corrupted God's community (Num. 25:7-8). The covenant of the kingdom with David occurs in the context of David subduing his enemies and with the promise of future rest from all his enemies (2 Sam. 7:1, 9-10). Thus, as can be seen, enmity forms a common promissory element in each redemptive covenant of the OT.

The element also finds its counterpart in the NT as Christ inaugurates the new covenant. The forces of evil gather against Christ throughout his life as he seeks to do his Father's will in bringing the covenant promises of the OT to their fulfilment. The enmity reveals itself in the form of the devil's temptations in the wilderness, the Pharisees and Sadducees opposition to his ministry, the evil spirits' resistance to his miracles; as his death approaches, the enmity comes in the form of Judas the disciple-turned-betrayer, Caiaphas the high priest, Pontius Pilate the Roman Governor and Herod the puppet king, as they take their stand against the Lord's Anointed (cf. Ps. 2:2); there are also the crowds taunting him with a final temptation to come down from the cross. Yet, as God's Anointed King, Jesus resists them all, triumphing over the world, sin, death, and the devil. As the NT authors confirm, he disarms the rulers and authorities in his death and puts them to open shame (Col. 2:15), destroying the one who held the power of death, the devil himself (Heb. 2:14); in his resurrection, he abolishes death and brings life and immortality to light (2 Tim. 1:10); in his ascension, he leads a host of captives (Eph. 4:8); in his heavenly session, he reigns over his enemies, putting them under his feet one by one until he destroys the last enemy—death itself (1 Cor. 15:25-26).

In sum, the promise of enmity is a substantive element in OT covenants, one that comes to a climax in the person and work of Christ as he does battle with the world, sin, death, and the devil to establish the new covenant. While the covenants in each dispensation have distinct epochal administrations, they are all of the same substance—they each speak to the God-initiated enmity between the offspring of the serpent and the offspring of the woman, climaxing in a final offspring who defeats the serpent himself.

2. The promise of offspring

Also common to the biblical covenants is the promise of an offspring. In the covenant of restoration, God promises a continuous line of offspring from the woman (Gen. 3:15). This substantive element is developed in the covenant of preservation with Noah, where God commands him to multiply and fill the earth (Gen. 9:1-2). The idea of continuity and multiplication of offspring continues in the covenant of promise with Abraham, Isaac, and Jacob, where the patriarchs are promised that the multiplication of their offspring will be as innumerable as the stars in the heavens (Gen. 15:5; 26:4), the sand on the seashore (Gen. 22:17), and the dust of the earth (Gen. 13:16; 28:14). While in Egypt, God brings these promises to an initial stage of fulfilment in Israel's multiplication and growth (Exod. 1:7). After Israel enters into covenant with God at Sinai (Exod. 19:3-6), the promise of fruitfulness is conditioned upon their obedience to God's laws (Deut. 28:4, 11). In the covenant of salt/peace with Aaron, the contributions are given as a 'perpetual due' to Aaron and his sons; the covenant of salt will be forever (Num. 18:8, 11, 19), which implies a continual lineage of offspring in the priesthood. In the covenant of the kingdom with David, there is the promise of an eternal dynasty (2 Sam. 7:12-13), which entails a son who will live forever.[21] When those covenant promises come to fruition in the person of King Solomon, the language employed to describe the magnificence of his reign recalls the patriarchal covenant promises: 'Judah and Israel were as many as the sand by the seas' (1 Kings 4:20; cf. Gen. 22:17). The promise of offspring is also present in the prophets as they predict the dawning of new covenant realities: Isaiah prophesies of a restored Israel being 'the offspring of the blessed of the LORD, and their descendants with him' (Isa. 65:23); Jeremiah prophesies of a day post-exile when God will give his people one heart, 'for their own good and the good of their children after them' (Jer. 32:39); Ezekiel prophesies

---

21. This is also implied in the promise of Genesis 3:15 since the ultimate son of the woman will defeat the serpent who brought death into the world.

of God's people returning to dwell in the land under one king, a new David, 'they and their children and their children's children' (Ezek. 37:25); and Hosea prophesies of a recommitment by God to see his people multiply again to be like the sand of the sea, which cannot be counted (Hos. 1:10). Thus, as can be seen, offspring is a common promissory element of the various covenants in the OT.

The element of offspring also continues in the new covenant. At its dawning, Jesus forms a new people of God with his disciples (Mark 3:13-19), and then, through his apostles, expands the people into an international body of believers through the preaching of his gospel (Luke 24:46-47; Acts 1:8). Jesus views this new band of covenant members as his 'brothers' (Heb. 2:12; cf. Ps. 22:22) but also as his 'children' (Heb. 2:13; cf. Isa. 8:18), the 'offspring of Abraham' (Heb. 2:16; cf. Isa. 41:8-9). This is so because Christ is *the* Offspring of Abraham (Gal. 3:16). Playing on a referential ambiguity of the singular noun 'offspring', the Apostle Paul argues that all the 'offspring promises' were ultimately about one Offspring—Christ. This is why Paul can say that, in Christ, believers are 'all sons of God, through faith'; we are 'Abraham's offspring, heirs according to promise' (Gal. 3:27, 29). The connotation of offspring is also present in Paul's explanation of how Christ's work affects the 'many' united to him by faith (Rom. 5:15-21). In contrasting Christ to Adam, the concept of posterity naturally comes into purview.

In sum, the promise of offspring forms a substantive element of each covenant administration in the OT, continuing in the NT.

3. The promise of a son

In the OT covenants, the general promise of an offspring contains a specific promise of a son. This is seen as early as the first promise of Genesis 3:15. The individual who will come to fight the serpent arises out of the corporate 'seed' (זֶרַע) of the woman. As such, since the offspring promised is a male descendant—a 'he' not a 'she'—a *son* is promised. A line of sons who carry forward the promise of Genesis 3:15 is reflected throughout the OT, often in connection to a covenant established with an individual. In the covenant of restoration made with Adam, Seth is chosen to replace Abel after he is murdered by Cain (Gen. 4:25); Seth goes on to form a godly line of male descendants in Enosh, Kenan, Mahalalel, Jared, Enoch, Methuselah, Lamech, and Noah (Gen. 4:26-5:27). In the covenant of preservation, Noah has three sons (Gen. 5:32), with Shem, his second-born, being the chosen son to continue the line of the offspring of the woman (Gen. 9:26-27; 11:10-25). From Shem eventually comes Terah, who has three sons, with Abram, his second-born, being chosen to carry on the line of the offspring of the woman (Gen. 11:27-12:3). In the covenant of promise, Abraham has two sons, Ishmael and Isaac. Although Isaac is the second-born son of Abraham, he is the son promised from Abraham and Sarah's own bodies, and so is chosen to be the son of promise (Gen. 15:4; 17:16, 19, 21). Isaac later has twin boys Esau and Jacob, with the progenitor rights passing from Esau to Jacob because of some human conniving on Jacob's part, but also, and ultimately, because of divine counsel on God's part (Gen. 25:23-34). In the context of the patriarchal covenant of promise, Judah has two sons from Tamar, Perez and Zerah, with the latter being chosen over the former (Gen. 38). From the time of Israel in Egypt, the son promise recedes into the background, while the covenant promise to the nation of Israel comes to the foreground. The nation takes the mantle of 'God's son,' whom he rescues out of slavery (Exod. 4:22-23). However, once settled in the Promised Land, with the monarchy established under Saul, the son promise returns to the foreground. In the covenant of the kingdom, God promises David a son from his 'own body' (מִמֵּעֶיךָ; 2 Sam. 7:12)—the exact same phrase as contained in the Abrahamic covenant (מִמֵּעֶיךָ; Gen. 15:4). The promise is met in Solomon, a son from David's own body (2 Sam. 12:24-25). Thus, as can be seen, the specific promise of a son is present in the main OT covenants.

In the NT these son promises find their 'Yes' and 'Amen' in Christ (2 Cor. 1:20). He is the individual son-seed who arises out of the corporate son-seed Israel, as predicted in the *protoeuangelion* announced in Eden (Gen. 3:15). He is the promised son of the

Abrahamic covenant, of whom Isaac was only a type. As noted, the apostle views Christ as *the* Offspring (singular) that God promised to Abraham (Gal. 3:16). He is also the promised son of the Davidic covenant with whom God would establish an eternal kingdom, the one descended from David according to the flesh (Rom. 1:2-3).

In sum, the promise of a son from within the general offspring of God's people forms another substantive element that is common to the OT covenants, and one which finds it fulfilment in Christ, *the* promised Son.

4. The promise of a royal son

The sons promised in the line of the woman's offspring are royal sons. As redemptive history unfolds, this fact is at first implicit but then later becomes explicit. The implicit revelation of a royal son is seen when the *protoeuangelion* promise of Genesis 3:15 is set against Adam's role in the covenant of works. Adam was God's son, made in his image and called to obey his Father in heaven (Gen. 1:26-28; 5:1-3; Luke 3:38). As God's son, Adam held public office as the head of the covenant of works, functioning in three roles: prophet, priest, and king. As prophet, he was to speak God's will to God's world; as priest, he was to mediate blessing to God's world from God's garden-sanctuary; as king, he was to rule God's world from Mount Eden. However, in the Fall, Adam failed as God's son, abdicating his role as prophet, priest, and king. As a result, the covenant of works was breached, and the avenue for confirmed righteousness and immutable communion with God was closed to Adam's posterity. But God did not abandon Adam or his posterity in his sin. He promised another covenant, a new covenant—the covenant of grace (Gen. 3:15). At the heart of this covenant was the promise of another son, a son who would come to do what the first Adam should have done. In this respect, he would be a second Adam, doing what the first Adam should have done when the serpent entered the garden—crush him in the head by a tree. And since God promised victory over the serpent, this son would be a last Adam, meaning that there would be no need for another (third) Adam. Now, if he would be a second and last Adam, he would have to be more than just another Adam. For if the first Adam, in his unfallen state, was unable to overcome the serpent's power and temptation as the king of creation, then the promise of another (second) Adam in an unfallen state was hardly going to produce a different outcome. Instead, for the second and last Adam to be successful, he would need divine intervention—he would need to be a God-man of sorts. The figure promised in Genesis 3:15, then, is best understood against the backdrop of the first Adam. As such, the second and last Adam—the God-man—must be a Son of God in some measure, and so function in the same roles as the first Adam, as a prophet, priest, and king. Thus a *royal* son—a king—may be deduced by good consequence from the 'mother promise' of Genesis 3:15.

This idea of royalty is also implied in the covenant of preservation with Noah, in which God commands Noah to be fruitful, multiply, and fill the earth like Adam before him (Gen. 9:1; cf. 1:26-28). The command is accompanied by a promise that fear and dread will fall upon every living creature under Noah's rule (Gen. 9:2), which speaks to his kingly status. The idea of kingly rule continues implicitly in the chosen line, with Noah's blessing on Shem as the one whom Canaan (Ham) will serve (Gen. 9:25-26). However, it is in the covenant of promise with Abraham that the royal theme becomes explicit, when God states openly to Abraham and Sarah that kings will come from them (Gen. 17:6, 16). If kings come from Abraham, then he is of royal ascent and his sons of royal descent. This theme develops in the patriarchal covenant as redemptive history unfolds. Jacob blesses his son Judah with a promise that includes royal status: the sceptre will not depart from him, nor the ruler's staff from between his feet; tribute will be brought to him, and the obedience of the peoples will be his (Gen. 49:10). In the context of the covenant of law with Israel, Balaam prophecies of a king in Israel whose kingdom shall be exalted (Num. 24:7); a star and sceptre (both royal symbols) will arise out of Jacob/Israel (Num. 24:17). Later, Moses makes provision for such a king within the theocracy of Israel when he gives the stipulations and requirements for a king (Deut. 17:14-20). At God's behest, Samuel the prophet-priest facilitates the transition from judgeship to kingship in Israel, first with Saul (the people's choice) and then with David (the Lord's choice). That the royal line will continue through David's offspring and not Saul's is confirmed in the covenant of the kingdom made with David (2 Sam. 7:12-16). God will establish his eternal kingdom with a son from David's line. Solomon initially raises hopes but then disappoints, and so the prophets look to the future for the rise of another Davidic king. Isaiah connects him to a virgin birth (Isa. 7:14), prophesying that a child will be born and a son given upon whose shoulders the government of David will rest forever (Isa. 9:6-7). He will be from the root of Jesse (Isa. 11:1), and thus of royal lineage; he will also be the servant of the Lord, and thus of humble beginnings (Isa. 53:2). Through the prophets Jeremiah and Ezekiel, God reiterates the same Davidic promise, only this time it is tied more directly to new covenant conceptualities. In Jeremiah, God promises to raise up for David 'a righteous branch' in the context of making a new covenant with Israel (Jer. 23:5; 30:9; 33:15, 17, 26). The same occurs in Ezekiel: in the context of establishing his (new) covenant of peace with Israel, God promises that his servant David will be king over his people again in the land (Ezek. 37:24-26).

With the coming of Jesus, the promise of a royal line within the offspring of the woman is brought into sharp focus. Matthew's Gospel begins with a genealogy directly connected to the royal line, from Abraham to David, from David to Christ (Matt. 1:1-17). However, the surprising part of the genealogy is that, strictly speaking, Jesus does not descend from the royal line; he is born of Mary but not begotten by Joseph. Nevertheless, following the angel's advice, Joseph takes Mary to be his wife, effectively adopting Jesus into the royal line of David.[22] Hence the title with

---

22. We are not informed from which tribe Mary descended, but from OT law we may deduce that it was most likely the tribe of Judah. In the book of Numbers, Moses made provision for the fatherless daughters of Zelophehad to receive their inheritance on the condition that they married within their tribe (see Num. 27:1-11; 36:6-9; Josh. 17:3-6). With respect to Mary, Jesus may receive royal status from the tribe of Judah via his mother in a general sense, but it is via Joseph that he receives legal entitlement to the throne of David.

which Joseph is addressed is also given to Jesus: 'son of David'. The fact that only Joseph and Jesus receive the title in the Gospels (Matt. 1:20; 9:27; 12:23; 15:22; 20:30; 21:9, 15; 22:42) marks them out directly as heirs of the Davidic promise.

In sum, the promise of a royal son forms a substantive promissory element in the OT covenants, one that finds its conclusion in Jesus, the Son of David. Put differently, the substance of the OT covenant promises is King Jesus.

5. The promise of worldwide blessing

A final substantive promissory element in the biblical covenants is that of worldwide blessing. In the covenant of works, blessing was promised to the world through Adam's personal, perfect, and perpetual obedience to the law of God. But with his Fall, it did not eventuate. So God promised a new Adam, the second and last Adam, through whom such blessing would come (Gen. 3:15). While the mother promise of Genesis 3:15 does not contain an explicit reference to worldwide blessing, it is implied in the context. If the serpent was the prime instigator in robbing the world of blessing, and if the promised second and last Adam will defeat him, then by implication the potential for worldwide blessing is restored. In the covenant of preservation with Noah, worldwide blessing becomes more discernible. The covenant that God forms with Noah and his family before and after the flood (Gen. 6:18; 9:9-11) ensures the blessing of life for the whole world. With Japheth's inclusion in the tent of Shem (Gen. 9:27), there is a subtle hint of blessing overflowing beyond the chosen offspring. However, it is in the covenant of promise with Abraham that worldwide blessing becomes most explicit. The patriarch is spotlighted as the conduit through whom all the families of the earth will be blessed (Gen. 12:3; 22:18). The promise is reiterated in the patriarchal covenant with Isaac and Jacob (Gen. 26:4; 28:14). In the covenant of law with Israel, worldwide blessing recedes into the background as the covenant promises become more focused on blessing Israel in the land upon condition of their obedience (Deut. 28:1-14). However, the idea of worldwide blessing is still present, at least implicitly, in the descriptor given to Israel as 'a kingdom of priests' (Exod. 19:6), which suggests a mediatorial role between God and the nations. In the covenant of the kingdom with David, there is no explicit mention of worldwide blessing (cf. 2 Sam. 7:12-16), and yet the nations are promised as his inheritance while the kings of the earth are encouraged to pay homage to him (Ps. 2:8-12). Moreover, when the covenant promises become effective in the early period of Solomon's kingdom, surrounding nations are blessed. There is peace all around as Solomon, the prince of peace, reigns, and the Queen of Sheba comes from the ends of the earth and returns home blessed from Solomon's bounty (1 Kings 10:13).

In the new covenant, the substantive promissory element of worldwide blessing, present in the OT in different epochs of redemptive history, comes to fulfilment in the coming of Christ. The Apostle Paul identifies Christ as *the* Offspring through whom blessing comes to all the families of the earth who believe in him (Gal. 3:8-9, 14, 16, 29; cf. Gen. 12:3; 22:18; 26:4; 28:14). Jesus's ministry and the subsequent preaching of his gospel to the nations becomes the conduit through which worldwide blessing is administered (Luke 24:46-47). God's light and salvation now extends to the ends of the earth (Acts 13:47; cf. Isa. 49:6).

In sum, worldwide blessing forms an integral promissory element in OT covenant promises, one which finds its fulfilment in Christ, the Offspring of Abraham, through whom universal blessing is found.

One Saviour, one salvation

As demonstrated above, the substance of the covenant of grace—in the promise of enmity, offspring, royal son, and worldwide blessing—is differently administered across the various dispensations of redemptive history. It is in this sense that Presbyterians affirm that the OT covenants of restoration with Adam, preservation with Noah, promise with Abraham, law with Moses/Israel, priesthood with Aaron/Phinehas, kingdom with David/Solomon are all of the same *substance*. That is, they all concern organically connected promises that come to fruition in the person of Jesus Christ—*the seed of the woman, the offspring of Abraham, the royal son in David's line, the one who brings enmity with the serpent to its climax and conclusion, and thus ushers in worldwide blessing*. While the covenants may convey different economies of redemption across various epochs of history, they are all of one substance. Each and all concern God's plan to redeem a people for himself through his Son, Jesus Christ. Paul states it like this: '... the gospel of God, which he promised beforehand through his prophets in the holy Scriptures, concerning his Son ...' (Rom. 1:1b-3a). In short, the substance of the covenant of grace is Christ, the Son of God, the Mediator of God's grace in both the old and new dispensations. It is in this respect that Presbyterians speak of one covenant of grace in substance being differently administered by Christ across both dispensations. In the old dispensation, he ministers his grace under the shadow of promises, types, and sacrifices; in the new dispensation, he ministers his grace in the full revelation of his person and work and the ordinances of baptism and Lord's supper (cf. WCF 7.5; 7.6; 8.6). Another way of saying this is that people in both dispensations are saved the same way: by grace through faith in Christ. OT saints looked to Christ in faith *prospectively*; NT saints look to Christ in faith *retrospectively*—together, they look to Christ in faith *substantively*.

Theologians have employed two important distinctions in this respect.[23] First, they have understood Christ as *incarnandus* (the one who would come in the flesh) and as *incarnatus* (the one who has come in the flesh). Saints in the OT believed in the Christ to come (*Christus incarnandus*), while saints in the NT believe in the Christ who has come (*Christus incarnatus*). This means that Christ is at work in both dispensations, which he can be by way of his role as the eternal Mediator of the covenant of redemption.[24] In this covenant, the eternal Son covenanted himself to be the

---

23. See Harrison Perkins, *Reformed Covenant Theology: A Systematic Introduction* (Bellingham, WA: Lexham Press, 2024), Chapter VIII, 'The Unity of the Covenant of Grace in Christ' (esp. 196-8).

24. This is the covenant of redemption/peace between the Father, Son, and Spirit, also known as the *pactum salutis*.

Mediator of the elect given to him by the Father before the foundation of the world (Eph. 1:4-5; 2 Tim. 1:9). This brings us to a second distinction that theologians employ. Theologians have understood Christ not as *fideiussor* (one who is a conditional surety for a debt to be paid) but as *expromissor* (one who is an unconditional surety for a debt to be paid). In the eternal covenant of redemption, Christ became the *expromissor* Mediator for his elect people, the lamb slain before the foundation of the world (Rev. 13:8). Since he is such a surety before time and then in time, Christ is the same yesterday (in the old dispensation), today (in the new dispensation), and forever (in the age to come) (Heb. 13:8). That is to say, as the eternal Son, Christ has been active in redemptive history ministering his saving grace from the typical administrations in the OT to the final administration in the NT. In short, Christ is the *expromissor* Mediator, *incarnandus* and *incarnatus*, of the covenant of grace.

This is why Christ can speak of himself, along with NT writers, as being present and active in the first dispensation. Christ says that Abraham saw his day and rejoiced (John 8:56); Paul writes that the gospel was preached (not just promised) to Abraham (Gal. 3:8) and that the congregation with Moses in the wilderness drank from a spiritual Rock that followed them, and that Rock was Christ (1 Cor. 10:4); Paul goes on to say that the rebellious among OT Israel put 'Christ to the test' (1 Cor. 10:9)[25]; Peter speaks of NT Christians being 'saved through the grace of the Lord Jesus, just as they [our fathers in the OT] will [be saved]' (Acts 15:11); the writer to the Hebrews mentions how Moses by faith 'considered the reproach of Christ greater wealth than the treasures of Egypt' (Heb. 11:26); and Jude states that Jesus acted as Savior and Judge in the OT: 'Jesus, who saved a people out of the land of Egypt, afterward destroyed those who did not believe' (Jude 1:5). So, the substance in the covenant of grace across both dispensations is one and the same because Christ is one

---

25. Some manuscripts say 'the Lord' in place of Christ, but the point still holds since 'Lord' is a common title for Christ in the NT.

and the same across those dispensations.[26] Of course, sameness in substance does not mitigate difference in circumstance or administration. With respect to redemptive history, Christ's mediation of grace progresses from typical shadow in the old dispensation to antitypical substance in the new dispensation—to Christ himself. As Paul writes in Colossians 2:17: 'these are a shadow of the things to come, but the substance belongs to Christ'. The point that Presbyterians wish to make, however, is that there is no such thing as an 'empty shadow'. Every shadow is connected to a substance. In other words, OT types are not empty types; they are not mere pointers; they are not *signa nuda* (bare signs).[27] Rather, they are *sign*ificant for their time in redemptive history. As Vos comments, 'The bond that holds type and antitype together must be a bond of vital continuity in the progress of redemption.'[28] With a statement like this, Vos stands in the

---

26. Wilhelmus à Brakel, *The Christian's Reasonable Service. Volume 4: Ethics and Eschatology*; trans. Bartel Elshout; ed. Joel R. Beeke (Grand Rapids, MI: RHB, 1995), 4:447-56: "Since Christ is one and the same in both the Old and New Testaments, and since in the New Testament Christ is a vicarious Surety in the absolute sense of the word, then He has also been so in the Old Testament" (4:451).

27. Examples of 'empty types' are seen in expressions of both 1689 Federalism and Progressive Covenantalism. Samuel Renihan is representative of the former when he writes, 'Thus through typology the new covenant, the covenant of grace, was present in the covenants of the Old Testament while remaining distinct from them' (idem, *The Mystery of Christ: His Covenant and His Kingdom* [Cape Coral, FL: 2020], 37). Richard Lucas is representative of the latter when he writes: 'old covenant types are of a different substance than their new covenant antitypes. The difference is not simply one of degree or quantity, but through escalation the antitype has an *a fortiori* (lesser to greater) qualitative difference from the type' (idem, 'The Past and Future of Baptist Covenantal Theology: Comparing 1689 Federalism and Progressive Covenantalism', *SBTJ* 26.1 [2022]: 116-63).

28. The relationship between symbols/signs and types is a complex one in need of careful parsing. Vos brings some helpful clarity:

> A symbol is in its significance something that profoundly portrays a certain fact or principle of relationship of a spiritual nature in a visible form. The things it pictures are of *present existence* and *present application*. They are in force *at the time* in which the symbol operates. With the same thing, regarded as a type, it is different. A typical thing is prospective; it relates to what will become real or applicable in the future.... The main problem to understand is, how the same system of portrayals can have served at one and the same time in a symbolical and typical capacity. Obviously this would have been impossible if the things portrayed had been in each case different or diverse, unrelated to each other. If something is an accurate picture of a certain

Reformed hermeneutical tradition of the Westminster Confession of Faith, which affirms that 'the virtue, efficacy, and benefits' of the gospel were applied to saints in the OT as much as to saints in the NT '*in and by* ... promises, types, and sacrifices' (WCF 8.6; emphasis added). Put differently, the *ordo salutis* was operative as much in the provisional, shadow form of the *historia salutis* as it was in the final, realised form of the *historia salutis*.

In sum, when it comes to the redeeming work of Christ across both dispensations, the creed of Presbyterians is "One Saviour, one salvation."

With respect to the covenant of grace and its continuity, we may consider two more aspects.

B. Structure of the covenant

While the *substance* of the covenant speaks of Christ, the *structure* of the covenant speaks of those to whom Christ is offered in the covenant promises: a chosen representative and their offspring. In each of the biblical redemptive covenants, a genealogical principle is affirmed: with Adam (Gen. 3:15), with Noah (Gen. 6:18; 9:8-9), with Abraham (Gen. 12:3; 13:15-16; 15:4-5, 13-16; 17:2, 7-10, 19, 21; 22:16-18), with Isaac (Gen. 26:3-4), with Jacob (Gen. 28:13-14; 35:11-12), with Israel (Exod. 20:6; 34:7; Deut. 5:10; Jer. 32:18), with Aaron (Num. 18:6-8, 11, 19; 25:12-13), and with David (2 Sam. 7:12). The issue we are concerned with here is whether the genealogical principle, so clearly evident in each of the biblical covenants, *continues* in the new covenant.

---

reality, then it would seem disqualified by this very fact for the pointing to another future reality of a quite different nature. The solution of the problem lies in this, that the things symbolized and the things typified *are not different sets of things*. They are *in reality the same things*, only different in this respect that they come first on a lower stage of development in redemption, and then again, in a later period, on a higher stage. Thus what is symbolical with regard to the already existing edition of the fact or truth becomes typical, prophetic, of the later, final edition of *that same fact or truth*. From this it will be perceived that *a type can never be a type independently of its being first a symbol*. The gateway to the house of typology is at the farther end of the house of symbolism. (Geerhardus Vos, *Biblical Theology: Old and New Testaments* (Edinburgh: Banner of Truth, 1975 [1948]), 144-5 (emphasis added).

Baptists of many stripes (Anabaptists, General Baptists, Particular Baptists, Progressive Covenantal Baptists, etc.) claim that with the coming of the new covenant there is a change to its structure, that is, a change in the membership of that covenant. Stephen Wellum is representative of the general position when he writes, 'one cannot understand the *new* covenant without acknowledging the massive *structural* changes that have taken place'.[29] For Baptists, the structural change relates to the tribal system and the genealogical principle. In the OT covenants, there was a tribal structure, with children being admitted by virtue of their parents—this naturally led to a 'mixed' people of God in the OT since not every circumcised child grew up to believe in the covenant promise of a Redeemer. However, in the new covenant a structural change occurs: the tribal nature of the people of God ends, with children no longer admitted by virtue of their parents. This naturally leads to a 'pure' people of God in the NT since only those who repent and believe are admitted into the covenant community. Thus, according to the Baptist argument, with respect to the genealogical principle, there is a sharp discontinuity between the testaments and across the dispensations. In the OT, the children of covenant members are included—at least at the national level; in the NT, the children of covenant members are excluded—at least at the ecclesial level. This exclusion ensures the purity of the people of God in the new covenant. The problem with the Baptist argument on this point, however, is that the biblical evidence is wholly opposed to it. A close look at OT and NT texts proves the case.

---

29. Stephen J. Wellum, 'Baptism and the Relationship between the Covenants', in *Believer's Baptism: Sign of the New Covenant in Christ* (Nashville, TN: B&H Academic, 2006), 143-4. Particular Baptists of the seventeenth century present a variation on this. They bifurcate the Abraham covenant into two covenants: a spiritual covenant and a national covenant. Children were included in the national covenant and received its sign of circumcision; children were not included in the spiritual covenant of which circumcisions was a sign and seal of righteousness for Abraham alone. For example, see Nehemiah Coxe, *A Discourse of the Covenants that God Made with Men before the Law* (1681), reprinted in *Covenant Theology: From Adam to Christ*, eds. Ronald D. Miller, James M. Renihan, and Francisco Orozco (Palmdale, CA: RBAP, 2005).

First, OT prophecies about the *new covenant* employ the language of the genealogical principle; that is, they presuppose the 'tribal' system. When speaking of the new covenant and its results, Moses and the three major prophets of Isaiah, Jeremiah, and Ezekiel each employ the language of 'and to your children' in some form or other (Deut. 30:6; Isa. 65:23; Jer. 32:39; Ezek. 37:24-25). If the establishment of the new covenant entails a radical repeal or cessation or discontinuance of the genealogical principle then it is not a little strange that these OT prophets employ language that will become null and void at the dawning of the new covenant. The counterargument that the texts concern *spiritual* descendants of believers in the new covenant fails at a contextual and logical level. Contextually, the passages indicate physical children; see especially the opening words of Isaiah 65:23: 'They shall not labour in vain or bear children for calamity.' Logically, to understand the offspring as being spiritual descendants whose hearts God will circumcise (e.g., Deut. 30:6) creates a tautology: by definition, a spiritual descendant already has their heart circumcised. With respect to Jeremiah 31 and the promise of the new covenant, Baptists make wrong deductions from verses read in isolation. For example, they argue that while in the old covenant one generation bore the consequences of sin for a previous generation, in the new covenant the tribal nature of the people of God will end. They base their argument on Jeremiah 31:30: 'But everyone shall die for his own iniquity. Each man who eats sour grapes, his teeth shall be set on edge.' However, to conclude from this verse that parental representation and the genealogical principle will no longer be applicable is a *non sequitur* based on a misreading of the text. The proverbial saying one verse earlier in Jeremiah 31:29 is not a proverb introducing a new arrangement among the people of God; rather, it is a complaint that will no longer be uttered by God's people after they see his righteous judgment in each person dying for their own sins. Indeed, Baptists miss the fact that Jeremiah's language of each person dying for their own sins is borrowed from Moses' language in the old covenant: 'Fathers shall not be put to death because of their children, nor shall children be put to death because of their fathers. Each one shall be put to death for his own sin' (Deut. 24:16). Conceptually, and in part linguistically, Jeremiah's words are virtually the same as Moses'.[30] In other words, what Jeremiah says will be part of the new covenant is as old as Moses and the old covenant. Any argument that Moses is speaking to the future realities of the new covenant era in Deuteronomy 24 is refuted on the grounds that the Mosaic principle is applied by Amaziah in his reign during the era of the old covenant (2 Kings 14:6). Furthermore, whatever the newness of the new covenant means in Jeremiah 31:31-34, it cannot entail a change to the genealogical principle, since in the following chapter (within the context of the prophecy about the new covenant) the prophet employs the covenant refrain: 'to them and to their children after them' (Jer. 32:39). To restate the genealogical principle in one chapter is meaningless if in the previous chapter the prophet has just announced its obsolescence. In sum, the Baptist argument from Jeremiah 31 fails for its wrong deductions and lack of contextual exegesis.

Second, Peter's use of the covenant refrain 'and for your children' in Acts 2:39 indicates continuity of the genealogical principle not discontinuity, and on the very day of new covenant inauguration. Before looking at the meaning of the text in relation to Genesis 17, let us simply note that if the move from old covenant to new covenant entails a sharp discontinuity with respect to the genealogical principle—in the Baptistic framework, an abrogation through reinterpretation—then Peter's choice of language in his Pentecost speech to a crowd of Jews is unfortunate at best and misleading at worst. For how else would a Jew interpret the words 'For the promise is for you and your children', if not in the genealogical framework of the OT covenants? At no point in his Pentecost sermon does Peter expound on the old covenant and the supposed change to the structure in the new covenant, as apparently foreseen by Jeremiah among other prophets; nor

---

30. Apart from the interchangeable words 'sin/iniquity', these two clauses are identical: Deuteronomy 24:16: אִישׁ בְּחֶטְאוֹ יוּמָתוּ; Jeremiah 31:30: כִּי אִם־אִישׁ בַּעֲוֺנוֹ יָמוּת.

does Peter explain how the genealogical principle takes on a new meaning in the covenant. Rather, he employs the covenant refrain without explanation.[31] Moreover, if Peter means *spiritual* children with his use of 'and your children', then the phrase is redundant given his additional words 'and for all who are far off'. Children of believing Jews would come within this latter category since, being outside of the new covenant, they too 'are far off'. Indeed, the final clause 'everyone whom the Lord our God calls to himself' is sufficient to qualify 'for you and for all who are far off'. The only reason, then, for Peter to include the children must be in the context of covenant continuity. Furthermore, the real problem with the Baptist argument is its failure to read Acts 2:39 against the backdrop of the Abrahamic covenant in Genesis 17. In his sealing of the covenant with Abraham, God commands the patriarch to circumcise himself, his children, and all foreigners in his household (Gen. 17:12-13). On the day of Pentecost, Peter informs the Jews gathered in Jerusalem that the promise of the gospel—which is none other than the new covenant itself—is 'for you and your children and for all who are far off' (Acts 2:39). The three groups of people—adult Jews, their children, and foreigners—match exactly the three categories outlined in the Abrahamic covenant. God makes his covenant of promise with Abraham, with his children, and with foreigners bought with his money. If the day of Pentecost marks the great divide between the old and new covenants, and thus a marked change in the structure of the new covenant compared to the old with respect to the tribal system and the genealogical principle, then why does Peter speak in terms that convey continuity not discontinuity? The answer is plain: while Peter sees the fulfilment of the *substance* of OT covenant promises in the ascension of Christ and the outpouring

---

31. Later in Acts, when a seismic redemptive-historical shift occurs in God's covenant dealings with Israel—when Gentiles are included in the people of God alongside Jews—God sends a vision and an angel to explain and confirm the change (Acts 10:9-16; 11:13). The shift from the inclusion of children in the old covenant to their exclusion in the new covenant is surely of the same magnitude, and yet no supernatural phenomena are given to explain this new arrangement of God's covenant dealings with his people.

of the Spirit, Peter sees no change in the *structure* of the new covenant. Hence, he can assert that baptism—a sign of the new covenant of which circumcision is the counterpart, old covenant sign—is applicable for believing adults, their children, and all who are far off.

Third, the household baptisms in Acts suggest continuity not discontinuity of the genealogical principle. Of first note is the relative infrequency of recorded baptisms in general in the NT: there are only twelve recorded occurrences (Acts 2:41; 8:12, 13, 38; 9:18; 10:48; 16:15, 33; 18:8; 19:5; 1 Cor. 1:14, 16), which is somewhat surprising given the preponderance of baptism for the burgeoning NT church. Of these twelve occurrences, four are household baptisms (Cornelius's, Acts 10:47-48; retold again in 11:14[32]; Lydia's, Acts 16:15; the Philippian jailor's, Acts 16:33; and Stephanas's, 1 Cor. 1:16; cf. 16:15). This constitutes one third of the recorded baptisms in the NT, which indicates that household baptism in the first generation of the church was common practice. The number carries significance when set against the Baptist argument for the newness of the new covenant. According to some Baptists, what is new in the new covenant is the structure and nature of the covenant community. For them, the tribal system of households was made obsolete—completely and absolutely; children were no longer included by virtue of their parents. And yet, we are to believe that one third of all recorded baptisms in the NT are *coincidentally* household baptisms. Admittedly, there is no mention of children in these households, and yet to imagine their complete absence seems more than a little far-fetched. But even if there were no children present, the fact that household baptisms occur at the dawning of the new covenant is still a problem point for the Baptist argument. For, once again, as with Peter's speech on Pentecost, the occurrence of such baptisms makes little sense if the newness of the new covenant entails the

---

32. Luke records that Cornelius gathered his relatives and close friends in his home (Acts 10:24). After the Holy Spirit falls on all who were present (Acts 10:44), they were baptised (Acts 10:47-8), thus constituting household baptism of a kind.

complete discontinuity of an OT system that had households and parental presentation at its core. Indeed, to have four household baptisms occur in a short period of time indicates a miraculous phenomenon. As Witherow notes, the Baptist 'requires the reader of Scripture to believe that there were no children in any of these households—that every member of these [four] families was capable of faith—and that, at the very time the head of each house believed, all the other persons in the house believed also'.[33] In contrast, the only paradigm in which household baptisms makes sense is that of covenantal continuity. Moreover, while Baptists contend that paedobaptists cannot produce a single verse that speaks to infant baptism, neither can they with respect to the baptism of children who are born to Christian parents who repent, believe, and then receive the ordinance of baptism. The book of Acts and NT epistles cover a period of about sixty years of the apostolic era, and yet there is not a single recorded instance—not even a hint—of a child from a Christian home being baptised upon profession of faith.[34] Timothy would surely present an ideal example, especially given the kind of things Paul reminds him of in his Christian experience (learning the Scriptures from an early age from his mother and grandmother, 2 Tim. 3:14-15; the gift of teaching given him by the laying on of hands by the elders, 1 Tim. 4:14; and of Paul, 2 Tim. 1:7). Yet there is no mention of Timothy making a good profession of faith in baptism as a believing adult. The argument for a proof text thus cuts both ways. In sum, the fact that, at the dawning of the new covenant, household baptisms occur at all, alongside individual baptisms, supports the argument for covenant continuity not discontinuity.

Fourth, the Apostle Paul assumes the inclusion of children in the new covenant community. In his letters to the churches in Ephesus and Colossae, Paul includes children among those to whom he writes. In Ephesians 1:1, he addresses his epistle 'To the saints who are in Ephesus, and are faithful in Christ Jesus.'

---

33. Witherow, *Scriptural Baptism* in *I Will Build My Church*, 201.
34. Witherow, *Scriptural Baptism* in *I Will Build My Church*, 203-4.

Later he exhorts individuals within the congregation of 'saints' to live out their God-given roles in ways that are 'worthy of the calling' to which they are called (Eph. 4:1). Wives are to submit to their husbands and respect them (Eph. 5:22, 33), while husbands are to love their wives as Christ loved the church and as they do their own bodies (Eph. 5:25-26, 28, 33); children are to obey their parents (Eph. 6:1), while fathers are not to provoke them to anger but bring them up in the discipline and instruction of the Lord (Eph. 6:4); bondservants are to obey their masters (Eph. 6:5-8), while masters are to treat them with good will and in a nonthreatening manner (Eph. 6:9). The same format occurs in Paul's letter to the Colossians, where the apostle includes children in the 'saints and faithful brothers in Christ at Colossae' (Col. 1:2; 3:20). It is noteworthy that Paul addresses the children in both churches without further qualification, as is the case with husbands, wives, bondservants, and masters. He does not speak to 'Children in the Lord' who have repented and believed in Christ; rather, they are simply, 'Children', which therefore includes every child in the church.[35] The observation is significant for what Paul goes on to say to the children. He states the fifth commandment to the children, 'Honor your father and your mother', and then supplies a parenthetic remark, '(this is the first commandment with a promise)', followed by the promise

---

35. In Ephesians 6:1 the prepositional phrase 'in the Lord' (ἐν κυρίωι) modifies the verbal clause 'obey your parents' and not the vocative noun 'Children' (Τὰ τέκνα). The 2LCF in 'The Appendix Concerning Baptism' attempts to narrow the child addressees to 'some believing children of believing parents', to whom the command with promise is given (see James M. Renihan, *To the Judicious and Impartial Reader: A Contextual-Historical Exposition of the Second London Baptist Confession of Faith*, Baptist Symbolics, Volume 2: An Exposition of the 1689 Baptist Confession of Faith [Cape Coral, FL: Founders Ministries, 2022], 606). But this reads into the text what is not there. If there is no qualification on husbands, wives, bondservants, and masters, there can be none for the children. The London confessors admit that elsewhere in Paul's epistles he does not assume all children of Christians are *believers* since in 1 Timothy 3 one of the qualifications of an elder is that his children believe, which assumes that not all men in the church have believing children. But this speaks to our point—in Ephesians Paul addresses *all* the children (believing and unbelieving), counting them *all* as members of the covenant.

itself: 'that it may go well with you and that you may live long in the land' (Eph. 6:2-3). Paul's words are a direct quotation (without citation formula) of Exodus 20:12. In context, the fifth commandment, like all the commandments in Exodus 20, were given as part of the covenant inauguration with Israel at Sinai (Exod. 19–24). For Paul to mention the promise alongside the commandment to the children in Ephesus can mean only one thing: *he views them as legitimate heirs of such a promise, and if so, then as legitimate members of the covenant community.* There is simply no other way to read Paul's application of an OT covenant promise to children in a NT church. On the Baptist framework, the move by the apostle is illegitimate unless every child in Ephesus has professed faith and then been baptised. Covenant promises only belong to covenant members, they argue, and since children of Christian parents are born outside of the covenant and only become members by repentance, faith, and baptism, the promise cannot be indiscriminately given to them. And yet, this is precisely what the Apostle Paul does, which means that the only basis he has for doing so is if he believes that every child in the church is a covenant member; and if they are a covenant member, then they have a right to the covenant sign—namely, baptism. In short, Paul's inclusion of children in his epistolary exhortations points up covenant continuity not discontinuity.

Fifth, the Apostle Paul's declaration that children of at least one believing parent are viewed as 'holy' (1 Cor. 7:14) speaks to a distinction between children of believers and children of unbelievers. The word 'holy' in Scripture is used in two ways: (1) in an essential sense of being; and (2) in a positional sense of consecration. In the first, holy may refer to God, unfallen angels, or the saints; in the second, it may refer to the Sabbath, high priestly garments, vessels and furniture of the tabernacle and temple, the promised land, etc.[36] In Exodus 19:6, God declares Israel will be a 'holy nation', set apart to win the world by being different from the world. Children within this nation were thus viewed as holy, like

---

36. Witherow, *Scriptural Baptism* in *I Will Build My Church*, 197.

their parents. To mark them out as his own, God places the seal of his covenant on their flesh (Gen. 17:13). It is this sense of 'holy' that Paul takes from the Jewish nation and applies to children in the Christian church. By virtue of the faith of at least one of their parents, they are not little pagans, but set apart for God and viewed as his own. This is not a denial of their inherent sinful nature as disobedient children of wrath (Eph. 2:2-3); rather, chosen by the grace of God, they are set apart from the world and counted as God's own. Now, if in the old dispensation such children received the covenant sign of belonging to God, then it logically follows that in the new dispensation children of believers receive the covenant sign of belonging to God. Of course, Paul is not arguing for infant baptism in this passage, but there is a principle at work that relates directly to it. Witherow states it succinctly: 'As the child of a Jew is to be treated as a Jew, so now the child of a Christian is to be treated as a Christian: if one parent is a believer, the children, in virtue of their connection with that parent, are to be reckoned holy.'[37] At this point Baptists are faced with a dilemma: do they view their own children as 'holy'? Presumably so, for the apostle's point is clear. But what does this mean in practice? That they come under the sound of the gospel on a regular basis? That they are raised in the instruction and discipline of the Lord? That they may say the Lord's Prayer at the dinner table in family worship? Though not stated in the text, these are all reasonable deductions by good consequence. But if Baptists make such deductions for the 'holy' state of children from believing homes—and they must make deductions in some form or other—then they ought to afford the same latitude to Presbyterians when they make their own deduction in relation to baptism. In sum, the holy state of children from a home with at least one believing parent suggests covenant continuity not discontinuity.

To conclude this section: just as the *substance* of the covenant of grace is the same across both dispensations, so too is the *structure* of that same covenant. The Presbyterian view allows for administrative development at both the substantive and

---

37. Witherow, *Scriptural Baptism* in *I Will Build My Church*, 198.

structural level. Substantially, types, promises, and sacrifices were the partial revelation of the gospel in provisional, shadow form; in the NT, Christ is the full revelation of the gospel in final, realised form. Structurally, in the OT, only men and boys received the sign of the covenant on their bodies; in the NT, men and women, boys and girls, receive the sign of the covenant on their bodies. But essentially, the substance and the structure do not change across the dispensations. There may be formal or circumstantial development in each case; there is no essential development. The same may also be said with respect to the signage of the covenant.

C. Signage of the covenant

Following on from the substance and structure of the covenant, we turn now to the *signage* of the covenant. If the argument thus far is sound, then the weight of the paradigm not only suggests that baptism is the new covenant sign of which circumcision was the old covenant sign, it requires it to be so. Circumcision as a physical sign symbolised various spiritual realities related to the covenant of grace in its shadow form. Under the old dispensation, circumcision was a cleansing rite, in which the old (flesh) was cut away to bring forth the new (flesh). It was a curse-bearing ordeal that led to a new beginning. As such, circumcision symbolised cleansing from sin (Isa. 52:1; Ezek. 44:6-7), regeneration (Deut. 30:6), repentance (Deut. 10:16; Jer. 4:4), and the sign and seal of righteousness received by faith (Rom. 4:11).[38] Baptism as a physical sign symbolises these same realities as they relate to the covenant of grace in its realised form. As a gospel ordinance, baptism symbolises union with Christ in his death, burial, and resurrection (Rom. 6:3-4; Col. 2:11-12), and all the benefits that ensue from that union, namely, cleansing from sin through forgiveness (Acts 2:38; 22:16; Eph. 5:26; Heb. 10:22), reception of the Holy Spirit (Acts 10:44, 47-48; 1 Cor. 12:13) and regeneration through circumcision of the heart (Col. 2:11; Titus 3:5), resurrection to new life through the powerful working of God (Rom. 6:4; Col. 2:12), and adoption and belonging through naming

---

38. Ferguson, 'Infant Baptism View', 87.

(Matt. 28:19). Thus it can be seen that NT baptism essentially points to the same spiritual realities as OT circumcision. As one Baptist scholar admits, 'circumcision means "essentially" what baptism means in the New Testament'.[39] This being so, a connection begins to emerge between circumcision and baptism, which brings us to a discussion of Colossians 2.

In Colossians 2, Paul speaks of our union with Christ by reference to circumcision and baptism. For Paul, OT circumcision serves as a picture of the inward change that we have experienced. By being 'in him', that is, in Christ, Christians have experienced these realities of spiritual circumcision (by the Spirit) a circumcision different to the physical one (made by hands) on the flesh (v. 11). These realities of spiritual circumcision come to us 'by putting off the body of the flesh' (cf. Col. 3:9; Rom. 6:6; 7:26), which itself comes 'by the circumcision of Christ'. The latter phrase may refer to the accomplished work of Christ's curse-bearing ordeal on the cross (i.e., his cutting-off, 'circumcision' experience that his infant circumcision prefigured[40]) or it may refer to the applied work of Christ circumcising the hearts of his people by the Spirit.[41] In either case, Paul indicates that external circumcision of the flesh served as a sign of the reality of internal circumcision of the heart, with Christ's circumcision work being the foundational cause, either objectively in accomplishment or subjectively in application. It is by our union with Christ that we experience this change; hence Paul's introductory words: *'In him* also you were circumcised.' In verse 12, Paul continues the theme of union with Christ as he ties the experience of internal circumcision to having been buried with Christ in baptism, in

---

39. Paul K. Jewett, *Infant Baptism and the Covenant of Grace* (Grand Rapids: Eerdmans, 1978), p. 96, cited in Ferguson, 'Infant Baptism View', 88.

40. This interpretation reads τοῦ Χριστοῦ as an objective genitive in the phrase τῇ περιτομῇ τοῦ Χριστοῦ. In support, Ferguson, 'Infant Baptism View', 88, and n. 25.

41. This interpretation reads τοῦ Χριστοῦ as a subjective genitive in the phrase τῇ περιτομῇ τοῦ Χριστοῦ. In support, Calvin, *Galatians, Ephesians, Philippians & Colossians*, Calvin's New Testament Commentaries (Carlisle: Paternoster Press, 1996), 332.

which we were also raised with Christ.⁴² In doing so, Paul suggests that baptism is the NT counterpart to OT circumcision.⁴³

The question is which kind of circumcision or baptism does the apostle have in mind in Colossians 2: the external mode or the internal meaning? In verse 11, it would appear to be the internal meaning, since he is speaking of the circumcision that believers have experienced in Christ via a circumcision made *without hands*. External physical circumcision was a sign of this internal spiritual circumcision, but the latter is in Paul's purview here, not the former. And if this is the case, then so too with baptism: Paul has internal Spirit baptism in the foreground of his purview, with external water baptism in the background, if present at all. The logic of verses 11 and 12 may thus be paraphrased as follows: 'In him you were circumcised with a spiritual circumcision made without hands, ... as a result of having been buried with him in spirit baptism'. This fits with what Paul says elsewhere in 1 Corinthians 12:13: 'For in one Spirit we were all baptised into one body—Jews or Greeks, slave or free.' In this respect, physical circumcision and water baptism, as signs appropriate to their respective dispensations, point to these realities. Thus, even if in Colossians 2 Paul is speaking more of *the things signified* by circumcision and baptism rather than of *the signs* themselves, the language of circumcision and baptism naturally brings the signs to mind and raises the question of how they relate. Since both point to the same complex of interconnected spiritual realities—namely, spiritual circumcision and union with Christ—a connection between the signs of circumcision and baptism is at least

---

42. On this logic, we read the participle 'having been buried' (συνταφέντες) as tied adverbially to the mainline verb 'you were circumcised' (περιετμήθητε). The participial clause relates to the main verbal clause as means: 'In him you were circumcised ... *by the means of* having been buried with him in baptism.' In other words, internal circumcision comes through union with Christ in the 'circumcision' of his death, burial, and resurrection.

43. Calvin, *Galatians, Ephesians, Philippians & Colossians*, 332: 'Christ ... accomplishes in us spiritual circumcision, not through means of that ancient sign, which was in force under Moses, but by baptism. Baptism, therefore, is a sign of the thing exhibited, which when it was absent was figured by circumcision.'

'THE WEIGHT OF THE PARADIGM'

implied. However, most Baptist scholars argue that since physical circumcision is fulfilled in spiritual circumcision, there is no intended connection between circumcision and baptism.[44] But this is overly simplistic, for two reasons. First, it fails to acknowledge that in Colossians 2:11-12 Paul speaks of both circumcision and baptism within the same one-sentence complex. The sentence structure conveys that some kind of relation must exist between circumcision and baptism. Second, while it is true that physical circumcision (as sign) points to spiritual circumcision (as the thing signified), it does not follow that there is no connection between circumcision (as sign) and baptism (as sign). If one acknowledges that water baptism symbolises spirit baptism—which is the same thing as spiritual circumcision (the thing signified)—then one must accept that a connection between circumcision and baptism exists on the redemptive-historical plane at some level, since both signs point to the same reality. In other words, the OT sign of physical circumcision, which points to spiritual circumcision, is replaced by the NT sign of baptism, which also points to spiritual circumcision. In this sense, baptism may be said to fulfil and replace circumcision *at the level of signage*.[45] Diagram 2 illustrates the point.

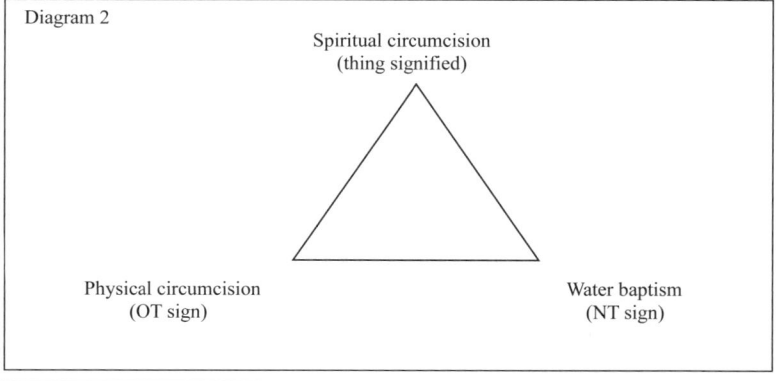

---

44. Wellum, "Relationship between the Covenants," 158-9.
45. Baptists argue that if this is the case, then the absence of any replacement theology in the Council of Jerusalem is conspicuous by its absence (e.g. Ware, 'Believer's Baptism', 46-7). However, as Sinclair Ferguson points out, the issues caused by the Judaizers ran deeper than simply responding with 'Baptism replaces circumcision'. The fundamental

While Baptists disagree with this scheme, the fact is that they (especially Particular Baptists) accept the same scheme with respect to Passover and Lord's supper, on the one hand, and the Sabbath and Lord's Day, on the other hand. For example, in the OT, the Passover meal (as a memorial sign to the typical Passover lamb) points to the death of Christ as a Passover sacrifice on the cross (as the thing signified). In the NT, the Lord's supper (as a memorial sign) also points to the death of Christ as a Passover sacrifice on the cross (as the thing signified), thus forming a connection with the Passover meal on the redemptive-historical plane at some level, as NT sign to OT sign. In this sense, the Lord's supper may be said to fulfil and replace the Passover meal *at the level of signage* (see Diagram 3).

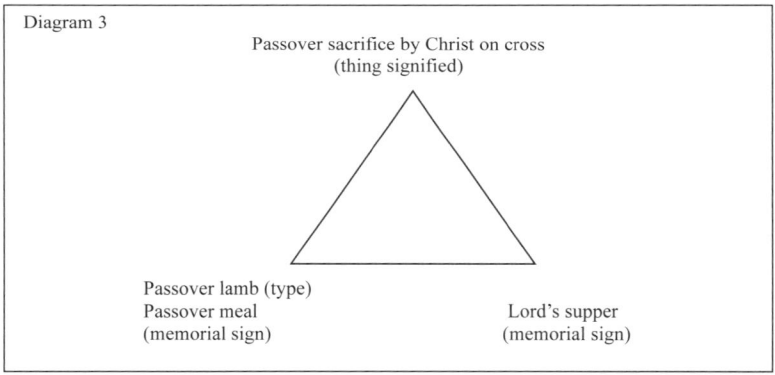

The same holds true with respect to the Sabbath. In the OT, the Sabbath (as sign) points to the eternal rest in heaven (as the thing signified). In the NT, the Lord's Day (as sign) points to the same reality of eternal rest in heaven (as the thing signified), thus forming a connection with the Sabbath on the redemptive-historical plane at some level, as NT sign to OT sign. In this sense, the Lord's Day may be said to fulfil and replace the Sabbath *at the level of signage* (see Diagram 4).

---

issue concerned the nature of the gospel, which would not have been easily resolved by simply referring to an ordinance of the gospel; 'one can replace circumcision with baptism yet retain the theology of the Judaizers' (Ferguson, 'Infant Baptism Response', 59; cf. also 88).

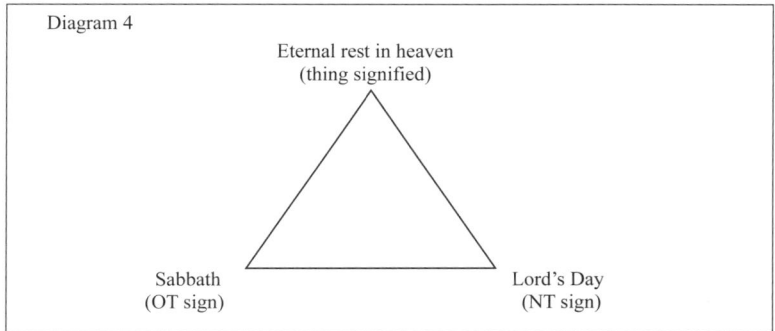

In each case there is some advance in the movement from OT to NT: with the Passover meal, the feast of unleavened bread is developed in the Lord's supper to include bread and wine; with the Sabbath, the day of observance changes in the Lord's Day from the last day of the week to the first day of the week; and with circumcision, the placement of the covenant sign on only men and boys is expanded in baptism to include men and women, boys and girls. If newness in the ordinances of Lord's supper and Lord's Day is acknowledged, then it must also be in the ordinance of baptism.

Conclusion

In summary, if the covenant of grace continues across both dispensations—moving from shadow to reality, from type to antitype—then the signage of that covenant must also continue. In the OT, the sign is circumcision; in the NT, with the dawning of a new dispensation, the sign becomes baptism. The book of Acts records the period of temporal overlap between the retirement of one sign and the introduction of another sign; hence why both are practiced for a time. However, once the church expands beyond the borders of Judea and Samaria and moves beyond the apostolic era, baptism becomes the permanent sign and seal of the new covenant.

Implications for baptism

Having established the continuity of the covenant of grace across both dispensations in its substance, structure, and signage, we conclude with two implications for Christian baptism. First, children of at least one Christian parent are legitimate recipients of baptism because the substance and structure of the covenant of grace does not change in redemptive history; and the reason it does not change is because the God of grace does not change (Ps. 102:26-27; Mal. 3:6; James 1:17). Second, in the old dispensation if God commanded that circumcision (as a sign of the covenant of grace) be placed on children of covenant members *before* they believed, why in the new covenant dispensation would the order of sign and faith be different? If the argument for the substance and structure of the covenant of grace continuing across both dispensations holds, then so too does the argument for the signage of that same covenant being placed on children prior to their expressing repentance and faith. Put simply, if God instituted the order of sign then faith in the provisional, shadow form of the covenant of grace in the first dispensation, why would he discontinue that order in the final, realised form of the covenant of grace in the second dispensation? To do so would be to change the constitution of the church from one dispensation to the next. Indeed, to do so would be to change (or at least infer change in) the character of God from one dispensation to the next.

The catholicity of baptism

In closing, we return to the divide over baptism with which this chapter began. Our proposal is that the solution to the baptismal divide is a return to covenant theology, a covenant theology grounded in careful exegesis of Scripture in its diverse parts across both dispensations and in the essential unity of all those parts across those same dispensations; more profoundly, the answer is found in a return to the God of the covenant, who in himself (*ad intra*), and therefore who in his relation to humanity (*ad extra*), is the same God of grace across both dispensations. When the Church catholic does this—when she returns to the one covenant of grace and thus to the immutable God of grace—then 'the weight of the paradigm' will indeed overwhelm, and she will again confess *ex animo*: 'one Lord, one faith, one baptism'.

CHAPTER NINE

The Zurich Consensus

The Lord's Supper and the Pursuit of Unity in an Age of Discord

Jon D. Payne

An unwavering commitment to theological fidelity should never diminish the charitable pursuit of Christian unity. In fact, it should always strengthen it. Ian Hamilton has not only taught this principle, he has also consistently modelled it throughout his long and faithful ministry. His gracious expression of reformed catholicity is a breath of fresh air in a culture where censorious partisanship is often mistaken for public courage or doctrinal clarity. Instead of taking a parochial and insular posture, Ian writes: 'We must see beyond ourselves to all who are fighting the good fight of faith and warring against our great enemy, the devil. We must cultivate a brotherly spirit towards all who love the Lord Jesus Christ in sincerity and truth.'[1] True believers, whatever their denominational stripe, contend with a common enemy and are united to the same Lord. Attitudes towards fellow believers should reflect this reality.

---

1. Ian Hamilton, "Pride and the Reformed Churches" in Banner of Truth Online Magazine, October 13th, 2001.

The 'brotherly spirit' to which Ian refers is not merely a form of Glaswegian affability or Highland courtesy. It is the Spirit-empowered impulse to treat fellow Christians with 'all humility and gentleness, with patience, bearing with one another in love, eager to maintain the unity of the Spirit in the bond of peace' (Eph. 4:2-3; cf. Gal. 5:22-23). Where the Spirit of God is present, so is love for the brethren.[2]

Ian Hamilton is a highly esteemed pastor-scholar. His sermons, lectures, and writings have had a wonderful ripple effect around the world. He has the reputation of being resolutely devoted to confessional orthodoxy, while maintaining a generous spirit of reformed catholicity. On a personal level, Ian is a beloved mentor and friend to me. I am thankful for his godly example, steadfast encouragement, and considerable influence in my life and ministry. Therefore, I am delighted to contribute to this *festschrift* in his honour, marking the occasion of his seventy-fifth birthday.

Highlighted in the pages that follow is a snapshot from the ministry of John Calvin. It is fitting to focus on the Genevan reformer. According to Ian, Calvin has 'inspired and shaped' his life and ministry 'more than any other human.'[3]

The Ecumenical Churchman

Calvin laboured tirelessly to unify the burgeoning Protestant churches in Europe. A major focus of his unifying effort centred on the doctrine of the Lord's Supper. Jesus instituted the Supper to unite his followers, not to divide them. Therefore, Calvin pursued confessional solidarity on the Lord's Supper with both Lutherans and those of a Reformed identity. He sought to bring harmony

---

2. Iain Murray explains: 'If love is the gift of the Spirit, it follows that an eminent degree of the Holy Spirit's working will be marked by eminent degrees of love between Christians. A narrow party spirit cannot coexist with a larger giving of the Spirit whose communion extends to the whole body of Christ. Exclusive attention to denominational interests may prevail among Christians in a period of spiritual decline; it never does so in days of enlarged blessing.' Iain Murray, *Revival and Revivalism*, Edinburgh: Banner of Truth Trust, 1994, 26.

3. Ian Hamilton, "Learning About John Calvin" in Banner of Truth Online Magazine, May 5, 2009.

between splintered Protestant movements on this hotly disputed issue. Lindberg states: 'It is the vision of the reform of the whole of Europe that contributes to Calvin's reputation as an ecumenical churchman.'[4] Contrary to popular opinion, Calvin was not an entrenched theological curmudgeon. He truly was an ecumenical churchman. A prime example of Calvin's irenic spirit, and his eagerness to foster confessional unity, is in the formation of the Consensus Tigurinus (1549).

The Consensus Tigurinus[5] (Zurich Consensus) is an agreement on the sacraments that was completed by 1549 by John Calvin (1509–64) and Heinrich Bullinger (1504–75). The succinct confession, constituted of twenty-six articles, chiefly addresses the theology of the Lord's Supper. Its aim was to unite the two major branches of the Swiss reformation.[6] Calvin and Bullinger 'understood the need for unity, but they also understood how deep the divisions within the Protestant world ran, and it is a measure of their desire for mutual support that they could put their names to a document on the Lord's Supper.'[7] Published in 1551, the agreement received the Latin title: *Consensio mutua in re sacramentaria ministorum Tigurnae Ecclesia et D. Ioannis Calvini ministri Genevensis Ecclesia*. It was fashioned amidst the

---

4. Carter Lindberg, *The European Reformations* (Oxford: Blackwell Publishing, 1996), 272-73.

5. The name is in reference to an ancient region of Switzerland, *Pagus Tigurinus*.

6. ed. Hans Hillerbrand, "Consenus Tigurinus" by Paul Robert Sanders in The Oxford Encyclopedia of the Reformation, volume one (Oxford: Oxford University Press, 1996), 414-415.

7. eds. Bruce Gordon and Emidio Campi, *Architect of the Reformation: An Introduction to Heinrich Bullinger, 1504-1575* (Grand Rapids: Baker, 2004), 20. Eire states that "The most basic division within the Reformed tradition was between the Swiss Reformed and the Calvinists. The Swiss Reformed claimed an older pedigree, holding Ulrich Zwingli and Heinrich Bullinger in the highest esteem. The Calvinists were upstarts of sorts, since John Calvin was a second-generation Reformer who derived his theology from the Swiss Reformed. The two branches of the Reformed family agreed on many substantial points of doctrine, but not all. The Calvinists would end up having a greater influence on Europe as a whole, and the term Calvinist came to be synonymous with Reformed in many places. Reformed orthodoxy, then, was to a great extent linked to Calvinism." Carlos M. Eire, *Reformations: The Early Modern World, 1450-1650* (New Haven: Yale University Press, 2016), 569.

rising tides of theological controversy. The Lord's Supper was at the centre of the storm, especially with respect to the Lutheran and Reformed branches of the Reformation.[8]

Historical Developments

Reformation confessions were not produced in a vacuum. They were written in uncertain times, amidst political strife and ecclesiastical discord. The *Consensus Tigurinus* was no exception. To understand the nature of the accord, therefore, one must be aware of the historical context.

Luther Contra Zwingli

In 1544 Martin Luther unleashed a new offensive against the Zwinglian view of the Lord's Supper in his *Kurze Bekenntnis vom Heiligen Sacrament* [tr. A Short Confession of the Holy Sacrament]. With echoes from the Marburg Colloquy (1529), the German reformer 'resurrected his vitriolic broadside'[9] against the Zurich church's symbolic memorialism.

The memorialism taught by Zwingli and maintained by Bullinger (Zwingli's successor at the Grossmünster) was deeply offensive to Luther. The Wittenberg reformer saw the Zwinglian view as a direct affront to the gospel. Indeed, for Luther, a denial of the real presence of Christ's body and blood *in, mit, und unter* the elements was a clear denial of Christ's gospel promises. The Lord's Supper was a divine mystery, and must be embraced by faith, not reason. Luther 'could not explain how Christ's body and

---

8. For further primary source material on the sacramental views of Calvin and Bullinger see, John Calvin, *Treatises On The Sacraments*; trans. from the original Latin and French by Henry Beveridge (Grand Rapids: Reformation Heritage Books, 2002) and Henry Bullinger, *The Decades of Henry Bullinger*, volume 2 (Grand Rapids: Reformation Heritage Books, 2004), 226-478. In addition, for a historical theology of the Lord's Supper in the Reformed Church see Hughes Oliphant Old, *Holy Communion in the Piety of the Reformed Church* (Powder Springs, GA: Tolle Lege Press, 2013).

9. ed. James T. Dennison, Jr., *Reformed Confessions of the 16th and 17th Centuries in English Translation, volume one, 1523-1552* (Grand Rapids: Reformation Heritage Books, 2008), 537.

blood could serve as vehicles for the Word that forgives sins and bestows life and salvation. But he was certain that with God even that is possible.'[10] Luther refused to spiritualise Christ's plain words: 'Take, eat; this *is* my body' and 'Drink of it, all of you, for this *is* my blood of the covenant, which is poured out for many for the forgiveness of sins' (Matt. 26:26-28):

> Luther thought it sufficient that Christ had said it ... [and] human reason cannot always fathom and can never master God's syntax. Therefore, the Wittenberg reformer thought that there is no reason why the Second Person of the Trinity, who had assumed human flesh and blood, could not offer his body and blood for the forgiveness of sins, life, and salvation if he wanted to do so.[11]

The Zurich reformers were unconvinced. So were their Swiss counterparts in Geneva. They insisted that Christ's humanity would be altogether ruined if Luther's teaching was correct. After all, how could Christ's true humanity be preserved while being simultaneously torn apart and placed on communion tables around the world? It was a fair question. Zwingli objected that it was impossible for the human body and blood of Christ to be present on altars throughout Christendom since the spatially circumscribed and localised human nature of Christ had ascended into heaven to be at the right hand of God.[12]

The eucharistic controversy between Luther and Bullinger raged unabated from the 1530's to 1550's.[13] It was Bullinger who

---

10. Robert Kolb and Charles P. Arand, *The Genius of Luther's Theology: A Wittenberg Way of Thinking for the Contemporary Church* (Grand Rapids: Baker, 2008), 199.

11. Ibid. On the ubiquity of Christ, Luther asserts that "according to his divinity Christ is everywhere. So I have written against Zwingli ... Christ is God and man in one person. Where I seek God, there I'll find him. Accordingly when we think of divinity we must turn our eyes away from time and space because our Lord God and Creator must be beyond space and time and creature." Luther's Works, *Table Talk*, volume 54 (Philadelphia: Fortress Press, 1967), 92-93.

12. Ibid.

13. The intense disagreement continues to be a major impasse between Lutherans and Reformed today.

became the manager of Zwingli's 'doctrinal legacy'[14] after his mentor's untimely death at the Battle of Kappel in 1531. It was far from pleasant finding oneself as Luther's theological opponent. The ardent German reformer did not hold back when criticising Zwingli nor Bullinger, either in formal public treatises or in conversation around the dinner table. Luther was relentless. Less than two years after Zwingli's death, Luther is recorded saying: 'I've bitten into many a nut, believing it to be good, only to find it wormy. Zwingli and Erasmus are nothing but wormy nuts that taste like excrement in one's mouth.'[15]

Five years later, in 1538, Luther attacked Zwingli and his camp, whom he argued possessed a 'speculative' view of the body and blood of Christ at the Lord's Table. The Wittenberg reformer regarded them as false brethren:

> First they taught that there is nothing but bread and wine [in the Lord's Supper]. Then they taught that the body and blood are present spiritually, that is, speculatively. Finally, they taught that they [the body and blood], are received bodily, but [only] in faith. These are nothing but philosophical ideas ... The landgrave, once desired that we call each other brothers, but I was unwilling, although Zwingli declared with tears that he wished to remain in our church and to have no separation between us. I hope he was punished on earth and has come to his right mind. There will always be perils in false brethren.[16]

Zwingli was not the only target of Luther's invectives. Luther states: "'Before the world existed, God said, 'Let there be a world,' and the world was. So, he says here, 'Let this be my body,' and it is; *nor is it prevented by the scoffing of Bullinger*, who says that because the body of Christ isn't seen it isn't present.'"[17] After Luther's sacramental offensive, the pastor of the Zurich Grossmünster reached out to Calvin for support. In 1546 Bullinger sent Calvin

---

14. Sanders, *Consenus*, 414.
15. LW, vol. 54, 72.
16. LW, vol. 54; 284.
17. LW, vol. 54; 89.

an unpublished manuscript of his *De Sacramentis,* and asked for advice and feedback on his work. The following year Calvin responded with copious annotations. A flurry of letter writing ensued over the next two years. It was during this time that the two reformed pastors 'developed a close relationship that transcended clear differences in their characters and theological inclinations.'[18] In a moving letter to the Zurich Reformer on 1 March 1548, Calvin writes:

> In whatever way I may hold the firm persuasion of a greater communication of Christ in the Sacraments than you express in words, we will not, on that account, cease to hold the same Christ, and to be one in him. Some day, perhaps, it will be given us to unite in fuller harmony of opinion.[19]

It is refreshing to witness such an irenic spirit penetrating the intense eucharistic battles of the day. Even so, coming to a consensus on the Lord's Supper would not happen overnight. The disagreements between Calvin and Bullinger were not insignificant. It is interesting to note that Calvin hardly mentions Bullinger's predecessor in his correspondence and tracts. Indeed, Calvin only refers to Zwingli a total of eight times in his 1200 surviving letters, and only six times in his numerous tracts.[20] Of course, this was no oversight. The intentional omission of the prominent Zurich reformer was due to Calvin's tireless efforts to unify the various branches of the Reformation. The name Zwingli touched a deep nerve in many, especially the Lutherans. Moreover, the Genevan reformer's 'opponents in the French-speaking lands invoked the name of Zwingli to attack his teaching.'[21] Consequently, in the documents and letters connected to the *Consensus,* Zwingli's name is conspicuous by its absence.

---

18. Lindberg, *European Reformations,* 258.
19. John Calvin, *Tracts and Letters,* volume five (Edinburgh: Banner of Truth, 2009), 160 (Italics mine).
20. Bruce Gordon, *Zwingli: God's Armed Prophet* (New Haven: Yale, 2021), 266-267.
21. Ibid., 267.

Unlike the Zwinglians, Calvin maintained that the true substantial (*substantia*) presence of Christ was received by faith in the eucharist. The bread and wine were more than bare signs. The Supper was not merely a memorial or remembrance of Christ's death. Calvin contended that when a believer receives the signs, he also receives that which they signify. Therefore, as a communicant partakes of the bread and wine, by faith, he truly receives Christ, and participates (*participes*) in his body. The eucharist is 'not just about memory, but the substance of Christ is received in the sacrament, and Christ's life is infused into believers.'[22] To be sure, the Genevan reformer vehemently rejected the Catholic and Lutheran views of the corporal presence of Christ in the Supper. Yet he insisted that Christ was truly present at communion, albeit spiritually, and received by the instrument of faith.

> I say therefore, that in the mystery of the Supper, by the signs of bread and wine Christ is *truly* delivered to us, *yea and his body and blood*, in which he hath fulfilled all obedience for purchasing of righteousness to us: namely that first we should grow together into one body with him: and then being made partakers *of his substance*, we may also feel his power in the communicating of all his good things.[23]

According to Calvin, true believers feed upon Christ, through faith, at the Lord's Table. The sacrament is life and nourishment to the Christian's soul.[24] This profound mystery is intended more for the believer's apprehension than for his comprehension:

---

22. J. Todd Billings, *Calvin, Participation, and the Gift: The Activity of Believers in Union with Christ* (Oxford: Oxford University Press, 2007), 98.

23. John Calvin, *Institutes of the Christian Religion* (Glasgow: Printed by John Bryce and Archibald McLean, jr., for Alexander Irvine, 1762) Book IV, xvi; 11; p. 657 (Italics mine).

24. Ian Hamilton echoes Calvin when he explains that, "Believers are expected to benefit from participation in the Lord's Supper. The Lord has not left us a spectacle to admire, but a Supper for us to eat and be spiritually nourished by. Just as we give our children food to nourish them, so the Lord has given his children food to nourish them … the sacraments are 'means of grace.' They are not bare or empty symbols, but vehicles for the Holy Spirit to bring us into sweeter communion with our risen Saviour, cf. 1 Cor. 10:16." *How should I Benefit from Communion?* in Banner of Truth Online Magazine; August 8. 2008.

> Let the sum be, that our souls are so fed with the flesh and blood of Christ, as bread and wine do maintain and sustain the bodily life …But although it seem incredible, that in so great a distance of places the flesh of Christ reacheth to us that it may be meat to us; let us remember how much the secret power of the Spirit surmounteth above all our senses, and how foolish it is to measure his unmeasurableness by our measure. That therefore which our mind comprehendeth not, let our faith conceive, that the Spirit truly knitteth in one those things that are severed in places.[25]

Here Calvin almost sounds Lutheran. The Genevan pastor's use of the terms *substantia, exhibere,* and *vera participes* were unacceptable to Bullinger.[26] For a consensus to be reached between the two Swiss pastors accommodation would be needed.

In an exchange of letters from 1547-1549, Calvin and Bullinger engaged in an irenic dialogue chiefly focused upon 'what, if anything, takes place during the celebration of the sacraments.'[27] Negotiations advanced throughout their correspondence, most positively in a letter from Bullinger to Calvin in November of 1548 - a letter in which he set forth twenty-four propositions on the Lord's Supper.[28] Six months later, in the Spring of 1549, Calvin and his mentor, William Farel (1498-1565) travelled to Zurich for an unannounced visit to edit and finalise the *Consensus Tirgurinus*.[29] The trip came only a few weeks after the sorrowful death of Calvin's cherished wife, Idelette.[30]

---

25. Calvin, *Institutes*, IV; xvi; 10.
26. Billings, *Participation*, 96-97.
27. Sanders, *Consenus*, 414.
28. Ibid.
29. Donald K. McKim and Jim West, *Heinrich Bullinger: An Introduction to His Life and Theology* (Eugene, OR: Cascade Books, 2022), 135.
30. In a letter to Pierre Viret on April 7th, 1549, Calvin expressed exceeding sadness over his wife's death. 'Although the death of my wife has been exceedingly painful to me, yet I subdue my grief as well as I can … and truly mine is no common source of grief. I have been bereaved of the best companion of my life, of one who, had it been so ordered, would not only have been the willing sharer of my indigence, but even of my death. During her life she was the faithful helper of my ministry. From her I never experienced the slightest hindrance. She was never troublesome to me throughout the entire course of her illness; she was more anxious about her children

Making use of Bullinger's *De Sacramentis*, Calvin's *Genevan Confession*, and the content of their constructive written exchanges, the Swiss pastors commenced work on a final draft of a confession. With astonishing efficiency, they completed the *Consensus Tigurinus* within two hours. In a letter to Martin Bucer (1491–1551), in June of 1549, Calvin comments: 'At the commencement of our deliberations, agreement seemed really hopeless. [But] light suddenly broke forth ... [and] we agreed without difficulty.'[31] Calvin and Bullinger's patient and persevering correspondence over the course of many years had borne the fruit of agreement.

The *Consensus* is constituted of twenty-six articles.[32] While the document is a cooperative work, the first twenty articles were penned by Calvin, and the last six by Bullinger. It would not go to the printing press, however, until March 1551. This occurred soon after the Genevan reformer strongly urged Bullinger, in a letter dated 17th of February, to publish the Consensus in light of 'individuals of a malignant, morose, and ill-natured disposition, [who] are making an ado about our union.'[33] The Lutherans, of course, were (and still are) highly displeased with the sacramental theology of the *Consensus*. It's been characterised as a muddled expression of 'Zwinglian Calvinism' in which the Lord's Supper is reduced to 'empty signs' and a 'real absence' of Christ.[34] In addition, the *Consensus* 'aroused deep suspicion' in some of the other Swiss churches, such as in Berne. The Bernese and others felt slighted for not being invited to participate in the discussions.[35]

---

than about herself.' John Calvin, *Tracts and Letters, volume 5, Letters, Part 2: 1545-1553* (Edinburgh: Banner of Truth, 2009), 216.

31. John Calvin, *Tracts and Letters, volume five, Letters, Part 2: 1545-1553* (Edinburgh: Banner of Truth, 2009), 235-236.

32. A full English translation of the *Consensus Tigurinus* is found in ed. James T. Dennison, Jr., *Reformed Confessions of the 16th and 17th Centuries in English Translation, volume 1, 1523-1552* (Grand Rapids: Reformation Heritage Books, 2008), 538-45.

33. John Calvin, *Tracts and Letters, volume 5, Letters, Part 2: 1545-1553* (Edinburgh: Banner of Truth, 2009), 305 .

34. John Theodore Mueller, "Notes on the Consensus Tigurinus of 1549," Concordia Theological Monthly, Volume 20, Article 73, December 1949, 903-909.

35. Bruce Gordon, *The Swiss Reformation* (Manchester: Manchester University Press, 2002), 176.

Not all were opposed to the new confession, however. In fact, it received high praise throughout Protestant Europe. The *Consensus Tigurinus* was adopted by the churches in 'Zurich, Geneva, Neuchatel, Bienne, Pays de Vaud, the Grisons (Graubunden), Basil, St. Gall, Schaffhausen, and Mulhausen.'[36] Dealing with their own set of issues, it took the church in Berne a bit longer to adopt the *Consensus*. But they finally approved it in September 1549. The *Consensus* was also commended by Martin Bucer, Peter Martyr Vermigli (1500–62), and many other English theologians.[37]

The Content of the Confession

As stated above, the *Consensus Tigurinus* is a confession written to unite the Swiss churches around a Reformed view of the sacraments (especially the Lord's Supper), and is 'generally recognised to be a compromise position for Calvin's sacramental theology in relation to that of Bullinger and his predecessor Zwingli.'[38] Regarding its content and structure, it sets forth positive teaching on the nature and benefits of the sacraments (articles 1-9), while also strongly refuting the sacramental views of Catholics and Lutherans (articles 10-26).

The Church and her 'spiritual government' exist to 'bring us to Christ.' He is the 'end of the law' the 'sum total of the gospel' and the 'ultimate end of a blessed life.' To deviate from this truth 'in the slightest point' always leads to erroneous views of the sacraments. One must 'start from Christ' to 'speak fittingly' of baptism and the Lord's Supper. [Articles 1-2]

---

36. Dennison, *Reformed Confessions*, 538.

37. Ibid.

38. J. Todd Billings, *Calvin, Participation, and the Gift: The Activity of Believes in Union with Christ* (Oxford: Oxford University Press, 2007), 96. Billings explains that when Calvin crossed theological swords with Lutheran Joachim Westphal in the 1550's, Calvin, "moves beyond the language of the Mutual Consent to that of 'true participation' in Christ, feeding upon the substance of Christ, along with other themes from his more mature eucharistic theology of the *Institutes* of 1539/43, the *Short Treatise*, and relevant commentaries. Indeed, the centrality of this language is shown by the title of Calvin's final treatise on the subject, The True Partaking of the Flesh and Blood of Christ in 1561." (99)

Christ, the eternal Son of God 'has taken upon himself our flesh, to bring to us, by right of adoption, what belonged to him by nature ... that we may be sons of God.' United to Christ by the regeneration of the Holy Spirit, the believer receives new life and the imputation of perfect righteousness. As our High Priest in the flesh, Jesus 'expiated our sins by the unique sacrifice of his own death.' Christ must also 'be reckoned as king, who enriches us with every kind of good thing, who rules and protects us by his power, who provides us with spiritual weapons that we may stand unconquered against the world and the devil, who frees us from all harm and who governs and guides us by the sceptre of his mouth.' In order for Christ to show us himself in these offices, and 'produce these effects in us, he must be made one with us, and grow together into his body.' In vital union with Christ, and indwelt by the Holy Spirit, the believer enjoys spiritual communion with Jesus, and is 'a partaker of all the blessings which reside in him.' To attest to this spiritual reality, Jesus instituted the preaching of the gospel and the sacraments of baptism and the Lord's Supper. [Articles 3-6]

The sacraments are 'marks and badges of Christian profession' and 'brotherhood.' They are meant to 'incite us to thanksgiving and exercise of faith and godly living.' They are 'contracts binding us to this.' Baptism and the Lord's Supper are also 'living pictures which influence our senses in a deeper way, as if leading up to the thing itself' helping us to better exercise our faith. What God has 'pronounced with his mouth, is confirmed and ratified as if by seals.' Therefore, there is 'no doubt that God grants within us by his Spirit that which the sacraments figure to our eyes and other senses.' While a 'distinction' must be drawn 'between the signs and the things signified' it is important that 'we do not disjoin the truth from the signs.' When the believer embraces by faith the promises offered in the sacraments, he truly receives 'Christ spiritually with his spiritual gifts.' [Articles 7-9]

The focus must not be upon 'the bare signs but rather to the promise attached to them.' It is through faith in Christ and his gospel promises that we become 'partakers of Christ.' The signs themselves cannot give us Christ. We should not 'gaze' upon them as if they did. 'The sacraments, separated from Christ, are nothing but empty masks.' Even so, in the sacraments 'a voice clearly resounds, telling us to hold fast to none other than Christ alone and to seek the grace of salvation nowhere else.' [Articles 10-12]

The sacraments 'will profit nothing unless God in all things makes them effective ... [for] the whole work of salvation must be ascribed to Him alone.' Therefore, it is 'Christ who truly baptises within, and who in the Supper makes us partakers of himself.' It is the 'Spirit alone' who 'begins and perfects faith' through the sacraments in the lives of his elect. Those who receive communion apart from true and saving faith do not receive Christ. 'For the signs are administered to the reprobate as well as to the elect, but the reality only reaches the latter.' [Articles 13-18]

The believer's communion with Christ is not exclusively tied to the sacraments. 'Even outside the use of the sacraments the reality which is figured remains firm for the faithful.' Moreover, the spiritual benefits that the believer receives are not tied exclusively to the moment of its administration. The fruit could come much later. [Articles 19-21]

The *Consensus* rejects 'those ridiculous interpreters who insist on what they call the precise literal sense of the solemn words of the Supper—This is my body, this is my blood.' The Lord's Supper should not be 'understood as though there was an intermingling or transfusion of substance. But we draw life from the flesh once offered in sacrifice and the blood poured out for expiation.' To 'affix Christ' to the elements 'by our imagination' leads many to 'make an idol' of them. The doctrine of the papists (transubstantiation) is a 'fiction' as much as all 'stupid fantasies and worthless quibbles which either derogate from his heavenly glory or do not really agree with the truth of his human nature.' The resurrected, ascended, and exalted Christ 'bearing the nature and fashion of a human body, is finite and contained in heaven as in a place.' Therefore, he cannot be dragged down from heaven, torn apart, and placed on tables. [Articles 22-26][39]

The summary above illustrates that the *Consensus* is a *via media* between Zurich and Geneva, and 'forges acceptable reformed terminology to describe a reformed doctrine of the sacraments.'[40] Bullinger's spirited rejection of the corporeal presence of Christ in the eucharist, contra Wittenberg and Rome, is balanced by Calvin's emphasis upon the eucharist's instrumentality and Spirit-wrought efficaciousness in the lives of the elect. Concessions were made by both reformers for the sake of unity. Sanders states that 'Calvin undoubtedly sacrificed some of the key terms he had developed between 1539 and 1545 to describe the Lord's Supper in particular.'[41] In some places the language of the *Consensus* is ambiguous, leaving room for varying perspectives among the Swiss churches, but inviting sharp and protracted criticism from the Lutherans.[42]

Models of Reformed Catholicity: Ancient and Modern

Calvin is not typically known for his irenic spirit and relentless pursuance of Christian unity. His tireless efforts to produce the *Consensus Tigurinus* provide evidence that both are true of him. Moreover, his propensity for warm-hearted friendship with fellow pastors from different Protestant movements underscores a remarkable catholicity of spirit. For example, Calvin and Philipp Melanchthon (1497–1560), Luther's right-hand man, were lifelong friends. The two magisterial reformers 'shared the desire to overcome the Lutheran/Swiss division over the Lord's Supper.'[43] Furthermore,

---

39. All quotes included in my seven part summary are from the English translation of the *Consensus Tigurinus* in ed. Dennison, *Reformed Confessions*, 538-545.

40. Sanders, *Consensus*, 415.

41. Ibid., 96.

42. According to Lutheran theologian Joachim Westphal (1510-74), "the Swiss Reformed claims to unity are a sham. In the *Farrago* [1552], Westphal draws upon the writings of Calvin, Bullinger, Zwingli, Peter Martyr, Carlstadt, [and] Bucer ... to develop a chart of twenty-eight different interpretations of the words 'This is my body.'" Billings, *Participation*, 97.

43. Lindberg, *European Reformations*, 258.

as has already been shown, the Genevan Reformer had a strong friendship with Bullinger, even though 'clear differences' in their theology were 'acknowledged.'[44] Calvin's friendships and quest for confessional solidarity in Protestant Europe were not based upon a narrow, inflexible, or unbending uniformity. Without neglecting doctrinal integrity, he was willing to make concessions, as well as foster unlikely friendships for the glory of Christ and ecclesiastical unity.

A modern example of generous catholicity is found in the man honoured in this festschrift. Ian Hamilton, like his favourite Reformation theologian, models an irenic spirit and a willingness to warmly engage those with different theological perspectives. More than that, he is willing to become their friend. Ian demonstrates a kindness and graciousness towards others which are sometimes lacking in Reformed circles, and which we would do well to emulate. In Ian's native country, there are over 1,500 castles. The one most visited is located in Edinburgh's old town. Dominating the skyline, the castle is perched high above the city with towering walls and fortifications. Medieval cannons face outward, reminding passers-by of the storied battles of former days. Sadly, it is too often the case that a reformed pastor's vision of ministry is to dwell within an impenetrable theological fortress, with cannons directed towards any who would differ theologically. Like Calvin, Ian shows us a better way.

Now, to be clear, Ian's catholicity, rightly, has limitations. He is no soft latitudinarian, and his generous spirit does not engender theological compromise or some form of doctrinal reductionism. Not in the least – the Glaswegian pastor is resolutely biblical, confessional, and presbyterian. He is undaunted and unwavering in his reformed convictions. He vigorously defends the truth in his preaching and writing. Nevertheless, in doing so, he maintains a catholic spirit and seeks to pursue gospel unity among true believers. Ian is right to remind believers that 'the church is called to display to a fallen world ... a power that humbles us before God

---

44. Gordon, *Swiss Reformation*, 176.

and unites us to fellow blood-redeemed sinners in the body of Christ.'[45] Elsewhere he adds:

> We are prone, instinctively, to think in terms of denominational loyalty. I am a Presbyterian and deeply thankful for my wonderful heritage, notwithstanding its many blemishes. My problem, and maybe it's not yours, is that I can only too easily cultivate a superior attitude to other Christians outside the Reformed tradition and inwardly, if not outwardly, think of them as 'children of a lesser God.' Please do not misunderstand me. I love the Reformed faith and believe it is the purest expression of God's revealed truth. It would be a delight to see fellow Christians from other traditions 'see the light' and embrace the Reformed faith and glory in the God who is the epicentre of it. But I need to be reminded constantly that the Reformed faith is not 'the faith.' It is, I certainly believe, the most God-honouring expression of 'the faith,' but there are many Christians who trust Christ, love the gospel, but who are outside … the Reformed faith. According to God's own Word, it is a test of our Christian faith that we love 'whomever has been born of him.'[46]

Here Ian is referring to the penetrating words of 1 John 5:1: 'Everyone who believes that Jesus is the Christ has been born of God, and everyone who loves the Father loves whoever has been born of him.' This command to love all true and professing Christians is not based on absolute doctrinal unity, but on union with Christ. Theological distinctives such as *credo* and *paedo* baptism will oftentimes keep Christians in separate churches this side of heaven. For the sake of order, this is not an altogether bad thing. However, one day, when Christ returns in glory with

---

45. Ian Hamilton, *Ephesians: The Lectio Continua Expository Commentary on the New Testament* (Grand Rapids: Reformation Heritage Books, 2017), 105.

46. Ian Hamilton, *Loving Our Brothers* in Banner of Truth Online Magazine, July 17th, 2007. He adds: "Christian love is not blind; but nor is it narrow-hearted or sectarian. The Reformed Christian believer has infinitely and eternally more in common with believers who are outside their tradition than with any pagan. We are brothers. We have the same Father. We are united, through faith alone, to the same Saviour. We are indwelled by the same Holy Spirit. We have the same 'high and holy calling.' And we are heading for the same eternal city, the New Jerusalem, where we will be, together, forever with the Lord."

the angels, the elect from every tribe, tongue, and nation (and denomination) will as one people be ushered into paradise and worship the crucified and risen lamb forever (Rev. 7:9-12). This breath-taking eschatological vision should inform and fuel every Christian's love for fellow believers. According to Ian, all Christians should 'imitate the large-heartedness' of Christ. Not in desertion of truth, but in submission to it:

> This is not an appeal for you or me to abandon long-cherished convictions, or even denominational allegiance. It is a fact, however, an uncomfortable fact ... that our Lord Jesus Christ welcomes (not tolerates only!) all who trust him as their only Lord and Saviour. Their theology may be defective, but if they are united to him, they are his—and if they are his, then they are yours and mine. I for one do not think it is an easy thing to imitate the large-heartedness of our Saviour towards his people. Why, many of them are not even Presbyterians! Some of them are Arminians. Some are Charismatics, with a woefully defective theology. And yet, they are Christ's. No less elected by the Father, washed in the blood of the Son, and sanctified by the Spirit.[47]

The production of the *Consensus Tigurinus* is a brief episode in the annals of Reformation history, which deserves to be better known than it is. It highlights a generous pursuit of Christian unity in turbulent times. According to Schaff, 'The negotiations reflect great credit on both parties, and reveal an admirable spirit of frankness, moderation, forbearance, and patience, which triumphed over all personal sensibilities and irritations.'[48] Despite clear theological differences, Calvin worked diligently and graciously with his Swiss counterpart in Zurich, driven by a passion for Christ and his Church.[49]

---

47. Ian Hamilton, *The Tyranny and Necessity of Narrowness* in Banner of Truth Online Magazine, October 28th, 2008. In this article Ian quotes "Rabbi" John Duncan's (1796-1870) personal credo: "'I'm first a Christian, next a Catholic, then a Calvinist, fourth a Paedobaptist, and fifth a Presbyterian. I cannot reverse this order.'"
48. Philipp Schaff, *The History of Creeds, Volume One* (Grand Rapids: Baker Books, 1996; first printed in 1931), 472.
49. Having said that, it must be acknowledged that the *Consensus* further

Ian Hamilton is animated by that same passion for catholicity. His life and ministry are a wonderful reflection of the Genevan reformer's catholicity and, greater still, of our Saviour's love.

---

deepened the chasm between the Swiss and the Lutherans, and did not resolve all the problems between Zurich, Berne, and Geneva. Our best efforts in ministry never deliver perfect outcomes in this life.

CHAPTER TEN

Training and Forming Ministers in the Catholic Calvinist Vision

Joseph A. Pipa, Jr.

I appreciate the opportunity to contribute this essay to the Festschrift honouring Ian Hamilton. I have known Ian for over twenty years. I have observed him as a husband and father, a pastor and preacher, and teacher and board member of a seminary. All who know him acknowledge him to be a humble Calvinist and catholic in his sympathies. He is often invited to minister in Baptist and Bible churches and treats all fellow Christian with love and respect. No better topic summarises the life and ministry of Ian than training and forming men who embody the vision of Catholic Calvinism. He serves as an adjunct professor and Trustee at Greenville Presbyterian Theological Seminary and recently, President at Westminster Seminary (UK).

I am framing my essay on how this training and forming takes place in the context of a seminary education. I will develop three planks for training and forming men for the gospel ministry in Calvinistic Catholicity: academic integrity; warm hearted piety; and ecclesiastical commitment. I derive these planks from the ministry of Ezra the scribe. In Ezra 7:9-10 the Holy Spirit informs us that 'the good hand of his God was upon him. For Ezra had set his heart to study the law of the LORD and to practice it, and to teach His statutes and ordinances in Israel.'[1]

As a Scribe, Ezra demonstrated the first plank, academic integrity. He was well-trained in the law of God. He had devoted his life to careful study of the Scriptures. He is described in Ezra 7:3 as a scribe 'learned in the words of the commandments of the LORD and His statutes to Israel.' He would have had a solemn grasp of revelation God had given to the Church at that time. We see the results of his study in in his exposition of the law in Nehemiah 8:1-8.

Note, as well, his godliness. He manifests the second plank in his piety. He exercised his ministry with heart devotion, committed to living the truth he was teaching. He set his heart 'to practice it (the law of the LORD).' Only after such study and commitment to piety, did he teach.

The third plank, ecclesiastical commitment, is seen in his motivation. Although not stated explicitly, Ezra acted out of concern for the church that had returned from exile. He made the arduous trip from Babylon to Jerusalem to teach the law of God. He loved the church. Note his prayer as well in 9:5-15.

Due to his three-fold commitment, God prospered his ministry (Ezra 7:6, 9). If we are to have a new generation of ministers whom God blesses, we must base our instruction on these three planks.

The First Plank

The first plank in training and forming men for the gospel ministry is academic integrity. The gospel minister needs to be as rigorously educated as a physician or lawyer. The level of training for the ministry nowadays is dismal in comparison to earlier generations. And even by today's standards, candidates for the ministry are woefully ignorant. In my denomination, (the Presbyterian Church in America), men regularly have difficulty passing the theological examination for ordination. The standard for knowledge of Greek and Hebrew is inadequate – the knowledge of the two languages

---

1. All scriptural quotations from NAU, 1995.

may be measured by a seminary degree that only requires a year's study in each language. A curriculum designed to meet the goal of academic integrity must be full-orbed and demanding. As to its rigour, Cunningham writes,

> If it be the great duty of the ministers of the gospel to explain and open up the Word of God in its true meaning and real import for the salvation of men, then it is manifest that their theological education should be principally directed to these two objects—first, that they acquire that information, form these habits, and be impressed with these general views and principles, which may constrain them ever after to devote their principal attention to the study of God's Word, and may afford them the best assistance in attaining most speedily and most certainly to a correct knowledge of the meaning of its statements; and second, that they become intelligently and accurately acquainted on scriptural grounds with those fundamental doctrines of revelation which out to pervade all their efforts to instruct their fellow-men, as bearing most directly and immediately upon the salvation of sinners, and which, when distinctly perceived, and firmly held, and faithfully applied, will preserve them from radical or fundamental error in the interpretation of any portion of Scripture.[2]

A seminary's curriculum should ground students in a working knowledge of the Bible. It should cover the full range of theological loci. It should reflect the symbiotic relationship of Biblical and Systematic Theology. It should instruct students in Church History and Historical Theology. The students, as well, must be aware of cultural trends and errors in order to heed the exhortation of Paul in Titus 1:9: 'He will be able to exhort in sound doctrine and to refute those who contradict it' (NASB). The seminary should equip him to defend the faith in his context.

The seminary should aim at training men to use Hebrew and Greek in the exegesis of the Bible. Today, the goal of many seminaries is to teach men enough Hebrew and Greek to enable

---

2. William Cuningham, *An Introduction to Theological Studies,* ed. J. Ligon Duncan III (Greenville, SC: A Press, 1992), 17, 18. In this book, he describes the curriculum that will accomplish these goals.

them to use language tools. Such an approach is inadequate. The church needs men able to exegete the Hebrew and Greek texts for themselves.

The Reformers emphasised Greek and Hebrew in their teaching. The commitment to study the Scriptures in the languages of the Scripture was essential to the Reformation. Today many ministers and seminaries tolerate the norm of a student finishing seminary without really knowing Greek and Hebrew. Yet, it was the knowledge of Greek and Hebrew that, in great part, the Spirit used to give birth to the Reformation. When Jerome translated the Latin Vulgate, he translated the word *'metanoeo'* which means 'repentance' with a Latin idiom that meant 'do penance.' And thus, for centuries the church based its doctrine of penance on a faulty translation. Only as men began to read the New Testament in Greek did they properly understand the biblical concept was repentance and not penance.

We have similar problems today when faulty English translations go unchallenged, and the Bible study notes teach error. The Westminster Confession of Faith insists that 'in all controversies of religion, the Church is finally to appeal unto them (the original languages of the Bible)' (WCF 1.8). The Reformers understood this and so they instructed men then in the languages as well as in Biblical and Systematic Theology.

Cunningham emphasises this need: 'Ministers of the gospel ought not in the execution of their function, which consists mainly in opening up and expounding the mind of the Spirit in the word, to be wholly dependent upon translators and commentators, but should be capable of understanding the original inspired writings.'[3]

With respect to pedagogy, the professor should teach his courses in a way that that prepares men for pastoral ministry and preaching. For this reason, he should have served as a pastor as well as being academically prepared. Moreover, the curriculum will have applied theology courses in which the student is given

---

3. Cunningham, 17.

the tools to be an effective pastor preacher, and churchman. Instructors teaching should be well trained and competent. They are to be knowledgeable in their field and committed to lifelong study in their field. A Calvinistic professor will aim at the glory of God in all his teaching. As Paul says of the preacher, he preaches for God in Christ (2 Cor. 1:17). This aim requires prayerfully preparing his lecture and teaching in dependence on the Holy Spirit.

The professor will reflect Calvinistic Catholicity, as well, in his lectures. He should expose his students to the breadth of Reformed traditions, by having them read widely in the various Reformed traditions, as well as other theological traditions. Moreover, he should expose them to the development of doctrines throughout church history. He should teach his students Calvin's dictum, 'Affirm truth wherever you find it.' Calvin writes:

> Therefore, in reading profane authors, the admirable light of truth displayed in them should remind us, that the human mind, however much fallen and perverted from its original integrity, is still adorned and invested with admirable gifts from its Creator. If we reflect that the Spirit of God is the only fountain of truth, we will be careful, as we would avoid offering insult to him, not to reject or condemn truth wherever it appears.[4]

The professor should require his students to do their best and master the material. He should examine in such a way that the students not only manifest their grasp of the content of the course, but also demonstrate an ability to integrate and apply it in ministry contexts. He will accomplish this goal by giving examinations in which students do not simply rehearse the facts but show their ability to think critically. In their essays, the students must be required to do good research, to use critical thinking skills, and to write well.

---

4. John Calvin, *Institutes of the Christian Religion*, ed. John T. McNeill, trans For Lewis Battles (Philadelphia: The Westminster Press, 1967) II. 2.15.

The Second Plank

The second plank in training and forming men is warm hearted piety. Ezra practiced what he learned and taught. Dabney maintains that the main reason for lack of growth in the Presbyterian church of his day was lack of piety:

> The real *desideratum* is not new methods, but fidelity to the old, a true revival in the hearts of minister and Christian themselves, a faith, that 'feels the power of the world to come,' a solemn and deep love for souls. What we most need is repentance, and not innovation.[5]

We call this commitment experimental or experiential Calvinism. As Ian himself teaches, a commitment to experimental theology is at the heart of Calvinism. What do we mean by experimental Calvinism? Murray Capill defines experimental theology:

> The word 'experiment' has to do with testing something. A scientist conducts experiments to test his hypotheses. Applied to theology, it refers to the work of testing the reality and truth of God's word in the hearts and lives of people. Truth is not left as a mere hypothesis—a detached, intellectual belief. Truth is applied to life; its reality and validity is shown and demonstrated; its presence in our lives is tested and proven.[6]

We do not learn truth as an end in itself, but rather as a means by which we know, love, and worship God. Charles Bridges writes that there must be 'an application of the didactic system to the sympathies of the heart.'[7] Each Christian should know the truth through his experience of it and let every experience be shaped by the truth. The preacher must preach known and felt truth. If one preaches known belief and felt truth, one will preach with passion. Preaching must come from the heart and experience of

---

5. R. L. Dabney, "A Thoroughly Educated Ministry" in *Discussions Evangelical and Theological* (1891; repr., London: The Banner of Truth Trust, 1967), 2.656.

6. Murray Capill, *Preaching with Spiritual Vigour :Including Lessons from the Life and Practice of Richard Baxter* (Fearn Ross-shire, Scotland: Mentor, 2003), 15.

7. Charles Bridges, *The Christian Ministry*. (London: The Banner of Truth Trust, 1967), 259.

the pastor to the heart and experience of God's people. John Owen says that preachers must experience in their own souls the power of what they preach:

> Without this they will themselves be lifeless and heartless in their own work, and their labour for the most part will be unprofitable towards others. It is, to such men, attended unto as a task for their advantage, or as that which carries some satisfaction in it from ostentation and supposed reputation wherewith it is accompanied. But a man preacheth that sermon only well unto others which preacheth itself in his own soul. And he that doth not feed on and thrive in the digestion of the food which he provides for others will scarce make it savoury unto them; yea, he knows not but the food he hath provided may be poison, unless he have really tasted of it himself. If the word do not dwell with power in us, it will not pass with power from us. And no man lives in a more woeful condition than those who really believe not themselves what they persuade others to believe continually. The want of this experience of the power of the gospel truth on their own souls is that which gives us so many lifeless, sapless orations, quaint in words and dead as to power, instead of preaching the gospel in the demonstration of the Spirit.[8]

On principle, the Puritan preachers would never enter the pulpit without first having preached the sermon to themselves and warmed their hearts with its truth. Having applied it to themselves, they were on fire with what they had to preach. Thus, the well-trained minister must have warm piety. The seminary shapes this commitment through spiritual formation. The seminary community must foster piety. The men who teach must model vibrant, biblical piety. They must be Ezra-like men, committed to practicing what they believe and teach. When one teaches for the glory of God, one reflects God in one's teaching. A teacher must teach his course experimentally. Moreover, the professor should teach in a manner that shows his personal dependence on God.

---

8. John Owen, *The Works of John Owen*. 16 vols. (London: The Banner of Truth Trust, 1967), 16:76.

The seminary also labours to help students grow in godliness. Each student must be an active member of a local church. The seminary should expect the daily practice of private devotions and family worship.

To foster piety, the professor must be involved with the students outside the classroom. In the American colonies, and today in some Reformed denominations, the church used the parsonage model for training ministers. Sometimes it would be less formally organised; a young man would go and live with a minister to learn informally from him through reading and joining in pastoral labours. Oftentimes, though, the arrangement was more formal and a young man would attach himself to a pastor to read divinity. There would be a set curriculum. The candidate would read and discuss with his mentor and thus prepare for the ministry. The student would live with the pastor and see his personal and family piety. The advantage of this method is the pastor plays an active role in the spiritual formation of the student.

However, formal instruction at a seminary is a more effective method to train larger numbers of men. Nevertheless, in the seminary context, we must not neglect the essential, personal involvement in the lives of our students. The professor must be accessible, not only to help with academic questions, but also as a counsellor and one who prays for and with his students. Moreover, he must model for them what he teaches in the classroom. Like Paul, he must be able to say, 'Be imitators of me, just as I also am of Christ' (1 Cor. 11:1 NASB).

One aspect of this mentoring is having students in the home. As a minister must exercise hospitality, the professor, as he is able, should open his home to his students. Demonstrating what hospitality is like and allowing students to experience a Christian family. Moreover, the teacher should keep contact with men after they graduate as a friend and counsellor. If personal relationships are nurtured while the students are in school, the students will be comfortable to reach out to their mentors with personal and pastoral problems and questions.

The Third Plank

The third plank in training and forming men is ecclesiastical commitment. The Calvinistic professor should love the Church of the Lord Christ and want to serve the church. The seminary must not view itself as a graduate school, but rather as a handmaiden to the church, preparing men to love and serve the church. Moreover, the professors should be churchmen, involved in the courts of the Church. The students should know the traditions of the church and be able to trace out the development of doctrine through the ages. Hence, it is important that men being trained and formed know Church History and appreciate how God in his providence led the church organically to develop the doctrines revealed in the Bible. Bavinck writes:

> A given proposition is a dogma in itself, apart from any recognition, if it rests on the authority of God. Nonetheless, it is intended, and has an inherent tendency, to be recognised by us as such. Truth always seeks to be honoured as truth and can never be at peace with error and deception. It is, moreover, of the greatest importance for every believer, particularly for the dogmatician, to know which Scriptural truths, under the guidance of the Holy Spirit, have been brought to universal recognition in the church of Christ.[9]

Moreover, a Reformed seminary must maintain confessional integrity. It must be thoroughly Calvinistic, committed to teaching all things in conformity with the Reformed Standards of the school. Bavinck writes,

> The power of the church to lay down dogmas is not sovereign and legislative but ministerial and declarative. Still, this authority has been granted by God to his church, and it is this power that enables and authorises her to confess the truth of God and to formulate it in speech and writing ... the confession of the church supplies us with an excellent—not infallible—means to find our way amid many and varied errors to the truth of God laid down in his word.[10]

---

9. Herman Bavinck, *Reformed Dogmatics,* ed. John Bolt, trans. John Vriend (Grand Rapids: Baker Academic, 2004), 1.30.
10. Bavinck, *Reformed Dogmatics*, 1.31.

However, the seminary ought to teach the doctrines of the confessional standards in a way that the students will know the exegetical bases of the doctrines. The faculty should be catholic in affection and communicate a love for the church to its students. Presbyterianism has historically been committed to what Dabney calls 'broad scriptural catholicity.'[11] He continues, 'It is the most liberal of all churches, receiving all true penitents to membership, of all shades of doctrinal opinion, have not *shibboleth*, communing with all, unchurching none, who teach the essential rudiments of salvation.'[12] For example, Reformed churches accept baptism by immersion, while great majority of Baptists churches do not accept sprinkling or pouring as legitimate mode of baptism.

The teacher should avoid sectarianism by not emphasising minor hobby-horses. The professor should exhibit a love for all who are in the visible catholic church. He should exhibit humility, when dealing with those with whom he disagrees. Moreover, the students must be trained to be churchmen, committed to serving Christ and his people through involvement in the courts of the church. They should be taught the principles of church government, the polity of the church in which they will serve, and how to conduct themselves in the church courts.

Conclusion

Commitment to these three planks will enable the seminary to train and form men who embody the vision of Catholic Calvinism. There is no better exemplar of a seminary shaped by these planks than old Princeton. She is an apt model for us, since she is the mother and grandmother of the majority of conservative Presbyterian seminaries. A commitment to the three planks is embodied in the *'Plan of a Theological Seminary'* adopted in 1812 by the General Assembly that established Princeton. In it the Assembly stated the purpose of the Seminary:

---

11. R. L. Dabney, "A Thoroughly Educated Ministry" in *Discussions Evangelical and Theological*, report 1891 (London: The Banner of Truth Trust, 1967), 2.653.

12. Ibid, 2.653.

It is to form men for the Gospel ministry, who shall truly believe, and cordially love, and therefore endeavour to propagate and defend, in its genuineness, simplicity, and fulness, that system of religious belief and practice which is set forth in the Confession of Faith, Catechisms, and Plan of Government and Discipline of the Presbyterian Church; and thus to perpetuate and extend the influence of true evangelical piety, and Gospel order.

It is to provide for the Church an adequate supply and succession of able and faithful ministers of the New Testament; workmen that need not to be ashamed, being qualified rightly to divide the word of truth.

It is to unite, in those who shall sustain the ministerial office, religion and literature; that piety of the heart which is the fruit only of the renewing and sanctifying grace of God, with solid learning; believing that religion without learning, or learning without religion, in the ministers of the Gospel, must ultimately prove injurious to the Church.

It is to afford more advantages than have hitherto been usually possessed by the ministers of religion in our Church, to cultivate both piety and literature in their preparatory course; piety, by placing it in circumstances favourable to its growth, and by cherishing and regulating its ardour; literature, by affording favourable opportunities for its attainment, and by making its possession indispensable.

It is to provide for the Church, men who shall be able to defend her faith against infidels, and her doctrines against heretics.

It is to furnish our congregations with enlightened, humble, zealous, laborious pastors, who shall truly watch for the good of souls, and consider it as their highest honour and happiness to win them to the Saviour, and to build up their several charges in holiness and peace.

It is, finally, to endeavour to raise up a succession of men, at once qualified for and thoroughly devoted to the work of the Gospel ministry; who, with various endowments suiting them to different stations in the Church of Christ, may all possess a portion of the spirit of the primitive propagators of the Gospel, prepared to make every sacrifice, to endure every hardship, and to render every service which the promotion of pure and undefiled religion may require.[13]

Princeton seminary effectively trained and formed men who embody the vision of Catholic Calvinism. The record of history shows how successful the school was for over one hundred years in providing men who served the church faithfully around the world. Ian Hamilton as pastor and theological educator exemplifies the three virtues we have commended as necessary in forming men for the ministry. May all we who engage in seminary education, by God's grace, follow in his steps.

---

13. David B. Calhoun, *Princeton Seminary; Volume 1 Faith and Learning 1812-1868* (Edinburgh: The Banner of Truth Trust, 1994), 416, 417. In the Plan the General Assembly worked out what the school must accomplish in its curriculum (pages 423-424).

CHAPTER ELEVEN

A Confessionally Catholic Calvinism?

Chad Van Dixhoorn

This essay seeks a resolution to the conundrum that is Ian Hamilton: the warmly committed confessional Calvinist who practices a generous catholicity. Historical textbooks and enthusiastic ecumenists do not have a category for confessionally Calvinistic catholics, and yet our Glaswegian presbyterian presents a confirmed case. Some effort ought to be made to understand the phenomenon, not least because it is contagious: those who know Ian, find themselves wanting to be confessionally Calvinistic catholics too.

Ian Hamilton is a teacher of the Bible who considers attentively the great Christian tradition, and so this essay fittingly begins with an early Christian confession. The Nicene Creed is famous for its four-part description of the church as one, holy, catholic and apostolic. The display of these attributes in the history of Christ's church has been more, or less visible at varied times and places, and in different traditions of the church, including those claiming as their heritage the Protestant Reformations of the sixteenth and seventeenth centuries.

Protestant Catholicity

In considering these attributes of the church, it must be readily admitted that Lutherans, the Reformed, and even the 'radical reformers,' have not always shared amicably the one baptism bequeathed to the church, and we have fought long about how to partake of one bread. We dispute, too, about the subjects of baptism and the substance of the Supper's elements. Thankfully, when it comes to the oneness of the church, a solid case can be made that we have found more unity in the gospel of our Saviour than we have in the symbols of the gospel. Likewise, there is a wide acceptance among Protestants of the importance of a pursuit of holiness for the good health of the church, even if that pursuit is sometimes missed through quests for immediacy, and sometimes marred by quietism or complacency. Not only are we committed to defining the church as one, and as holy, but as protestants we are also eager to defend the apostolic credentials of the church. We seek apostolicity in a commitment to the revealed doctrine of all apostolic writings, coming from God as the interpretive climax of the whole of Scripture. Our opposites find their apostolicity via a narrowly defined succession of supposedly Petrine ordinations in a local episcopate in Rome.

What then of catholicity? The catholicity, or universality, of the church is also helpfully highlighted by the Nicene Creed as one of the main characteristics of Christ's church. It is often claimed that Roman Catholics have a corner on catholicity. In spite of the oxymoronic concept of a 'Roman' Catholicism - a locally sourced, and thus restricted, universality - apologists for communions remaining in fellowship with the pope have long made it their case that the catholicity of their church is obvious, expressed as it is both chronologically and geographically. For better or for worse, loyalists to Rome have retained many liturgical and governmental traditions over the centuries, at least until the later twentieth century. Through missionary endeavours, some of them marked by extraordinary courage, Roman communions have long offered a priestly presence on every continent, including, since

1976, Antarctica. This appearance of catholicity is maintained in spite of the variety evident in regional Roman churches, the rivalries characteristic of monastic orders, and the inconsistency of papal policies.

Among Protestants, however, we do not find even the appearance of such catholicity. Protestant churches are to be found on every continent, but they are often characterised by 'worship wars,' and considerable variety in church governance. Even after setting aside those churches in modernist, or unbelieving traditions, there remains significant diversity in doctrine. There are many Protestant denominations, and countless non-denominational churches, many of them independent of any network, or affiliation, with any other church. So where is Protestant catholicity to be found?

Protestant catholicity is expressed wonderfully, at least in part, in the way in which we view others, an acceptance as genuinely Christian of all those throughout history, and around the world, who worship the Triune God and trust Jesus Christ as Saviour. Certain branches of the Protestant world, such as the Presbyterian, want more than this: we believe in the importance of a catholic visible church, and not merely an invisible one. A catholicity that is seen, and not only one that is evident in the way in which we view others. And yet a catholicity of viewpoint should not be overlooked as an inconsequential second best, for it is of great import.

This Protestant catholicity of viewpoint is Christlike, for it includes in its number all those for whom Jesus intercedes in his high-priestly prayer in John 17. Protestant catholicity in this form offers the oldest kind of Christian catholicity, for it includes all those saints and Christian churches who lived prior to, or today live unaware of, Roman attempts to monopolise catholicity. Protestant catholicity is eschatologically oriented, for it considers as brethren all those whom we expect to see in heaven. Protestant catholicity is also generous—at its best the most genuinely 'catholic'—for it recognises that there are those within the Roman communion itself who are our brothers and sisters—sinners who in spite of the confused and erroneous teaching of their church do in fact worship the Triune God and cling to Christ's redeeming work as their only hope.

It is no secret that in liberal and pietistic protestant traditions, catholicity has been understood differently. Among these groups with their overlapping constituents, catholicity is conceived in terms of a shared ethic, shared experience, or shared affections. Christians everywhere rightly rejoice when we see or sense common commitments and experiences. Nonetheless, it is better, and certainly truer to the historic roots of the Lutheran and Reformed branches of the Reformation, to see in these privileges not the basis of a true catholicity, or the definition of such catholicity, but the necessary consequences of the true catholic faith—of maturing life committed to the worship of the Triune God and trusting ever more fully in the person and work of Christ. As it happens, liberal and pietistic definitions of catholicity, focusing as they do on experience, also tend to miss many other necessary consequences of a properly grounded Protestant catholicity: not only do we recognise other Christians across time and space, and share with them many experiences, but we also share an appreciation for our extensive family history, and we share a humility that makes us listen to church councils, great scholars and courageous saints of the church, eager to hear what the Spirit may have taught others, before we ourselves seek to teach those around us, or decide we must differ with them.

So broad is this Protestant catholic vision that one might be tempted to call it a 'mere Christian'[1] catholic vision. 'Protestant catholicity' remains a better term than 'Christian catholicity' since Protestants have a wider view of catholicity, and a more generous view of other Christians, than do consistent non-Protestants. I am mindful that such a statement may not itself appear generous, but in its support, one only has to compare the Westminster Confession of Faith's discussion of the Communion of the Saints—a puritan articulation of Protestant catholicity, no

---

1. C. S. Lewis, Mere Christianity, Fontana Books, Glasgow, 1989.

less, with the never-rescinded decrees and canons of the Council of Trent. Roman ecclesiology has (until the ambiguities of recent years) anathematised from both the catholic church militant and triumphant, those who are not loyal to the papacy and its teachings. It is true, of course, Roman soteriology, however, has long had a universalistic streak—something that Samuel Rutherford explained in lectures to his students. This tendency, growing ever stronger in recent years, attributes salvation to all persons, including those who have no knowledge of Christ or who are even his sworn enemies. Such soteriology does not temper the ecclesiology; it only leads to the confusion that evidences itself in Roman Catholic scholarship and leadership. If true catholicity is more than Roman provincialism, and less than Roman universalism, then its Protestant manifestation and definition (at least as defined here) is not only the more Christlike, historic, heavenly and generous understanding of the church's catholicity, but also the more orthodox.

Calvinist Catholicity

Thus far I've been reflecting on Protestant catholicity. Those who know the brother honoured in these essays will know that his ministry and friendships amply display his commitment to Protestant catholicity, or as he might put it in confessional terms, to the Communion of the Saints. The persons Ian Hamilton befriends and the places where he is invited to preach are marked by the wide expanse of those saints who are in communion with Christ, and thus with each other. Nonetheless, Ian expends his efforts in the cause of 'Calvinist Catholicity' in particular, and not merely for what we might term a Protestant Catholicity in general. The reasons for this commitment, I would suspect, are manifold, reflecting both Ian's training, background and personality, and his doctrinal and ministerial commitments. Even after my years of worshipping and then serving with Ian (or perhaps because of those years) I would not pretend to explain fully to readers the reasons why Ian commends Calvinist Catholicity. However, I will venture to offer some reasons consistent with his other commitments.

In the first place, while Reformed Protestants seek to cultivate a generous understanding of catholicity, we also ought to understand that the core commitments of Protestant catholicity are best cultivated, maintained and defended within a context that promotes biblical worship, doctrine and government. Thoughtfulness about the worship of the Triune God, seeking to praise him in a way that he approves and that aims at his glory, constitutes one leg of the sturdy stool on which the Reformed faith stands. This worship, in turn, is only possible through understanding biblical doctrine, the next leg of the stool—not least a rich grasp of the excellencies of Christ, whose Spirit makes us alive, uniting us to Christ by faith, and who then calls us from that moment to worship the Father through the merits of the Son. The third leg of the Reformed stool is government or discipline, which acknowledges that Christians must seek to worship God as those who seek purity in heart and life. There is a Calvinist consensus on these points, even if there are differences in the way in which we seek to glorify God in worship, teach his Word, and foster holy living through good shepherding.

But secondly, if Calvinism is good for gander, is it not all the more important for the goose? Ian is not simply a Reformed Christian, but a Reformed minister. While a minister can worship with and minister to the widest variety of Christian churches, he cannot as easily minister in practice with an equally wide variety of Christians and churches. If he is to care about worship as a Reformed Christian, how much more if he is teaching about worship in a Christian seminary, for he must do so amongst students who encourage him to explain what he is convinced the Bible teaches about the subject. If he is not only to pray as a member for labourers in the harvest, but to work as a presbyter in approving men for missionary service, he must have specific commitments about ecclesiology and polity, for he cannot be indifferent to the kind of pastoral care and rule which a missionary will seek to exercise over new converts under his charge. If he as a Christian is to pray and long for the church to grow, and grow strong in his or her own land, how much more should the minister seeking to plant or revitalise a church that studies and appreciates the full counsel of God – knowing that the whole of the Word is needed for the thriving of a church? After all, he knows that some ways of worshiping God are sincere but shallow. Some government of the church amounts to little more than ministries of manipulation. Some ways of explaining the gospel are confused, and do not present the person and work of Son and Spirit in all their glory or lead saints and sinners to a loving Father with the Christian fruits of joy and peace.

Of course, this gospel can be shared by anyone who worships the Triune God and trusts in the gospel of his Son. It can be taught by those who have not thoughtfully considered church government and a full range of biblical doctrines, but who nonetheless enthusiastically centre their message and lives on this gospel. It can be taught, and is routinely taught, by evangelicals, in the classical sense of the word. We rejoice in such zealous evangelical gospel preaching. But for a Reformed minister, God-directed commitments regarding worship, government and doctrine are not optional extras among a buffet of ministry priorities. Rather they together offer the best means to promote the one, holy, catholic and apostolic church. And a Reformed minister is operating out of humble conviction, rather than bigotry or personal preference, when he concludes that this is best done in a Calvinistic church context and mode.

Ian Hamilton is not only committed to the Reformed faith as a means of promoting proper catholicity. He is committed to Reformed catholicity in particular. This too is important. Protestant catholicity recognises other Christians in many contexts. A Reformed catholicity recognises not only Protestant Christians in many contexts, but other Reformed ministers in different Reformed denominations. A Reformed catholic church member prays and works for his or her church to draw closer to other churches. A Reformed catholic minister does the same. But additionally, both within and without his denominational context, he seeks opportunities to cooperate in missionary endeavours, ministries of mercy, seminary instruction, encouragement through conferences, shared scholarship, and more. Calvinist catholicity is maximally generous towards other ministry partners, not sectarian in spirit. When separation is required on this side of glory, he supports but grieves it. A Calvinist Catholicity informing one's ministry knows more than the communion we have with Christian saints, or the appreciation we have for evangelical scholars and pastors; it celebrates and utilises the maximum cooperation possible between Reformed churches and evangelical ministries.

Calvinists and Confessions

This Calvinist Catholicity has long been evident in Ian Hamilton's ministry. Surely it is one of the reasons why Ian's ministry has blessed so many, and perhaps it is one of the reasons why his ministry has been so blessed. But as I mentioned as I began this essay, Ian is also known for his commitment to confessionalism, as evidenced in his most scholarly work, *The Erosion of Calvinistic Orthodoxy*. Ian has stressed that it matters not only whether Presbyterians have a confession, but how they hold it. 'To have and to hold' is important in more than one context. It might be tempting to see this work as representative of only an early stage of Ian's ministry. But the author issued a revised edition of the work in his sixties that only strengthened his thesis. So, the question remains: how does Calvinistic confessionalism sit with Calvinist catholicity? Or is this the great tension of his life and ministry?

For many committed to catholicity, even amongst Calvinists, a confession is more of a liability than benefit; it is something to work around, not work with. Better by far, it is thought, to reduce the amount of doctrine one teaches, to go with the flow, to find a touchpoint among Christians in a common admiration for inspiring figures, or a rich but not-very-closely-studied heritage, as a shared inspiration. But Ian resists all this and leans into a robustly confessional faith. If the tension between confessionalism and catholicity is real, he seems not to have noticed. In what remains of this essay, I will suggest that Ian, and others with him, have found in a warm confessionalism a better way of being a Calvinist, and ultimately, a better way of being catholic.

Boundary lines for Christian communions have been drawn in four main ways. Functionally, they are delineated by popular opinion, by major figures, by universities or seminaries, and by confessions and catechisms. The first has always been present, but has risen to real prominence more recently. Popular opinion has been most impactful in drawing boundaries within twentieth-century fundamentalism and evangelicalism. This has been especially true with voluntary, or parachurch organizations. Radio preachers, conference speakers, and seminary decision-makers have found themselves censuring others (or self-censuring!) based on the responses of their listeners and readers. Most of these organizations used brief or informal statements of faith that articulated the core of their doctrine, and then to a greater or lesser degree, allow popular responses by way of the post, or monetary donations, to inform the larger range of doctrines that would be taught. In his brilliant study of Fuller Seminary and the evangelical movements and persons that contributed to its founding, George Marsden noted that 'Standards of the informal creeds could be enforced by appeals to popular opinion.' But his shrewd observation on this fact is significant for catholicity: 'Before that court, even more than before a formal ecclesiastical court, the truly fundamental was difficult to distinguish from the peripheral.'[2] The boundary lines offered by public opinion were blurry, and unstable. Today, in the age of the internet where the public has access to unprecedented amounts of information delivered at an unprecedented speed, as well as the ability to speedily comment and respond, public opinion will likely play an increasing role in policing the boundaries of Christian communions, both parachurch organizations and churches.

Long before popular opinion was truly popular—before the term 'celebrity' had currency—Christian communions were often defined by well-known figures. Within Roman Catholicism major theologians could be more influential than church councils. Martin Luther personified orthodoxy for much of the Lutheran

---

2. George Marsden, *Reforming Fundamentalism: Fuller Seminary and the New Evangelicalism* (Grand Rapids: Eerdmans, 1987), 132.

communion prior to the Formula of Concord, and for many Lutherans long after. Within the Reformed communion, John Calvin, Ulrich Zwingli, and other international, national and local reformers did the same. For later Calvinistic baptists, Charles Spurgeon substituted for doctrinal standards. So did J. Gresham Machen in America, and Dr Martin Lloyd-Jones for the free-church culture of the British Isles. Sinclair Ferguson has long been quoted as an oracle, defining what it meant to be presbyterian or Reformed. For two decades, Tim Keller or John Piper has embodied what it means to be Calvinist, or a Christian, for countless Protestants.

Of course, university divinity professors and seminary faculties have also been useful in establishing boundaries. Limiting ourselves to American history, one only needs consider the way in which Harvard College and then Yale functioned informally as shapers, promoters, and enforcers of orthodoxy for early American congregationalists. Presbyterian seminaries would later do much the same, most famously in the case of 'Old Princeton,' but also, for many decades, Westminster Theological Seminary in Philadelphia. These three means of drawing boundaries, the popular, the personal, and the institutional, are not mutually exclusive. In our own day most of these are at play among self-styled Calvinists and other Christians too. And among the Reformed, these often function alongside of—or instead of—the oldest means by which Protestants defined their communions: confessions.

One of the significant features of the Protestant Reformation, and one not discussed enough, was the making of confessions. Naturally, not one Protestant Confession existed at the beginning of the 1500s. Over 90 Reformed confessions and catechisms— not including Lutheran ones—had been printed by the end of the 1500s. In their attempt to recover the best of the Christian tradition, and to reform the church according to the Bible, Protestants were eager to explain to all who would listen, a wide range of doctrines that they held in common. In some places the Reformation was a slow process, and the confession to which Ian

Hamilton subscribes—along with this author and many others—only received its final polish in 1647, 130 years after Martin Luther first wrote his Ninety-Five Theses on penance, indulgences and papal authority.

Just as the great creeds of the church were designed to express a catholic Christianity, so the great Reformed confessions defined what it meant to be Reformed. And as it happened, these often underlined the importance of a catholic Calvinism. This can be seen in their structure, for many confessions and most catechisms of the Reformation followed or echoed the structure Apostles' Creed. This catholicity is visible in the doctrines of the creed, which invariably discussed the Christian doctrine of the Triune God at or near the beginning of the text. It is obvious in the language of these confessions, which often echoed wording from classic creeds and definitions of the first ecumenical councils. It is evident in discussions of the church, which routinely insisted that the church is universal, and not merely universal in the sense of a body of believers, or the elect, but as a universal visible church of Christ. These texts displayed catholicity in their commitment to a shared ethic, in questions and answers offering application of the ten commandments, in a shared vision of worship, in discussions of the Word and sacraments, in a call to fervent piety, in expositions of the Lord's prayer. These are evidences of catholicity, not examples of compromise. The framers of these texts were rarely trying to please everyone. They were pastors. They knew this was not possible. It is often said that confessions presented compromise (or compromised) statements of doctrine. It is more accurate to say that confessions presented common statements of doctrine; a faith held in common.

It is evident from these Calvinistic confessions that the Reformers were interested in more than the recovery of the gospel; they wanted to recover true worship, doctrine and discipline, for each precept and practice supports the other, whereas leakage in one dilutes the rest. Most of us can be tempted at times to trim the truth in order to make the gospel more compelling. The blessing of a confession is that it reminds us that our Lord is most honoured when we preach the whole counsel of God, even if it makes us or our message look foolish to non-Christians and compromised Christians. But this is not the whole story. For in addition to the explicit purposes and benefits of a creed to orthodoxy and catholicity, Reformed ministers also wrote confessions to keep the whole of the church from being held hostage by a part of it.

Naturally, those who use confessions will always be influenced by popular opinion, brand name conference speakers, and by trusted institutions, such as the *Banner of Truth Trust*. But for those who are not confessional, whether Catholic or Protestant, their secondary standards will always be functionally embodied in a few people—even though we know that professional ambitions and jealousies, as well as attempts to justify existence not by usefulness but through niche opinions—tend to drag away from an orthodox Calvinism. The histories of American seminaries are particularly instructive in this regard. The founders of Fuller Seminary proclaimed that they were starting a new Princeton, restoring the legacy of great men such as the Hodges, Warfield and Machen. But the influence of Fuller's star-studded faculty could not return the grand old denominations of America to their doctrinal moorings. What the Fuller founders did not consider, but which later historians have noted, is that the Princeton faculty had been tethered to a much older doctrinal standard—the Confession and Catechisms penned by the Westminster Assembly centuries before.

Our forefathers sought to be confessional because they knew that the changing opinions of even the best men are inadequate guides to the peace and purity of the church of Christ. Of course confessions are products of men, but these texts are well-known and tested, and by design hard to change. Earlier Calvinists relied on the weakness of confessions over the power of prominent institutions, the hope of pleasing crowds, or the glamour of popular personalities. Arguably this is still the best recommendation, and it would benefit Reformed people if we heeded more our confessional heritage, for these old texts, forged in the heat of controversy and sometimes hammered out in long debates over the teaching of Scripture, offer a strong anchor in the tumultuous waters of a changing culture.

Confessions and the "Ecclesial Imaginary"

This is once again to make a case for confessionalism. How does confessionalism live harmoniously with catholicity? Might confessions not only be compatible with, but contributive to, a Calvinist catholicity? The philosopher Charles Taylor coined the term, 'Social Imaginary,' to express the idea of a collective understanding in a society or a social group, a collective imagination, that enables us to share a sense of plausibility. It is in part as a result of this social imaginary that we find some things meaningful, worthy of guiding our priorities or actions. At the risk of abusing an oft-referenced term, I find something in Taylor's contribution that is helpful in my attempt to answer this question. It seems to me that confessions, where appreciated, have the capacity to expand our 'ecclesial imaginary.'

The experience of many Calvinists has long been that confessionalism can expand the churchly vision of those who honour and invest in these rich resources. When confessionalism becomes an aspect of a person's 'ecclesial imaginary,' one tends to see certain effects. People who have followed a leader, whether a local pastor or a prominent pundit, may continue to find in those figures significant external reference points. But once they have discovered a Reformed Confession or catechism, and a community that appreciatively deploys these texts, they also discover new glasses through which to see quirky positions, changing views and—importantly—those overly narrow alliances. A good confession equips the Calvinist, new or old, with a vision of friendship and cooperation not directed by the fleeting impressions of popular opinion, 'influencers,' or even seemingly stable institutions. They learn to utilise all three as potential reinforcers of Reformed orthodoxy and fraternity. But they know them to be poor substitutes and inadequate replacements for confessional texts and confessional communities of millions of Christians, down through the centuries.

It is true that there are those who abuse confessions; confessional hermits of one kind or another—cenobites or anchorites who narrow their vision as they go through life. But who can tell how much narrower they would have become without a confession. The Confessional Calvinist envisaged of the Ian Hamilton variety, by contrast, comes to imagine, or rather, to see, a wide fellowship because his creed tells him that Christians are everywhere that worship of the trinitarian God and faith in the gospel of Christ are found. The Christian with a confessional Calvinist's catholicity will not find his personal and ministerial fellowship limited by the endless labyrinth of guilt-by-association decisions made by the creedless fundamentalist or pragmatic evangelical; the Christian who struggles to distinguish between significant and trivial matters, and thus struggles to know with whom he can fellowship precisely because of his creedlessness. Confessional Calvinist catholicity disposes us to work with the thousands, hundreds of thousands, or millions, with a creed similar to our own. More than that, Confessional Calvinist catholicity ought to foster real respect for those who have creeds that are in some respects dissimilar, especially when they not only have such a text, but seek to hold it and use it. The Calvinist using his confession ought to have ever-growing instincts for Catholicity, because the great creeds of the Reformation summarise so much commonly held scriptural doctrine. The best confessions suggest that much is to be mined from the Scriptures, and it is in this shared journey into the Scriptures, coming ever closer to mind and heart of God revealed therein, that confessional Calvinist catholics find their deepest joys, strongest bonds, and clearest eyes to see and appreciate Christ and the many people he is calling to glorify himself, and to enjoy him forever.

Part Three
Historic Role Models

CHAPTER TWELVE

Augustine

The Original Catholic Calvinist

Peter Sanlon

My wife and I benefited immensely from attending Cambridge Presbyterian Church 2005-2010 while I did postgraduate work on Augustine's sermons. We found in Ian a model of warm-hearted pastoral ministry and wisdom which meant much to us when our first baby, Calvin, died in the womb. Ian visited us as young grieving parents in hospital, prayed with us and pointed to God's kindness and sovereignty. Over the years we remained friends and like so many others, I have as a pastor turned to him for advice when the weight of the ministry seemed too much for me. I see now that Ian's pastoral vision and his welcome of us to his church is precisely the spirit of Catholic Calvinism this book is an extended reflection upon.

John Calvin's grace-filled sovereign view of God, and his catholic instincts, to a significant degree, were demonstrated by and learned from, Augustine. Humility and catholicity would lead both Augustine and Calvin to prefer the title of 'Christian' to any that subdivided the Church. But to the degree that the term 'catholic' and 'Calvinist' have significance, Augustine was, at the risk of obvious anachronism, the original catholic Calvinist.

In preparing his commentaries 'it was Calvin's regular practice to make use of Augustine' and to have relevant works of Augustine 'in front of him.'[1] So shaped by Augustine's influence was the reformation that one study on Augustine's reception concludes, 'The appropriation of Augustine could at times appear to be an exercise in intellectual ventriloquism.'[2]

The catholic and warm-hearted vision of a sovereign gracious God which so typified Calvin is neither natural to the fallen human heart, nor inevitable in the era in which he lived. One must ask where did Calvin's theological-pastoral instincts come from? To be sure they were honed in pastoral ministry, ecclesiastical dispute and Biblical study. And yet many have been busy in those realms and maintained more of a party spirit, more of a censorious nature, more of a cold business-like administrative outlook, than Calvin. So, one must press further and ask—where lay the influence that shaped Calvin so?

A wide reading of Calvin cannot but alert any reader to his deep appreciation of Augustine—he cited him extensively, and even where the Latin African Father is not quoted, the topics treated and combination of literary style with spiritual instincts are reminiscent of Augustine. It is difficult to avoid the conclusion on reading Calvin and Augustine, that the Genevan reformer had his outlook, theology and instincts shaped at a foundational level, by Augustine. If the obvious anachronistic portrayal of Augustine as the 'Original catholic Calvinist' grates on readers, feel free to turn the lens around and read this chapter as a meditation on Calvin as being what I think he understood himself to be—a latter patristic Father of the Western church, born a millennium out of time. If Augustine was the original catholic Calvinist, perhaps Calvin was the final patristic theologian.

---

1. Anthony Lane, *John Calvin: Student of the Church Fathers*, T&T Clark, Edinburgh, 1999, 194.

2. Arnoud Visser, *Reading Augustine in the Reformation: The Flexibility of Intellectual Authority in Europe*, Oxford University Press, Oxford, 2011, 1500-1620, 138.

Augustine the Catholic

From the moment Augustine was ordained as presbyter, to his death, Augustine battled with the Donatists. Augustine's pastoral instincts towards a catholic view of church and ministry were forged in this multi-generational, protracted and complex theological dispute. The Donatist controversy in N. Africa had its roots in the temperament and passion of a Church that honoured earlier martyred leaders such as Cyprian and had sought to hold on to the Faith through multiple waves of Roman state persecution. Ministering in N. Africa obliged Augustine to familiarise himself with the history of the dispute. The ethos of catholicity Augustine would embody was not the modern spirit of appeasement and positivity towards all views. Augustine would commend a catholic vision of Church, but without coming to a view on Donatism which was willing to refute it as error, he would be unable to respond to pressing pastoral situations.

The Donatists comprised the vast majority of the Church in N. Africa. They were committed to the holiness, faithfulness and integrity of the Church. During times of persecution, numbers of ministers capitulated under fear of torture and death, to the state. Some sprinkled incense to Caesar as Lord—making light of their idolatry. Others lied to obtain certificates saying they had so acted. Others—the most egregious offenders—were '*traditores*,' ministers who as traitors handed over the Scriptures to Roman soldiers who demanded the sacred books for burning. The story of persecution under the Roman Empire was a long one of both martyrs who held true to the Lord through horrific tortures and executions, and those who in weakness compromised to hold onto comfort and life in this world. The issue of the Donatist Controversy arose when persecution ended. What then ought to be the Church's response to those who had denied the Faith in earlier persecution?

The majority of the Church in N. Africa had a pastoral instinct towards two positions. Firstly, laity who wished to be forgiven and welcomed back into the Church would need to undergo a severe and long period of penance to demonstrate the sincerity of their repentance. For many this period of penance would last a lifetime. The sacrament would be withheld, table fellowship declined, and pastoral support unavailable till one's deathbed. Secondly, clergy who had capitulated to persecutors had demonstrated that they were false brethren—not members of the true Church. Consequently, any sacraments or ordinations they had performed earlier in ministry were invalid and would need to be done again. Baptisms that had marked people's entrance to the Church had not been genuine, and so rebaptism by a Donatist minister would be required.

The Donatists were intoxicated with a sense of righteousness that can only be felt by those who have suffered injustice and seen others compromise without obvious earthly loss. Combined with the prestige and security that comes from being in the majority, this was a heady mix. Inevitably, the Donatists came to feel that they were the true Church—the only ones who Jesus would recognise as faithful. There was much evidence they could point to, in favour of this view. Confronting this outlook, Augustine sought to be a pastor and church minister. He not only engaged at a doctrinal, exegetical or speculative level of theology; Augustine was not satisfied with merely offering a correct definition of catholicity. Augustine looked beneath the surface of the Donatists' challenge to catholicity and diagnosed the heart of what it meant to view your party or sub-section of the catholic Church as uniquely faithful to Jesus.

Augustine argued that the Donatist outlook, as a spirituality that denied catholicity, emptied the heart of love and filled it with pride. We see this doctrinal charge most clearly in his sermons on 1 John. Augustine preached, 'Love is represented to us by the dove that came upon the Lord ... You who deny love have made a schism. Those who hate love, hate the dove. So, the dove convicts them. The dove came down on our Lord Jesus and He is the one who baptises (John 1:33). You dare to claim those he baptises as your own—you want to hold them to yourself. But for the person who enters the catholic church, baptism is not erased. The King's claim must be recognised, for he owns his own.'[3]

The Donatists felt that they were the one true church and they would hold to themselves the authority to rebaptise (properly) those who had fallen from grace in persecution. Augustine in his preaching pointed out the possessive presumption that gave rise to such actions—the Donatists put themselves in the place of Jesus and pushed aside his Spirit. Too often in contemporary debates ministers keep discussions at the level of externalities and practices. Augustine, in his defence of a catholic vision of church, felt it necessary to go deeper and expose the motives of the heart that drove some to think their party the only truly faithful church. In his focus on the heart's motivations he was in keeping with the New Testament diagnosis (Gal. 6:13; 2 Cor. 11:20; Titus 1:11).

The catholic ethos recognises that the sacraments are administered by Christ himself (through his officers) and with Christ's authority. To seek to claim them for our party is to resist the Spirit by whom Christ works in his people with greater freedom and generosity than we might naturally recognise. Augustine was not arguing for a vision of church that fostered unity at cost of overlooking sin. He knew the *traditores* had sinned—but he also knew that, 'We have a contract with God in the Lord's Prayer—if we want God to forgive our sins, we must forgive others. Lose love from your heart and you cannot forgive. Let love reside and you can forgive with peace and your heart does not become narrow.'[4] The lovelessness of the party spirit Augustine challenged was demonstrated in hearts that would not forgive the person who mourned and grieved their sin. Repentance was rejected in favour of status within the approved group—which while it made members feel proud and secure, Augustine discerned it did so in a loveless way that barred forgiveness from meeting the repentant sinner.

Augustine knew that some had left the church—such were described by the apostle John as 'anti-Christs.' Augustine's

---

3. Augustine, *Sermons on 1 John*, 7, 11.
4. Augustine, *Sermons on 1 John*, 7, 1.

concern was with those who wanted to confess their sin and return to the fellowship. 'Those who left and now return are not anti-christs—they are not against Christ because they cannot remain apart from Him.'[5]

Augustine held that pride is the initial movement of every sin[6] and by means of inculcating pride in people, the devil fashions people in his image[7] and debases the image of God.[8] A person who submits to martyrdom with pride rather than love, has not gained anything.[9] A Christian has God's image restored and in becoming like God who is love, 'will live in such a way as to not exalt himself over other people.'[10] Pride can motivate a person to do all the external things that a loving believer does—but 'love in a person pushes out pride.'[11] The love which Jesus implants in a believer is the kind of love that expresses the love God is—a love that loves not just those in our party or on our team, but also our enemies. Such love aims to transform and change. 'Pay attention to why Christ taught you to love your enemies. Was it so that they might remain enemies? If so then Christ was urging you to not love them, but to hate them. Look at how Jesus loved his enemies—he did not want them to remain enemies. He said, "Father forgive them"' (Luke 23:34).[12]

The logic of Augustine's catholic vision is inexorable—those who are not eager to forgive and welcome the repentant sinner, have allowed pride to displace love. The Holy Spirit is catholic in his love—this is seen not in institutions that support a temporal, organisational church or market a particular take on Christian ministry. The love of the Spirit is manifest wherever believers work and strive to forgive the repentant sinner. 'I have preached

---

5. Augustine, *Sermons on 1 John*, 3, 5.
6. Augustine, *Sermons on 1 John*, 8, 6.
7. Augustine, *Sermons on 1 John*, 4, 10.
8. Augustine, *Sermons on 1 John*, 8, 6.
9. Augustine, *Sermons on 1 John*, 8, 9: citing 1 Cor. 13:3.
10. Augustine, *Sermons on 1 John*, 8, 8.
11. Augustine, *Sermons on 1 John*, 8, 9.
12. Augustine, *Sermons on 1 John*, 8, 10.

these things so that you will not be restrained in loving your enemies.'[13] A catholic Christian will take all steps possible to enable sinners to repent and be welcomed into fellowship. Augustine's willingness to welcome repentant *traditores* earned him the opprobrium of the majority Church in his day, and was a stand he took at considerable personal cost. The catholic spirit of Augustine did not ignore or downplay sin, but neither did it tolerate a spirit that pridefully rested satisfied in splendid isolation from those who would benefit from being urged to repent and be welcomed into the grace we all need.

Augustine the Calvinist

As the foundations of reformation were laid there was in the 1500s an 'Augustinian Renaissance'[14] Princeton theologian, B. B. Warfield penned the famous observation: 'It is Augustine who gave us the Reformation. For the Reformation, inwardly considered, was just the ultimate triumph of Augustine's doctrine of grace over Augustine's doctrine of the Church.'[15] The high value Calvin placed on patristics in general and Augustine in particular is what opened the door to Calvin being such a catholic reformer. Calvin 'was doubtlessly a great patristic scholar. In comparison with his contemporaries, his knowledge was in many respects unique. This special patristic knowledge gave his theology its special hallmark. For his many followers worldwide, this may still mean that the patristic element genuinely belongs to Calvinist theology and can preserve it from plain and unhistorical Protestantism. The *testimonium patrum* [testimony of the fathers] links the Reformation with the church's catholic tradition through the ages.'[16]

---

13. Augustine, *Sermons on 1 John*, 8, 11.
14. George, Timothy, *Theology of the Reformers*, Nashville, Broadman Press, 1988, 48.
15. B.B. Warfield, "Augustine," in *Calvin and Augustine*, ed. Samuel G. Craig (Philadelphia: The Presbyterian and Reformed Publishing Company, 1956), 322.
16. Van Oort, J., 2015, *Notes on Calvin's knowledge, use, and misuse of the Church Fathers*, HTS Teologiese Studies/Theological Studies 71(3).

In the *Institutes* Calvin made extensive use of Augustine, with over half of his citations being specifically systematic theological in character.[17] This suggests that Augustine was relied on by Calvin not merely to highlight the continuity of the reformation with the Early Church, nor because Calvin agreed with Augustine. The best explanation is that Calvin—a man who had never himself studied theology in a formal university context, had via his humanist reading habits, found in Augustine the teacher from whom he would learn the Christian ethos.

What was it about Augustine's theological vision that so impacted Calvin, that today we can speak of 'Augustinian Calvinism' and even at the risk of appearing anachronistic, can meaningfully describe Augustine as a Calvinist? The crucial under-girding aspect of Augustine's theological vision was surely that he had a capacious, sovereign, grace-filled view of God. From this flowed all else. We find this immense vision of God most explicitly in Augustine's *Confessions* and his anti-pelagian writings. The immensity of God captures Augustine's heart as he opens his *Confessions*:

> What are you, then, my God? What are you, I ask, but the Lord God? For who else is lord except the Lord, or who is god if not our God? You are most high, excellent, most powerful, omnipotent, supremely merciful and supremely just, most hidden yet intimately present, infinitely beautiful and infinitely strong, steadfast yet elusive, unchanging yourself though you control the change in all things, never new, never old, renewing all things yet wearing down the proud though they know it not; ever active, ever at rest, gathering while knowing no need, supporting and filling and guarding, creating and nurturing and perfecting, seeking although you lack nothing. You love without frenzy, you are jealous yet secure, you regret without sadness, you grow angry yet remain tranquil, you alter your works but never your plan; you take back what you find although you never lost it; you are never in need yet you rejoice in your gains, never avaricious yet you demand profits. You allow us

---

17. Han, S. (2010), *An investigation into Calvin's use of Augustine*, Acta Theologica. 28, 76.

to pay you more than you demand, and so you become our debtor, yet which of us possesses anything that does not already belong to you? You owe us nothing, yet you pay your debts; you write off our debts to you, yet you lose nothing thereby.[18]

The respect Augustine had for God translated to an immense respect for God's word and preaching. 'Preaching, through exegesis, discussion and argument, attempts to make plain the meaning of your words, while subjecting itself always to the authority of your book.'[19] The emotional, sensory and affectionate impact of God's grace on Augustine which has made *Confessions* so vital a work of the Church arose from Augustine's efforts to preach the Psalms. As he immersed himself in the Psalms, he began to experience in prayer and writing, the spirituality of David. Augustine's vision of God required that a minister have a deep and experiential encounter with God:

> Filled with terror by my sins and my load of misery I had been turning over in my mind a plan to flee into solitude, but you forbade me, and strengthened me by your words. To this end Christ died for all, you reminded me, that they who are alive may live not for themselves, but for him who died for them. I will contemplate the wonders you have revealed. You know how stupid and weak I am: teach me and heal me. Your only Son, in whom are hidden all treasures of wisdom and knowledge, has redeemed me with his blood. Let not the proud disparage me, for I am mindful of my ransom. I eat it, I drink it; I dispense it to others, and as a poor man I long to be filled' with it among those who are fed and feasted. And then do those who seek him praise the Lord.[20]

In the Pelagian Controversy Augustine sharpened the articulation of grace already present in *Confessions*.[21] He set the Pelagian error—which gave too much honour to human will and discipline—in the context of other heresies:

---

18. Augustine, *Confessions*, Translated by Maria Boulding, New City Press, NY, 1997, 1, 4.
19. Augustine, *Confessions*, 13, 34.
20. Augustine, *Confessions*, 10, 70.
21. Augustine, *Confessions*, 10, 60.

Let all who with a catholic heart stand in horror of these wicked and damnable doctrines in this threefold classification avoid the snares and plots of that fivefold classification. And let them exercise caution between the two, avoiding Mani without falling in with Pelagius and again not pulling back from Pelagius so that they join the Manichees. Or if they are already caught in one group or the other, let them not snatch themselves from either of them in such a way that they rush into the other. Of course, the two appear opposed to each other, since the Manichees show who they are by their blaming those five errors, while the Pelagians hide behind their praise for them. For this reason all who are in conformity with the rule of the catholic faith condemn and avoid both. For they give glory to the creator at the birth of human beings for the good creature of flesh and soul-something which the Manichee refuses to do. But they do this in such a way that they admit that infants need a saviour on account of the defect passed on to them by the sin of the first human being—something which Pelagius refuses to do. Thus they distinguish the evil of shameful concupiscence from the good of marriage so that they do not, like the Manichees, blame the source of our birth and do not, like the Pelagians, praise the source of our shame. They maintain that the holy and righteous and good law was given by the holy and righteous and good God through Moses—a point which Mani denies in opposition to the apostle. But they claim that the law reveals sin without taking it away and commands righteousness without giving it—a point which Pelagius in turn denies in opposition to the apostle.[22]

Such was Augustine, the Church Father Calvin chose to be discipled by. A capacious vision of God that emphasised his grace and required creatures to engage with him in heartfelt desire and passion. John Calvin with his famous reticence to speak of self would never be happy to see his name used as a label for a church, party or outlook. However, to the extent that his leading theological instincts were learned from Augustine, he would perhaps have reluctantly accepted that were there any such thing as a Calvinist, the capacious vision of God was first present in

---

22. Augustine, *Answer to the Two Letters of the Pelagians*, Translated by Roland Teske, New City Press, NY, 1998, 3, 3.

Augustine, the original Calvinist, who like Calvin was of the view that their convictions were nothing more than that of the church Catholic.

A Vision of God

Augustine's vision of God was supremely that of a sovereign God who graciously provides for his Church. His desire—shared by Calvin—was that people see how glorious God is and respond to Him in a heartfelt, experiential way. Anticipating Calvin's close relating of God and humanity, and our dependence on God for all things, Augustine wrote: 'If a human wants to become something, he or she must turn to God, our Creator. We grow cold as we move away from him, warm as we draw nearer to Him.'[23] Such an experiential expression of our dependence on God was learned by Calvin as he pondered Augustine's writings and exhibited in words such as:

> This sense of the power of God is for us a fit teacher of piety, from which religion is born. I call 'piety' that reverence joined with love of God which the knowledge of his benefits induces. For until men recognise that they owe everything to God, that they are nourished by his fatherly care, that he is the Author of their every good, that they should seek nothing beyond him-they will never yield him willing service. Nay, unless they establish their complete happiness in him, they will never give themselves truly and sincerely to him.[24]

We remain thankful for Calvin's legacy. And we are grateful for Calvin's mentor in the spirit of Catholicity—Augustine.

---

23. Augustine, *Expositions of the Psalms*, Vol. 3, New City Press, NY, 2001, Ps. 70 Exp. 2, 6.
24. Calvin, *Institutes*, 1, 2, 1.

CHAPTER THIRTEEN

John Calvin and Catholicity

W. Robert Godfrey

John Calvin (1509–64) was a great reformer of the church, working for its life and ministry as well as developing its theology. He was adamant that the faithfulness of the church was vitally important for the lives of Christians and for society. He shared the conviction of Cyprian that he who would not have the church as his mother would not have God as his Father.[1]

Calvin's concern for the church was reflected in the attention he gave to it in his *Institutes of the Christian Religion*. Over thirty percent of that work develops his positive doctrine of the church and carefully examines the sacraments and the history of the church. It delineates the ways in which the church in its historical development deviated from biblical teaching. But Calvin was not only a historian or theologian of the church. He was also a very active servant of the church. He was a pastor and preacher as well as founder and teacher of the Genevan Academy, which educated future ministers. His work for the church extended far beyond Geneva, ranging from official activities to informal advice to churches throughout Europe. His writing and work reflected his concern for the church, and particularly for its catholicity.

The world into which Calvin was born had a particular understanding of the catholicity of the church. The pope as the

---

1. John Calvin, *Institutes*, 4, 1, 4.

bishop of Rome and the successor of Peter claimed to be the head of the church on earth and the guarantor of the church's orthodoxy, unity, and catholicity. When Calvin as a young man embraced the cause of reformation, that renewal movement had already rejected the papacy as the divinely established head of the church on earth—indeed many had concluded that the pope was the antichrist, rather than the vicar of Christ. Luther had initially hoped that the pope might lead the reform of the church, and when he found that the pope rejected that call for reform, he turned to the civil magistrate to lead the reform in the spirit and tradition of the work of the Emperor Constantine. Luther hoped that the civil magistrate, like Constantine, would call for an ecumenical council to meet and reform the church.[2]

By the time Calvin began his work as a second-generation reformer, reformed churches had been established in many parts of Europe. In some areas the reform of the church had been led by the civil magistrates and had been established in law. In other areas the reformed churches faced opposition from civil governments which continued to support the Roman Catholic Church. In his work Calvin faced a twofold challenge. The first

---

2. Turning to the civil authorities for leadership in reforming the church was a return to the dominant form of ecclesiastical direction and control through most of the history of the church. See Peter Heather, *Christendom, The Triumph of a Religion, A.D. 300-1300*, New York (Knopf), 2023. He summarised the thesis of his remarkable study: "Despite what it liked to pretend (and some of its apologists still do), papal religious authority was an astonishingly late phenomenon within the developing European Christian tradition. Bishops of Rome, as the heirs of St Peter, had enormous prestige from an early date, and other Christians leaders periodically sought their opinion on important religious matters. They did not feel remotely bound to follow those opinions, however, if they disagreed with them. Correspondingly, as this book explores, emperors and kings exercised much greater actual religious authority than any pope for many centuries after Constantine, and not just in practice but also by right, since it was generally accepted that Christian rulers were directly appointed by the Almighty. Only in the eleventh century did long-standing papal prestige evolve into an initial formal claim that popes should exercise general religious authority, while it took most of the following century for this claim to become accepted in practice" (xv). The papal system and its full sacramental soteriology as defined at the Fourth Lateran Council of 1215 (see Heather, 507ff) was only about 300 years old when Luther confronted it.

was to explain theologically why the Protestant churches were not schismatic sects breaking the unity and catholicity of the church, but rather showing how the churches reformed by the Word of God were in fact the true church, united in truth and faith. The second was to help the Protestant churches despite their differences to cooperate with one another as fellow Christians.

In the *Institutes* Calvin grounded his approach to the catholicity of the church in the insistence that Christ alone was the head of the church on earth. Christ was not an absent or inactive head, rather he was a present and active governor of his church, directing it by his Word and Spirit. He wrote, 'The church is called "catholic," or "universal," because there could not be two or three churches unless Christ be torn asunder...which cannot happen! But all the elect are so united to Christ...that as they are dependent on the one Head, they also grow together into one body, being joined and knit together...as are the limbs of a body....'[3] Connection to Christ as head is the essential ground of unity for the church.

In his *Catechism of the Church of Geneva* (1545) Calvin catechised the faithful on this point. He explained the reference in the Apostles Creed to a catholic church in this way: 'What is the meaning of the attribute catholic or universal? By it we are taught that, as there is one head of all the faithful, so all ought to unite in one body, so that there may be one Church spread throughout the whole earth, and not a number of Churches (Eph. 4:3; I Cor. 12:12, 27).'[4] Here too we see his emphasis on Christ's headship being the real unity of all Christians. This catholicity of the church was expressed both in the invisible church of the elect and regenerate as well as in the visible, institutional church:

> For we have said that Holy Scripture speaks of the church in two ways. Sometimes by the term 'church' it means that which is actually in God's presence, into which no persons are received but those who are children of God by grace of adoption and true members

---

3. *Institutes*, 4, 1, 2.
4. *Calvin: Theological Treatises*, ed. J.K.S. Reid, Philadelphia (Westminster), 1954, 103.

of Christ by sanctification of the Holy Spirit. Then, indeed, the church includes not only the saints presently living on earth, but all the elect from the beginning of the world. Often, however, the name 'church' designates the whole multitude of men spread over the earth who profess to worship one God and Christ. By baptism we are initiated into faith in him; by partaking in the Lord's Supper we attest our unity in doctrine and love; in the Word of the Lord we have agreement, and for the preaching of the Word the ministry instituted by Christ is preserved. In this church are mingled many hypocrites who have nothing of Christ but the name and outward appearance. There are very many ambitious, greedy, envious persons, evil speakers, and some of quite unclean life. Such are tolerated for a time either because they cannot be convicted by a competent tribunal or because a vigorous discipline does not flourish as it ought.[5]

Calvin saw clearly that the catholicity of the church was expressed in both the purity of the invisible church and the reality of weaknesses in the visible church.

While Calvin clearly distinguished the invisible church from the visible church, he devoted almost all his attention in the *Institutes* to the visible church as the institution in which Christians must live. Christ was seen as actively the head of the visible church:

Now, therefore, the church still has, and will always have, him present. When Paul wishes to show the way in which he manifests himself, he calls us back to the ministries he uses. The Lord, he says, is in us all, according to the measure of grace which he has bestowed on each member [Eph. 4:7]. For that reason, 'he appointed some to be apostles … others pastors, others evangelists, still others teachers,' [Eph. 4:11]. Why does Paul not say that Christ has set one over all to act as his vicegerent? For that the occasion especially demanded, and it ought in no way to have been omitted, if it had been true. Christ (he says) is present with us. How? By the ministry of men, whom he has set over the governing of the church… To men he assigns nothing but the common ministry, and a particular mode

---

5. *Institutes*, 4, 1, 7.

to each. Why did he, in that commendation of unity, after he had mentioned 'one body, one Spirit ... one hope of calling, one God, one faith, one baptism' [Eph. 4:4-5], not immediately also add, one supreme pontiff, to keep the church in unity? ... Let that passage be diligently pondered ... we should not follow any other pattern than that which the Lord himself has given in his Word.[6]

Calvin's point here about Paul's letter to the Ephesians is true of all the New Testament letters which are addressed to all Christians with the clear assumption that because of the grace that they have in Christ as head (Eph. 4:7), they will be able to understand, embrace, and follow apostolic teaching. What is true of all Christians is particularly true of the church's ministers who have the responsibility to teach the Word and lead the church according to it. The acceptance of the apostolic teaching of the New Testament was foundational to the character of the true church for Calvin. This stood in sharp contrast to the false church, particularly the Roman Catholic Church led by the papacy. Of that church Calvin wrote:

> Instead of the ministry of the word, a perverse government compounded of lies rules there, which partly extinguishes the pure light, partly chokes it. The foulest sacrilege has been introduced in place of the Lord's Supper. The worship of God has been deformed by a diverse and unbearable mass of superstitions. Doctrine (apart from which Christianity cannot stand) has been entirely buried and driven out. Public assemblies have become schools of idolatry and ungodliness. In withdrawing from deadly participation in so many misdeeds, there is accordingly no danger that we be snatched away from the church of Christ.[7]

While the papal church was the dominant false church that the reformers confronted, anabaptists and anti-trinitarians also were separated from the true church. Since there are true churches and false churches in the world, it is critical that Christians have clear criteria by which to distinguish the true from the false. Calvin

---

6. *Institutes*, 4, 6, 10.
7. *Institutes*, 4, 2, 2.

carefully discussed the marks of—the crucial evidence for—the true church. He wrote that a church is true 'if it has the ministry of the word and honours it; if it has the administration of the sacraments, it deserves to be held and considered a church. For it is certain that such things are not without fruit. In this way we preserve for the universal church its unity, which devilish spirits have always tried to sunder; and we do not defraud of their authority those lawful assemblies which have been set up in accordance with local needs.'[8] These marks point to the fundamental character of the local churches where the preaching of the Gospel and the administration of the sacraments actually take place.

While highlighting the two marks of the true church, Calvin recognised that there would be some differences on less important points of doctrine and practice among various churches. He wrote:

> Some fault may creep into the administration of either doctrine or sacraments, but this ought not to estrange us from communion with the church. For not all articles of true doctrine are of the same sort. Some are so necessary to know that they should be certain and unquestioned by all men as the proper principles of religion. Such are: God is one, Christ is God and the Son of God; our salvation rests in God's mercy; and the like. Among the churches there are other articles of doctrine disputed which still do not break the unity of faith ... We should agree on all points. But since all men are somewhat beclouded with ignorance, either we must leave no church remaining, or we must condone delusion in those matters which can go unknown without harm to the sum of religion and without loss of salvation.[9]

For Calvin distinguishing between necessary articles and secondary ones was proper and unavoidable for maintaining the catholicity of the church. Calvin nowhere enumerated a comprehensive list of necessary articles of faith in contrast to

---

8. *Institutes*, 4, 1, 9. While many later Reformed theologians added discipline as a third mark of the true church, Calvin limited the marks to two. While church discipline was very important to Calvin, he perhaps felt that it was too subjective to qualify as a clear mark of the church.

9. *Institutes*, 4, 1, 12.

articles which are true but not essential. Perhaps in the nature of the case such a list would be impossible. It is intriguing, however, that Calvin did offer a significant list in his defence of the basic unity of the Reformed and the Lutherans. In 1556 Calvin wrote his treatise *Second Defense of the Faith concerning the Sacraments in answer to Joachim Westphal*, to refute what he saw as sacramental extremism in some Lutheran theologians. He believed that such extremism was corrupting the true Lutheranism of Luther and Melanchthon, with which the Reformed had cherished agreements. He prefaced his treatise with an introductory letter addressed 'to all honest ministers of Christ, and sincere worshippers of God, who observe and follow the pure doctrine of the Gospel in the churches of Saxony and lower Germany.' In that letter Calvin enumerated the extensive agreements in doctrine and practice that united the Reformed and moderate Lutherans. He wrote:

> In regard to the one God and his true and legitimate worship, the corruption of human nature, free salvation, the mode of obtaining justification, the office and power of Christ, repentance and its exercises, faith, which, relying on the promises of the Gospel, gives us assurance of salvation, prayer to God, and other leading articles, the same doctrine is preached by both. We call on one God the Father, trusting to the same Mediator; the same Spirit of adoption is the earnest of our future inheritance. Christ has reconciled us all by the same sacrifice, in that righteousness which he has purchased for us, our minds are at peace, and we glory in the same head.[10]

Here Calvin was using and specifying elements of his idea of necessary articles. It is interesting that Calvin saw basic agreement with the Lutherans on key matters of worship and repentance, areas where some later Reformed theologians were critical of the Lutherans.[11] Throughout his career Calvin repeatedly acted on the basis of his distinction between necessary

---

10. John Calvin, "Second Defence of the Faith concerning the Sacraments in answer to Joachim Westphal," in *Tracts and Treatises on the Doctrine and Worship of the Church*, Grand Rapids, Michigan (Eerdmans), 1958, vol. 2, 251.

11. For a thorough review of Calvin's views of Luther, see R. Scott Clark, *Subtle Sacramentarian' or Son? John Calvin's Relationship to Martin Luther*, The Southern Baptist Journal of Theology, 21.4 (2017), 35-60.

and unnecessary articles. He also encouraged his followers, in situations where they could not thoroughly reform the church, to cooperate in establishing a good Protestant church in general. He tried to restrain those who tended to adopt an 'all or nothing' or perfectionist approach to the life of the church. Calvin's wise distinction was embraced by most of his followers, as can be seen, for example, in the Westminster Confession of Faith. There we read: 'This catholic church hath been sometimes more, sometimes less visible. And particular churches, which are members thereof, are more or less pure, according as the doctrine of the gospel is taught and embraced, ordinances administered, and public worship performed more or less purely in them.'[12] Some true churches are purer and more faithful than others.

One way to see the practical work of Calvin for the unity of the church is to examine the concerns of his letters.[13] Many of these letters were related to issues in the Swiss churches. He wrote to Berne trying to advance cooperation where at times there were tensions with the church of Geneva. He also addressed issues in Neuchatel and Basle. He wrote most often to Heinrich Bullinger, Zwingli's successor in Zurich. He discussed many matters with him affecting churches throughout Europe as well as various issues in the Zurich churches.[14] He even at times wrote to the churches and city council of Geneva. His greatest achievement with the Swiss churches was the *Consensus Tigurinus* (1551) which he reached with Bullinger, on the meaning of the Lord's Supper.[15] This agreement cemented ties between Geneva and Zurich in the Reformed community but increased suspicions of Calvin on the part of many Lutherans.

---

12. Westminster Confession of Faith, chapter 25.4.

13. A good selection of his most important letters is available in English in *Select Works of John Calvin: Tracts and Letters*, ed. H. Beveridge and J. Bonnet, Grand Rapids, Michigan (Baker), 1983, vols. 4-7.

14. For reflections on Calvin's relationships with different kinds of friends, see W. Robert Godfrey, *Calvin and Friends*, in John Calvin, For a New Reformation, ed., D. Thomas and J. Tweeddale, Wheaton, Illinois (Crossway), 2019, 131-158.

15. See Chapter by Jon D. Payne: 'The Zurich Consensus: The Lord's Supper and Unity in an Age of Discord.'

Calvin wrote regularly to Melanchthon, usually urging him to be more active in promoting better relations between the Reformed and the Lutherans. (Calvin seemed not to know the difficulties Melanchthon increasingly faced with the Gnesio-Lutherans and the serious limits of his influence.) Calvin was certainly concerned about the progress of the reformation in the Holy Roman Empire. When Martin Bucer, the great reformer of Strassburg, asked him to write a defence of the reform to present to the emperor and the imperial diet meeting at Speyer in 1544, Calvin responded with one of his great treatises, *The Necessity of Reforming the Church*.[16] He presented the case on behalf of all the Protestants at the diet.

Calvin followed the reform of the church in England with great interest. He wrote to Thomas Cranmer, the Archbishop of Canterbury, as well as to the Protector Somerset and to King Edward VI. He was involved in the efforts to convince John Hooper to become a bishop in the Church of England despite Hooper's serious reservations about unreformed elements in the church. Calvin's interests extended to the reform of churches far to the north and to the east. He wrote encouragement to the King of Sweden and dedicated his commentary on the twelve minor prophets to him in 1559. He also wrote to various political and ecclesiastical leaders in Poland and dedicated his commentary on Hebrews in 1549 to the King of Poland, and his commentary on the Acts of the Apostles in 1560 to Nicholas Radziwill of Lithuania.

Frequently Calvin wrote to those in France. Some of these letters were eloquent exhortations and encouragements to prisoners for the faith awaiting execution. He helped the Reformed Churches in France in their synodical organisation. He wrote to many powerful nobles who identified with the Reformed cause. He was the principal author of the *French Confession of 1559* for the Reformed churches there. Calvin's extensive correspondence—

---

16. See John Calvin, *The Necessity of Reforming the Church*, Orlando, Florida (Reformation Trust), 2020.

which went far beyond what has been summarised here—sought to advance the cause of truth, unity, cooperation, and a willingness to compromise on minor issues. In a remarkable way Calvin combined a strong and clear vision of what the church ought to be according to the Scriptures with an eager concern to see the unity of the church despite some differences.

Of some importance is his appeal both to church leaders and to civic government leaders to advance the true reform of the church. These appeals reflect a significant tension in Calvin's thought. He wanted the church to have a measure of independence from the state to follow the Scripture's teaching. This had been Calvin's goal in Geneva—never fully attained—when he sought the right of the church to exercise spiritual discipline over its members independent of state involvement. At the same time Calvin believed that the Christian magistrate should support and enforce true religion. Tensions arose if the state failed to do its duty adequately. While this problem may have been less obvious during the Reformation, it was still a noticeable problem even then.

After Calvin's time the Protestant churches of Europe became increasingly divided and regionally isolated. Civil governments established and protected their national churches. Most churches accepted, at least de facto, their civil governments as the ultimate guarantors of the unity, catholicity, and orthodoxy of the church. Through the centuries various Protestant theologians and churchmen lamented divisions in the churches and hoped through various ecumenical efforts to unite the churches. But divisions multiplied and most Christians came to accept with some regret an understanding that various denominations were real if imperfect parts of the true church.

In light of the many denominational divisions of churches today and particularly of the secularisation of civil governments in the west, one might well ask if Calvin's views on the catholicity of the church have any real contemporary usefulness. One early modern Reformed theologian, Abraham Kuyper (1837–1920), sought to address that question in his own reflections on the catholicity of the church. He believed that he was clarifying Calvin's doctrine of the church in rejecting its unbiblical connection to the state.

Kuyper was a leading figure in a great renewal of Calvinism in the Netherlands in the nineteenth and early twentieth centuries. At various times he served as a pastor, elder, theologian, and professor. He led a separation from the state Reformed church in the name of orthodoxy and discipline and the creation of a new denomination. He also founded a university, edited periodicals, reinvigorated a Christian political party, served in parliament, and was prime minister for four years. In all his labours in the church and in the state, he sought to rethink the character and role of Calvinism in an increasingly post-Christian world. He was both a profound and creative theologian and a popular leader of a large Christian movement.

Kuyper believed that as society lost a sense of the sovereignty of God, the greatest danger it faced was the emergence of various forms of human tyranny. In particular he warned of the danger of state tyrannies which would proclaim that all freedoms, rights, and institutions derive as a gift from the state. He seems now to have been prophetic, writing as he did before the rise of communism and fascism in the twentieth century.

Kuyper's antidote to all tyranny was his teaching of 'sphere sovereignty,' which insisted that the various spheres or institutions of society—for example, the church, the state, or the family - each derive its character and responsibility directly from God, not from some other institution. As this applies to the church, the church ultimately must give account only to God for its teaching and life. No civil government or pretended church authority over churches can replace the responsibility of churches to God alone. As this applies to the state, the state must limit itself to the administration of justice, not seeking to make judgments on true churches where it has no competence. Kuyper took this distinction so seriously that he led the successful effort to revise the *Belgic Confession* (1561), the historic confession of the Reformed churches in the Netherlands, particularly Article 36 on 'The Civil Government.' The revision removed the language that obligated the civil government for 'removing and destroying all idolatry and false worship of the Antichrist.' Unity and catholicity were the responsibility of the church alone.

In his notable *Lectures on Calvinism*[17] delivered at Princeton University in 1898, Kuyper expressed his view of the church which he believed made Calvin's teaching more consistent. He stressed the foundational importance of the invisible church for its visible life:

> In its essence, for the Calvinist, the Church is a spiritual organism, including heaven and earth, but having at present its centre, and starting-point for its action, not upon earth, but in heaven ... The real, heavenly, invisible Church must manifest itself in the earthly church. If not, you will have a society, but no church. Now the real essential Church is and remains the body of Christ, of which regenerate persons are members. Therefore the Church on earth consists only of those who have been incorporated into Christ, who bow before Him, live in His Word, and adhere to His ordinances; and for this reason the Church on earth has to preach the Word, to administer the sacraments, and to exercise discipline, and in everything to stand before the face of God.[18]

Kuyper, who follows the *Belgic Confession*, Article 29, in seeing discipline as a third mark of the church, seems to have expected a greater visible purity to the church than Calvin did. Kuyper, like Calvin, ties the church to the active headship of Christ, but ties that headship strongly to the local church and the involvement of all members: 'So the sovereignty of Christ remains absolutely monarchical, but the government of the Church on earth remains democratic to its bones and marrow.'[19] In Kuyper, more explicitly than in Calvin, and perhaps more in keeping with apostolic teaching, the local churches are the places where Christ effectually exercises his headship.

---

17. Abraham Kuyper, *Lectures on Calvinism*, Grand Rapids, Michigan (Eerdmans), 1975. These lectures were long one of the few writings of Kuyper available in English. Now there is a major multi-volume translation project underway under the general title *Abraham Kuyper: Collected Words in Public Theology*.

18. *Lectures*, 59, 62f.

19. *Lectures*, 63.

Local churches for all their devotion to Christ and to his Word will inevitably develop a variety of differences:

> By virtue of this starting-point [the principle not of compulsion, but of liberty], there was no other church-power superior to the local churches, save only what the churches themselves constituted, by means of their confederation. Hence it followed of necessity that the natural and historic differences between men should also, wedge-like, force their way into the phenomenal life of the church on earth. National differences of morals, differences of disposition and of emotions, different degrees of depth of life and insight, necessarily resulted in emphasising first one, and then another side of the same truth. Hence the numerous sects and denominations into which the external church-life has fallen by virtue of this principle.[20]

For Kuyper these differences are neither a tragedy nor the end of the catholicity of the church; they are inevitable in a fallen world and will be overcome only when Christ returns in glory to judge the church as its Head. For Kuyper what he calls the multiformity or pluriformity of the church does not weaken or diminish it, but contributes to its vitality. Here too he is significantly different from Calvin. Kuyper wrote:

> After the experience of three centuries it must be confessed that this multiformity, which is inseparably connected with the fundamental thought of Calvinism, has been much more favourable to the growth and prosperity of religious life than the compulsory uniformity in which others sought the very basis of its strength.[21]

The remarkable diversity and vitality of the history of American churches would seem to commend Kuyper's contention.[22] By

---

20. *Lectures*, 64. Kuyper and the Dutch Reformed churches are presbyterian in their polity but emphasized the original jurisdiction of the local churches and their participation in broader assemblies, and so are significantly different from Scottish Presbyterianism.

21. *Lectures*, 64f.

22. Indeed it may well be that diversity and vitality are linked throughout the history of the church. Consider this statement by the distinguished historian Judith Herrin: 'Although Christianity provided the medium for both the unity of faith and the unity of culture in the Late Antique world, it was not by means of a uniform and

contrast the established churches of Europe often seem to lack vitality and have not maintained their orthodoxy. Nevertheless, Christians should avoid divisions wherever possible and should pursue unity under the Word of God.

Kuyper's revision of Calvin's teaching on catholicity reduces Christian guilt about the dividedness of the visible church, but increases Christian responsibility to build the true church, to reflect on the necessary articles of the faith, and to cultivate a catholic spirit toward all true churches. Whether or not Calvin living in our modern world would have agreed with Kuyper's approach is a good question for historical and theological discussion. Regardless of the answer, we should all heed Calvin's words of encouragement and of warning:

> Happy indeed is that attainment of unity of faith [cf. Eph. 4:13] when all—from the highest to the lowest—aspire toward the Head! …By his word, God alone sanctifies temples to himself for lawful use. And if we rashly attempt anything without his command, strange inventions forthwith cling to the bad beginning and spread evil without measure.[23]

---

monolithic force. On the contrary it was immensely varied and reflected the different regions into which it had spread in the course of six centuries. Over such a long time span and vast area, local peculiarities that distinguished one regional church from others were bound to develop, especially when Christendom consisted more of a loose confederation of believers than a tightly regulated organisation. In this process political and geographical factors, and autonomous and disparate growth combined. If these are ignored or given insufficient weight, we lose sight of the central dynamism of Christianity, which rests precisely on a unity through variety. In the early centuries Christians developed their own idiosyncratic and independent types of devotion; episcopal, patriarchal, and papal authority were established very slowly, and communities reserved the highest degree of loyalty, obedience, and affection for their local leaders. Thus uniformity of ritual and even of belief was impossible, indeed in some cases it was undesirable.' Judith Herrin, *The Formation of Christendom*, Princeton (Princeton University Press), 1987/2021, 90

23. *Institutes*, 4, 1, 5.

CHAPTER FOURTEEN

John Owen

Catholic Calvinist

Benedict Bird

If one were to describe John Owen as a 'catholic Calvinist', the controversial element, in his eyes, would not have been the first term, but the second. He always regarded himself as a member of the catholic church, and denied any intention 'in the least [to] disturb, break, or dissent from the *Catholick Church*.'[1] Unwarranted divisions between Christians were 'the chief cause of Offences unto them who are yet strangers from Christianity.' The 'Principal *Cause*' of such divisions was 'no other than the Ignorance or Misapprehension … of the *true nature of that Evangelical Unity*' which Christ requires.[2]

Some definitions are needed. What did Owen understand by 'catholic' and 'catholic church'? The term derives from καθολικός, meaning entire, whole, universal. But what and who are within the

---

1. John Owen, *A Discourse concerning Evangelical Love, Church Peace, and Unity* (1672), 15:102, original capitalisation and italics. Citations of Owen's works herein refer to the twenty-four volume William Goold edition (London: Johnstone & Hunter, 1850-55), except for the Latin work Θεολογούμενα Παντόδαπα which Goold did not include. Goold's orthography is used in quotations except where the original first edition presentation is significant, notably Owen's unwillingness—*vide supra*—to cede the term 'Catholick' (capital C) to the Romanists.

2. *Discourse concerning Evangelical* Love, 15:105, original capitalisation and italics.

ambit of that universe? Does it consist of all persons, churches and teachings that go by the name 'Christian'? Or is Christian *ecclesial catholicity*, and the duty to practise and uphold it, bounded by the limits of doctrinal orthodoxy?

Assuming that doctrinal orthodoxy is relevant to the question of catholicity, the enquiry moves on to the connection between the terms 'catholic' and 'Calvinist'. What is Calvinist doctrine, and is it the appropriate measure of orthodoxy for setting the bounds of *doctrinal catholicity*?

Applying the term 'Calvinist' to Owen, as noted above, is controversial: not least, because it is not evident that he ever described himself as a Calvinist.[3] He cites Calvin with approval in many places, though much less than he cites Augustine.[4] When an autonym was required, he was content with 'Reformed', 'Protestant' and 'Catholic'. Calvin's views coincided with much of the Reformed consensus in the mid-seventeenth century. But neither Owen nor his contemporaries regarded Calvin's writings as the last word in Reformed orthodoxy, or 'Calvinism' as synonymous with it.[5] As the term 'Calvinist' is commonly used today with reference to Reformed orthodoxy, we may suppose that

---

3. In a couple of places, Owen notes that 'Calvinist' was a term applied to those 'of his persuasion' by disparagers, particularly Lutherans: "Amongst Protestants, at least the one half account all men of my persuasion Calvinistical, sacramentarian sectaries," *A Countrey Essay for the Practice of Church-Government There* (1646), 8:47; and similarly, "Amongst Protestants [we are accused of] being *Reformatists*, or as they call us, *Calvinists*, [and] condemned for schismatics by the *Lutherans*, and for sacramentarian sectaries," *Of Schism: The True Nature of it Discovered and Considered* (1657), 13:94. The term 'Calvinist' appears around twenty times altogether in Owen's works. In every instance he is noting its use as a label by others, most frequently in contradistinction to the Lutherans in Germany.

4. See chapter by Peter Sanlon, 'Augustine: The Original Catholic Calvinist.'

5. See, for example, Richard Muller, *Post-Reformation Reformed Dogmatics, The Rise and Development of Reformed Orthodoxy: Prolegomena to Theology*, vol. 1 (2003), 30; and Muller, *Calvin and the Reformed Tradition* (2012), 44-8; Gavin McGrath, 'Puritans and the Human Will: Voluntarism within Mid-Seventeenth Century English Puritanism' (PhD diss., Durham, 1989), 63; John Coffey, Alister Chapman, and Brad Gregory, eds., *Seeing Things Their Way: Intellectual History and the Return of Religion* (2009), 164; Willem van Asselt, *Introduction to Reformed Scholasticism* (2011), 8, 201; Dewey Wallace, *Shapers of English Calvinism, 1660–1714* (2011), 9-10; Susan Moore, 'Reformed Theology and Puritanism', in *Cambridge Companion to Reformed Theology* (2016), 202; Stephen Hampton, *Grace and Conformity* (2021), 30-2.

with certain caveats Owen would have been willing to employ it. But with what caveats?

It follows, therefore, that to describe Owen as a 'catholic Calvinist' raises a good many questions. A supplementary enquiry would be whether Ian Hamilton, an avowed admirer of Owen and his works, would wish to be regarded as a 'catholic Calvinist' in the same sense that Owen would have been willing to endorse. No doubt Ian would add some caveats of his own. This paper must be confined to Owen's answers. These will be elicited from some of his many works, in every genre and decade of his writing, that address the nature of the true catholic church and its doctrine.

Some of these works were occasioned by the need to defend those who dissented from the *un*catholic demands for conformity made by those in the re-established national church.[6] Others were written in opposition to groups such as the Socinians, who preferred a narrow biblicism to the doctrines that had been broadly accepted as orthodox throughout church history.[7] Others warned of the threat to true catholicism presented by resurgent Roman Catholicism, a threat that intensified post-Restoration as the later Stuarts became less and less concerned to hide their sympathies.[8] Many of his other works examined particular theological *loci* such as atonement, justification and perseverance.[9] In these Owen demonstrates his doctrinal catholicity, affirming that which 'has been believed everywhere, always and by all', by drawing upon the teaching of a wide range of theologians, and important creeds and confessions, from different parts of the church down the centuries.[10]

---

6. For example, *Of Schism* (1657); *Discourse concerning Evangelical Love* (1672); *True Nature of a Gospel Church* (1689).

7. See *Vindiciæ Evangelicæ* (1655).

8. For example, *Animadversions on a Treatise Entitled Fiat Lux* (1662); *A Vindication of the Animadversions on Fiat Lux* (1664); *Sermon: The Chamber of Imagery in the Church of Rome Laid Open; or, an Antidote against Popery* (1682).

9. See for example *Salus Electorum, Sanguis Jesu, or The Death of Death in the Death of Christ* (1648); *The Doctrine of the Saints' Perseverance* (1654); *The Doctrine of Justification by Faith* (1677); *Πνευματολογία, or A Discourse on the Holy Spirit* (1674).

10. This understanding of catholicity—"*Quod ubique, quod semper, quod ab omnibus creditum est*"—was expressed by Vincent of Lérins in the early fifth century: see Sinclair Ferguson and David Wright, eds., *New Dictionary of Theology* (1988), 131.

Particular attention will be given to Owen's *Discourse concerning Christian Love*, published in June or July 1672. This was a few months after he had had at least one meeting with Charles Stuart junior, at which Owen had expressed gratitude for the recently-granted Indulgence. Charles intended this to benefit Roman Catholics primarily, but it restored some freedom of worship—for a matter of months—to dissenters as well.[11] In this *Discourse*, Owen defends the Reformed understanding of catholicity against opponents both Roman and at least nominally Protestant.

Definition of the Catholic Church

We begin with Owen's understanding of the 'catholic church', which differs little from Calvin's or the Westminster Divine's.[12] He distinguishes, as do they, and as does Scripture albeit *sine his nominibus*, between the catholic church invisible and visible. The invisible church comprises 'all the elect of God, of all that shall be saved in all ages and places, from the beginning of the world unto the end thereof.'[13] Together, these constitute:

> That *real living and spiritual body of [Christ]*, his Elect, Redeemed, justified, and sanctified ones, who are savingly united unto their Head by the same quickning and sanctifying Spirit, dwelling *in him in all fulness*, and communicated *unto them by him*, according to his Promise.[14]

Owen's emphasis on the Spirit, as the person of the Trinity who immediately effects the saving union between the elect and Christ upon their believing in him, is simultaneously notable and unsurprising, given the extensive attention that Owen gives to the work of the Spirit. It is not without good cause that he has been

---

11. Sarah Cook, *A Political Biography of a Religious Independent, John Owen* (PhD diss., Harvard, 1972), 331-35.

12. Cf. John Calvin, *Institutes*, 4.1.2; and *Westminster Confession of Faith* (1648), Chapter 25.

13. Χριστολογία: *A Declaration of the Glorious Mystery, The Person of Christ* (1679), 1:87. See also *The Branch of the Lord, the Beauty of Sion: or the Glory of the Church in its Relation unto Christ* (1650), 8:286.

14. *Discourse concerning Evangelical Love*, 15:78, original capitalisation and italics.

described as 'the theologian of the Spirit;' indeed, perhaps with even greater reason than that title has been extended to Calvin.[15] When Christ returns, all of the invisible church, comprising all of the elect 'in conjunction with the holy angels,' will form 'one mystical body, one catholic church'—at which point it will be invisible no more.[16] However in this age, since those belonging to the invisible church cannot be definitively identified, we must also speak of the visible catholic church, which is:

> More or less always visible by that *Profession of Faith* in [Christ], and obedience unto him, ... where-ever there are any *Societies* or *Numbers of men* who ordinarily profess the Gospel, and subjection to the Kingly Rule of Christ thereby.[17]

Owen emphasises that it is not by a bare profession alone that the visible church is delineated. It is 'their *Sincere faith and Obedience*' which mark out this church and its membership. Outside of this church 'there is no salvation to be obtained,' in that those who will not profess Christ as Lord, and who eschew his church, have no part with him.[18]

---

15. Sinclair Ferguson, *Theologian of the Spirit: John Owen*, in Tabletalk Magazine (2004); Ferguson, *The Holy Spirit* (1996), 12; Kelly Kapic, *Communion with God: The Divine and the Human in Theology of John Owen* (2007), 39-40.

16. *Sermon on 1 Corinthians 12:11: Ministerial Endowments, Preached at an Ordination, 3rd April 1678* (1678), 8:574.

17. *Discourse concerning Evangelical Love*, 15:78-79, original capitalisation and italics. See also *The Branch of the Lord*, 8:286, and *Of Schism*, 13:150.

18. Owen's congregational ecclesiology is apparent in his third particularization of the visible church, referring to "particular congregations," each a local church: *Of Schism*, 13:173-81. In a sense, the visible church is comprised of these. But the visible church does not itself represent "an instituted church," in a formal organizational sense, having authority over particular congregations, 13:137-38. If it were an instituted church it ought to be capable of gathering and engaging in "the joint performance of any exercise of religion, that they should hear one sermon together, or partake of one sacrament, or have one officer for their rule and government"; but this is "ridiculous to imagine." Hence "the universal [visible] church is not so called upon the same account that a particular church is so called. The formal reason constituting a particular church to be a particular church is, that those of whom it doth consist do join together, according to the mind of Christ, in the exercise of the...ordinances for his worship. And in this sense the universal church cannot be said to be a church, as though it had such a particular form of its own": 13:137. In other words, the unity of

The duty of catholicity

With these definitions in place, Owen considers the duty of catholicity owed by all members of the church. We have 'our first and principal regard' to those who are truly members of it, 'which the Lord Christ loved and gave himself for'—in other words, the invisible church.[19] To these we are bound in love, with 'that love ... planted in our hearts ... by that one and self-same Spirit, by whom the whole mystical body of Christ is animated.' Someone can scarcely claim to love Christ, yet not discern and love the whole body of Christ. But given that this church is 'invisible in its mystical form,' we are bound, secondly, to extend our catholicity and love to the visible church according to its 'outward profession.'[20] This is the 'visible kingdom of Christ' in any age, as distinguished from 'that world which lieth ... under the power of Satan.'[21]

As we seek to practise this duty of 'Christian *Love*, [and the] duty to live in constant *Communion*' with 'this *Catholick Church*...both towards the whole, and every Particular Member, as we have Advantage and Occasion,' there is a difficulty.[22] There are 'many who belong unto this church, by reason of some kind of profession that they make, [who] may justly be esteemed to

---

the visible catholic church derives from its common profession of Christ, not from having a common set or hierarchy of officers as the Romanists and Episcopalians pretended. Owen regrets that this simple ordering of particular churches, resembling "the first churches...planted by the apostles," did not remain acceptable to men as the church grew, *Discourse concerning Evangelical Love*, 15:88. Willem van Vasthuin puts it succinctly: "When looking at the primitive church and its history, [Owen] did not find any hierarchy of pastors, bishops, diocesans, archbishops, chancellors, archdeacons and commissaries; there was no ecclesial authority beyond that of the local congregation...Every congregation was a complete church in itself and could exist independently of other bodies of church government," 'John Owen as a Modern Theologian: A Comparison of Catholicity in Cyprian and Owen', in *John Owen between Orthodoxy and Modernity* (2019), 179.

19. *Discourse concerning Evangelical Love*, 15:79, 91, citing Ephesians 5:2.
20. 15:78, 81-82.
21. 15:82.
22. 15:86, original capitalisation and italics.

be the *world*, or of it.'²³ The visible church will always include some who are only nominally or ostensibly Christian. They may be properly regarded as Christians by the church on the basis of a charitable acceptation of their profession, while in fact they are still unregenerate:

> Whatever they *pretend* in shew at any time in the outward duties of *Devotion*, they have neither faith in Christ, nor *love* to the Saints: and so have part and fellowship neither in the *union* nor *communion* of the Catholick Church.²⁴

It follows that one part of the visible church may be predominantly or even wholly regenerate; another may be substantially unregenerate. Does the duty of catholicity extend equally and indiscriminately? How are demands by a church body for recognition and even submission—such as were being forcibly made in Owen's day—to be assessed? We find in his *Discourse* at least the following seven principles:

First, Owen prefaces his discussion with the reminder that 'love toward all mankind in general [is] required of us...Even towards the infidel, pagan, and Mohammedan world, Jews and Gentiles, we are debtors in this duty.'²⁵ This love should issue in compassion and prayer for 'so many perishing souls, originally made like ourselves, in the image of God, and from whom that we differ in any thing is an effect of mere sovereign grace.'

Secondly, he advocates a generous assessment of which churches should be regarded as being within the '*Catholic, visible Church*,' encompassing 'all who throughout the world outwardly own the Gospel.'²⁶ Necessarily he excludes those 'who openly reject the principal fundamentals of Christian religion (as denying the Lord Christ to be the eternal Son of God, with the use and efficacy of his death, as also the personal subsistence and deity of

---

23. 15:82.
24. *Of Schism*, 13:134, original capitalisation and italics; see also *Discourse concerning Evangelical Love*, 15:86.
25. *Discourse concerning Evangelical Love*, 15:70-71.
26. 15:82-83, original capitalisation and italics. On these 'fundamentals', see also *Of Schism*, 13:146.

the Holy Spirit).' To remain in communion with such a church is 'unlawful ... It is our indispensable duty to separate from them' if we are to 'approve ourselves faithful in our profession ... and to abstain from what [Christ] condemns.'[27]

But so long as churches 'own so much of the truths concerning one Lord, one faith, and one baptism as is sufficient to guide them unto life and salvation,' in that they instruct their adherents to 'subject ... their souls to Jesus Christ, ...observing the religious duties by him prescribed,' then we should expect that God will use them and his gospel for the 'conversion of souls.' We should be slow to assume that a church has strayed so far from orthodoxy that it cannot be regarded as being as within the visible church. Owen says:

> How far the *Errors* in Judgment, or miscarriages in sacred worship, which any of them have superadded unto the Foundations of Truth which they do profess, may be of so pernicious a nature as to hinder them from an Interest in the Covenant of God, and so prejudice their Eternal Salvation, God only knows. But...where Men in sincerity do improve the Abilities and Means of the Knowledge of Divine Truth wherewith they are intrusted, endeavouring ... a suitable *Obedience*, there are but few Errors of the Mind of so malignant a nature, as absolutely to exclude such Persons from an Interest in Eternal Mercy.[28]

Owen qualifies this by saying that we should not count within the catholic church those whose doctrine may be orthodox but whose practices are materially inconsistent with their profession, that is:

> ...whose *Lives and Conversations* are no way influenced by the Power of the Gospel, so as to be brought to some Conformity thereunto; or who, under the Covert of a Christian Profession, do give themselves up unto *Idolatry* and *Persecution* of the true Worshippers of God.[29]

All such idolators and persecutors are 'no otherwise to be esteemed but as Enemies to the Cross of Christ.' In applying these tests

---

27. *Discourse concerning Evangelical Love*, 15:93-94.
28. 15:85-86, original capitalisation and italics.
29. Ibid.

to the English established church, Owen advocated a charitable catholicity towards it:

> We look upon the *Church of England* ... to be as sound and healthful a part of the Catholick Church as any in the world. For we know no Place, nor Nation, where the *Gospel* for so long a season hath been *preached* with more Diligence, Power, and Evidence for Conviction; nor where it hath obtained a greater Success or Acceptation. Those ... who *perish amongst us*, do not do so for want of Truth, and a right belief, or Miscarriages in Sacred worship, but for their own Personal Infidelity and Disobedience. For ... we do not judge that there are such Errors publickly admitted among [its ministers], nor any such Miscarriages in Sacred Administration, as should directly or absolutely hinder their eternal Salvation.[30]

However much Owen disagreed with the ecclesiology and ways of worship of the episcopal church, he did not doubt that its constitution, and most of its parishes in practice, upheld the 'fundamentals' sufficiently for effective gospel proclamation.[31] Remarkably, he was willing to say this even of men who promoted the 1662 'Great Ejection' of those who would not conform to their strictures. That is not to say that all of its ministers were beyond reproach. Implicit in Owen's careful language is the possibility that some held to serious errors, albeit not 'publickly admitted;' and that some put serious obstacles in the way of the eternal salvation of its members, albeit not 'directly or absolutely' hindering their salvation.

Thirdly, domineering claims by 'a particular church of one single denomination' to be the entire catholic church should be rejected as 'absurd, foolish, and uncharitable.'[32] Such, says Owen, 'is the judgment of...the church of Rome.' It is a 'prodigy

---

30. Ibid.

31. In *Peace-Offering, in an Apology and Humble Plea for Indulgence and Liberty of Conscience* (1667), 13:551-52, Owen says that there is complete consistency between "our confessions," referring to the Congregationalists' Savoy Declaration of 1658 of which he was one of the principal draftsmen, and the doctrinal content of the Thirty-nine Articles of the Church of England.

32. *Discourse concerning Evangelical Love*, 15:84-85. See also *The Church of Rome No Safe Guide* (1679), 14:489.

of insolence' to deny 'any sort of Christians ... an interest in the love of God ... because they do not ... comply with those ways ... of outward church-communion which we approve of." Owen regarded the Roman church as the product of 'the pride and vanity of the declining Ages' following the fifth century, in which the church leaders 'styled themselves *Oecumenical* and *Catholick*,' and finally '*Papal*.'[33] The popes 'fell into a claim of a Sovereignty over the whole Body of Christianity, and every particular member thereunto belonging.' Inevitably, an organisation of this nature drew to itself men motivated by 'ambition, worldly domination, and avarice,' intent on pursuing 'their own incredible secular advantage.'[34] Compared with 'the internal spiritual beauty and glory of the true catholic church of Christ,' this portrayed but a 'deformed image.'

The papist leaders began 'imposing upon all persons and churches a necessity of the observation of [their] rites and ceremonies ... casting them out of communion who refuse to submit' and when that did not achieve full compliance, 'forcing men by carnal weapons, corporal penalties, tortures, and terrors of death, unto the embracement of [their] profession.'[35] The Roman church had shown itself to be doctrinally heretical and apostate, and a persecutor of the faithful.[36] As a body it had 'no institution in or warrant from the Scripture.'[37] As such it was like the self-instituted church of Israel 'after the defection under Jeroboam, [which] was no ... true church, nor any church at all.'[38] When a church spreads 'idolatry ... over the face of all [its] solemn assemblies, and [persecutes] those who desire to worship God in spirit and in truth,' it deserves 'the title of 'Babylon', [and] we are commanded to 'come out from among them.''

---

33. *Discourse concerning Evangelical Love*, 15:89-90, original capitalisation and italics.
34. *Chamber of Imagery*, 8:575.
35. *A Vindication of the Animadversions on Fiat Lux*, 14:225-26.
36. Owen considers the heretical and persecuting nature of the Roman church most extensively in *Animadversions* and *Vindication of the Animadversions*.
37. *Discourse concerning Evangelical Love*, 15:90.
38. 15:94, citing 1 Kings 12-13.

Even while writing thus, Owen warns against the tendency 'to judge and censure each other temerariously [rashly].'[39] The sort of party spirit, wherein all sides are 'conscious unto their own sincerity,' is 'an evil ... to be diligently watched against.' He continues: 'For us to judge and determine whether these or those churches are true churches or no ... and so condemn them in our minds (unless where open wickedness will justify the severest reflections), is to speak evil of the law, and to make ourselves judges of it.' Such judgments are only to be made 'when we are called thereunto in a way of duty,' for example in defending the church against false teachers.[40]

That said, fourthly, a Christian will not be guilty of schism if he separates himself from a church that denies the fundamentals of the faith, or persecutes those that adhere to them. Nor will he if he declines to join in worship with a church that *does* 'belong to the *Church Catholick visibly professing*,' but which has 'fallen into *sinful neglects*, disorders, and miscarriages, both in Doctrine, Discipline, and worship.'[41] Depending on the state of such a church, there will be 'a great *variety* in our Judgments concerning them and our Communion with them.' In other words, careful discernment will be required.

For example, where there are corruptions that are 'not... so heinous,' including some errors in doctrine, discipline and worship, then there may well be 'no sufficient Warrant unto any person immediately to leave their Communion.'[42] It may be that such person should see this is an opportunity:

> By divine Providence ... to exercise his *charity*, Love and Forbearance towards the persons ... whose Miscarriages at present he cannot Remedy. In such cases there is a large and spacious Field, for *Wisdom, Patience, Love*, and *prudent Zeal* to exercise themselves.[43]

---

39. 15:134-35.
40. 15:136, citing James 4:11-12.
41. 15:92-93, original capitalisation and italics.
42. 15:96-97, original capitalisation and italics.
43. Ibid.

Owen says that it is 'a most perverse imagination, that separation is the only cure for church disorders' such as those which he discusses. But he balances all this, by saying that if a church should:

> *Obstinately persist* in its Errors, Miscarriages, Neglects, and Mal-administrations; ... refuse to be warned or admonished, or ... bear with them that are yet found in it, whether Elders or Members, in peaceable Endeavors to reduce it unto the order of the Gospel, but shall rather hurt, persecute and seek their trouble for so doing, whereby their *Edification* comes continually to be obstructed ... through the loss of Truth and Peace; we no way doubt but that it is lawful for such persons to withdraw themselves from the Communion of such Churches.[44]

In all of these matters, prayerful self-examination is required, for there are many who 'make their own hasty conceptions to be the rule of all church ... communion, who, unless they are in all things pleased, can be quiet nowhere.'[45] Much wisdom is needed if we are neither to divide the body of Christ, nor to allow 'our own souls [to] be subverted' by those who are themselves being unfaithful to him.[46]

Fifthly, it is not schismatical to decline to join in worship where extra-biblical obligations are made the condition of communion. Failing to separate could amount to 'slothful negligence and carelessness in the great concerns of the glory of God.'[47] Christ commands churches to teach and observe 'all things whatsoever I have commanded you.'[48] The apostolic church practised this consistently, declining at the Jerusalem Council to 'appoint any one thing to be observed ... which the Lord Christ had not commanded,' and the early church endorsed the freedom of dissenting believers to 'meet in distinct assemblies ... for the celebration of holy worship,' rather than submit to practices

---

44. Ibid. See also *Of Schism*, 199-201.
45. *Discourse concerning Evangelical Love*, 15:96; see also 15:133-35.
46. 15:98.
47. 15:98.
48. 15:144, citing Matthew 28:19-20.

that were not commanded, even if 'not commanded' either.[49] This, known today as the 'regulative principle,' Owen defended in numerous works.[50]

Owen rejected the claims by the established church in his day that it was only requiring submission to ἀδιάφορα: 'things indifferent,' too insignificant to warrant objection.[51] Within this category were such requirements as the unfeigned consent by ministers to everything contained in the prayer book, observation of holy days, kneeling for the Lord's Supper, making the sign of the cross in baptism, and wearing of surplices.[52] Of these, Owen says:

> First to *invent* them, then to *impose* them, ... and then to judge and censure them as *Schismaticks*, as enemies to Love and Peace, who do not submit unto them, looks not unlike the exercise of an unwarrantable *Dominion* over the Faith and Consciences of the Disciples of Christ.[53]

Biblical catholicity requires that all must endeavour to 'keep the unity of the Spirit in the bond of peace.'[54] But responsibility for the disunity caused by such impositions lay with those who used their position of 'hav[ing] the most power' to impose them

---

49. 15:148-51, citing Acts 15 and Romans 14-15.

50. For example, *Of Communion with God* (1657), 2:150-52; *Of Schism*, 13:174-78; *A Discourse concerning Liturgies, and Their Imposition* (1662), 15:3-55; *A Brief Instruction in the Worship of God* (1667), 15:447-79; *Indulgence and Toleration Considered* (1667), 13:520-22; *Truth and Innocence Vindicated* (1669), 13:448-52; *Discourse concerning Evangelical Love*, 15:143-80; *An Enquiry into the Original, Nature, Institution, Power, Order and Communion of Evangelical Churches; with An Answer to the Discourse of the Unreasonableness of Separation written by Dr. Edward Stillingfleet* (1681), 15:229-30, 244-47, 340-41, 388-94. As for the 'normative principle' idea, that the church may add to what Scripture commands so long as it considers its additions to be edifying or adorning, Owen says "every *addition* is principally a *corruption* because it is an *addition*," *Brief Instruction*, 15:470-71 (original emphasis). It cannot be excused on the basis that it is a mere 'circumstance', if it is required to be "observed religiously," because if it is "to be observed in the worship of God, [it] is of the substance of [worship]."

51. *Discourse concerning Evangelical Love*, 15:145-47.

52. 15:158-64; see also *Of Schism*, 313.

53. *Discourse concerning Evangelical Love*, 15:149, original capitalisation and italics.

54. 15:151, citing Ephesians 4:3.

while refusing to allow dissenters to hold their own separate meetings.[55] Far from being the way of 'peace and love,' it was the 'fundamental cause of our divisions.'[56] The remedy was to return to the practice of the early church and make the only requirements for church membership 'baptism, with a voluntary credible profession of faith, repentance and obedience unto the Lord Christ in his commands and institutions.'[57]

Sixthly, we should be quick to assume that even in churches that are in various ways defective, there will be 'some [who] really belonging to the purpose of God's election, who ... shall at length be brought unto everlasting glory.'[58] Differences over 'church-constitutions or order,' for example, do not justify 'any want [lack] of love on our parts.'[59] It is 'the fondest imagination ... that we must of necessity want love towards all those with whom we cannot join in all acts of religious worship.' Even a church led by those with a 'worldly frame of spirit' may contain believers whose error in 'joining themselves unto such churches' ought not 'be any cause of the diminishing of our love towards them.'[60]

Even in apostate churches, Owen allows that there may 'remain a profession of the fundamental truths of the gospel,' such that they 'maintain the interest of Christ's visible kingdom in the world,' at least in the sense of containing many who 'secretly preserve themselves from being defiled' by the church's idolatry.[61] Citing the 'seven thousand who kept themselves pure from Baalish idolatry,' whom godly Elijah had overlooked, Owen warns that 'good men may sometimes be more severe in their censures for God than he will be for himself.'[62]

Owen's great concern is not to be found guilty of uncharitable judgments towards those who are in fact fellow subjects of the

---

55. 15:150-51.
56. 15:113, 151.
57. 15:154.
58. 15:83.
59. 15:92.
60. 15:91.
61. 15:94-95.
62. 15:95, citing 1 Kings 19.

kingdom of Jesus Christ.⁶³ To love and pray for them 'is the sum of the duty which is required in us towards them.' Such is the catholicity of spirit which Owen repeatedly advocated.

Seventhly, in all of these matters requiring discernment, it is vital to remember the theological foundation of true catholicity. The unity of the catholic church does not rest on human apprehensions or precisionist formulations of correct ecclesiology and doctrine, but on the spiritual reality that true believers in fact become 'one in the Father and the Son' through 'their participation of, and quickening by, the same Spirit that is in Christ Jesus, whereby they become his body, or members of it.'⁶⁴ We are spiritually one with Christ because, and only if, we have indwelling within us the same Spirit who indwells him.⁶⁵ There is no possibility of 'mutual usefulness' of one part of the body to another, or 'edification of the whole,' aside from 'the relation that the members have to the Head, and their union with him.'⁶⁶

Lacking this perspective and understanding, 'most men have pursued a shadow, …a vain figment of their own,' causing divisions and schisms by demanding that others conform to their 'outward rules and constitutions.'⁶⁷ Such demands, based on 'the commands of men,' can lead only to 'a kind of church tyranny.'

Thus, there can be no true unity except where the Spirit brings it about by regeneration; and, thereafter, by those 'united unto Christ [being] taught of God to believe the truths which are necessarily required thereunto.' There are fundamental truths to be believed, of which every man must be 'fully persuaded in his

---

63. 15:101-02.
64. 15:105-07.
65. Owen's emphasis on the necessity for every member of the true church to be indwelt by the Spirit leads Van Vlastuin to suggest that Owen was thereby adopting a "modern individualistic approach," at least compared with Cyprian who "starts with the corporative unity of the church" as the primary delineator of church membership: see 'John Owen as a Modern Theologian', 170, 182. This is not convincing.
66. *Discourse concerning Evangelical Love*, 15:105-07; see also *Two Discourses Concerning the Holy Spirit and His Work* (1693), 4:503-04.
67. *Discourse concerning Evangelical Love*, 15:105, 110.

own mind,' but then 'the whole mystery of the will of God, as revealed in the Scripture' is to be enquired into.[68]

This unity in the Spirit, and unity of faith, will issue in a unity of love, 'whereby all the members of the body of Christ are knit together among themselves.'[69] From this love comes the 'forbearance ... towards the infirmities, mistakes, and faults of others,' and the willingness of one member to 'communicate the spiritual supplies which he receiveth from the head, Christ Jesus, unto others ... unto their edification.' This is the gospel unity that 'we are to labour after' that binds together the catholic church unto the glory of God.

The doctrine of the Catholic Church

We have seen how Owen understood the catholic church, as it falls to be considered in its invisible and visible aspects; and how the duty of catholicity owed towards it requires that we be both generous and discerning. We conclude with a brief consideration of the relationship between this ecclesial catholicity, rightly understood, and doctrinal catholicity. It is a close—even somewhat circular—relationship. Scripture defines the ambit of the church; which in turn has a role in interpreting Scripture.

In one of the works in which Owen discusses this relationship, Θεολογούμενα Παντόδαπα, he considers the danger to doctrine that follows from undiscerning catholicity. When Christianity became the religion of the empire in the time of Constantine the Great, 'many took up the title of Christian who were still profane, superstitious, carnal, proud, greedy, luxurious—indeed, they rushed into the churches in crowds.'[70] It is unsurprising, says Owen that 'from this influx ... the doctrines of faith ... became

---

68. 15:108-09.
69. 15:109-11. See also Πνευματολογία, 3:588: "If among believers we will...love them only, delight in them only, be open and free in all effects of genuine kindness towards them who go our way, or are of our party, or are kind and friendly to us, or that never gave us provocations really nor in our own surmises, we are so far and therein worse than either Pharisees or publicans."
70. Θεολογούμενα Παντόδαπα (1661), 504, as translated by Stephen Westcott in *Biblical Theology* (1996), 660.

so rapidly corrupted in the churches.' The 'glory of the gospel was overshadowed, and superstitious practices flooded in.' This sorry influx included the worship of angels, prayers for the dead, images, purgatory, monasticism, priests and the mass. Along with these corruptions came 'shameful wrangles ... as church leaders strove for a wicked pre-eminence over their brothers.'[71] Says Owen:

> Let the Roman Church be our example: which, although it was a particular church it wished to be the universal, going beyond the bounds and nature of a particular church; but not attaining to the bounds and nature of the universal, it lost the whole nature of a church, with the result that it became neither particular nor catholic.[72]

In other words, false catholicity spawned false doctrine; false doctrine spawned a false catholic church: whereupon, having achieved dominance, this false church set itself up as the custodian and arbiter of doctrine. It was a circle of corruption that needed the Reformation for it to be broken.

Owen's account of the Roman usurpation continues in one of his works on the operations of the Holy Spirit, Σύνεσις Πνευματική. Rome had claimed for itself sole and infallible authority to declare Scripture to be the word of God; and 'when it is believed so to be, ...it *cannot* be understood, but according to the mind, judgment, and exposition of the same Church.'[73] This exclusivism was wholly inconsistent with the catholic illumination of true believers:

---

71. *Θεολογούμενα Παντόδαπα*, 506, trans. Westcott, *Biblical Theology*, 663.

72. My translation of *Θεολογούμενα Παντόδαπα*, 507: "Exemplo sit Ecclesia Romana, quæ cum particularis fuerit, voluerit autem esse Catholica, modum particularis & naturam excedens, Catholicæ autem non assequuta, totam amisit Ecclesiæ naturam, ut nec particularis sit neque Catholica." Westcott's translation is somewhat looser: "Let our great example be the Roman Church, which, although it had started as a local assembly, desired to gain a universal ascendency. By abandoning the nature and form of a true church, which is both particular and catholic, and instead conforming to the nature and form of the secular state, it ceased to be either particular or catholic, and thus to be a church at all," *Biblical Theology*, 664.

73. *Σύνεσις Πνευματική* (1678), 4:121, original capitalisation and italics. In *Animadversions on...Fiat Lux*, 14:93, he denies the claim that "With the Roman

> *Every Believer may in the due use of means appointed of God for that End, attain unto…all that knowledge of the mind and will of God revealed in the Scripture, which is sufficient to direct him in the life of God, to deliver him from the dangers of Ignorance, Darkness, and Error, and to conduct him unto Blessedness.*[74]

This catholicity is founded not on papal presumption, but on the work of the Spirit: who, having brought every believer into unity with Christ, proceeds to 'enlighten … our minds and enabl[e] our understandings to perceive and apprehend his mind and will as revealed in the Scripture.'[75] He is the 'supreme teacher … on whose wisdom, power, and authority, we ought principally to depend.'[76]

The Spirit's work of illumination is catholic in the sense of being fully sufficient for the salvation and sanctification of every believer. This does not mean that every believer receives the same degree of illumination; each receives what he needs:

> In those very *Foords* and appearing *Shallows* of this River of God, where the *Lamb* may wade, the E*lephant* may swim. Every thing in the Scripture is so plain as that the *meanest Believer* may understand all that belongs unto his Duty, or is necessary unto his happiness.[77]

Nor is it that believers are to be passive in their receiving of the Spirit's illumination. They are to read the Scriptures diligently, frequently and prayerfully.[78] Moreover, the Spirit has edified the church "in all ages" by ensuring that 'the doctrine of the gospel [is] preached *vivâ voce*.'[79]

In addition to these means of grace, the Spirit has 'stirred up and enabled sundry persons to declare by writing what their apprehensions were, and what understanding God had given them in and about the sense of the Scripture.' Here, Owen refers with

---

Catholics unity ever dwelt," saying "Never! The very name of Roman Catholic, appropriating Catholicism to Romanism, is destructive of all gospel unity."

74. Σύνεσις Πνευματική, 4:121-22, original capitalisation and italics.
75. 4:125.
76. 4:153.
77. 4:193, original capitalisation and italics.
78. 4:199-207.
79. 4:228.

approval to the writings of Ambrose, Chrysostom, Augustine, Œcumenius and others, as having given 'singular helps and advantages unto the right understanding of the Scripture.'[80] He names 'Bucer, Calvin, Martyr, Beza' as particularly eminent and useful in the Reformation era.[81] In other works, he draws discerningly from the writings of many other Church Fathers and mediaeval Schoolmen; Lutherans and Amyraldians; 'low' and 'high' parts of the English church; Dominicans and even Jesuits.[82]

All of these theologians 'the Spirit of God makes ... useful and prosperous according to the counsel of his own will.'[83] Some speak truth even despite being 'persons visibly destitute of any saving work of the Holy Ghost upon their minds;' others 'who are truly enlightened and sanctified by him do yet fall into sundry errors and mistakes.' None is infallible, nor 'absolutely secured from particular errors and mistakes, no more than we are from all actual sins by the work of the Spirit on our wills.'

So it is that Owen demonstrates his doctrinal catholicity, as he seeks to uphold 'the known doctrine of the ancient Catholick Church' and 'the Faith of the *Catholick Church* in all Ages.'[84] There is much valuable testimony in the writings of the church

---

80. 4:228-29. Owen is less complimentary about Origen. Cf. *The Nature of Apostasie* (1676), 7:68, where Owen refers to the "neglect of the gospel and its simplicity" and the teaching of "sundry things, perverse, curious, and contrary to the form of wholesome words committed unto them," by Justin Martyr, Irenæus, Clemens, Origen, Tatianus, Athenaguras, Tertullian, Lactantius, and others. Even so, he does not wish to "reflect with any severity on their names and memories who continued to adhere unto the fundamental principles of Christian religion."

81. This in itself demonstrates the problem with calling Owen a 'catholic Calvinist': the narrowing nature of the 'Calvinist' element tends towards rendering the expression oxymoronic.

82. In *The Doctrine of the Saints' Perseverance*, for example, Owen finds useful material in writings by Clement of Rome, Ignatius, Tertullian, Cyprian, Basil of Cæsarea, Macarius Ægyptius, Ambrose, Chrysostom, Augustine, Hilary, Prosper, Gregory I, Œcumenius, Gratian, Bradwardine, Aquinas and Álvarez (both Dominican), and Bellarmine and Suárez (both Jesuit).

83. *Causes, Ways, and Means*, 4:229-31.

84. *Πνευματολογία*, 3:245, 292, original capitalisation and italics. For similar expressions, see *Vindication of the Discourse Concerning Communion with God* (1674), 2:326; *Two Discourses Concerning the Holy Spirit*, 4:387, 500-501; *The Doctrine of Justification by Faith*, 5:209, 258, 368; *Sermon on 1 Corinthians 12:11*, 9:444.

fathers and their successors which can be 'read with profit and advantage.'[85] So too may the ecumenical creeds, including the Apostle's Creed:

> That *ancient Symbol* commonly esteemed *Apostolicall*...having also warrant from the Word of God, and being of *singular use* to hold out unto all other *Churches* of the world our apprehensions of the minde of God, in the chief heads of Religion.[86]

Even so, however much 'wisdom and skill' men may have demonstrated in declaring 'the truths that are taught in the gospel, by sound and wholesome words of their own, ...all of them, as to their propriety and significancy, are to be tried and measured by the Scripture itself.'[87]

Conclusion

John Owen was a practising catholic, in that his understanding of the boundaries of the church, both invisible and visible, was generously, discerningly and biblically shaped. That understanding constrained him to labour for loving communion with and throughout the whole church of God, while at the same time defending it against the wolves in sheep's clothing that both circled it and arose from within. He sought to commend orthodox doctrine, always drawn from and tested against Scripture, but as interpreted and approved by the whole Church of all ages. This careful catholicity required a clear comprehension of the way that God refines, reforms and revives his Church: allowing questions and even heresies to arise; then raising up men who, disdaining mere partisan or private advantage, search the Scriptures for answers and discernment that brings glory to God. To that same end, may we seek to learn from Owen's teaching and example.

---

85. *The Doctrine of the Saints' Perseverance*, 11:24, citing with approval Jean Daillé, *A Treatise Concerning the Right Use of the Fathers*, trans. Thomas Smith (1651).

86. *Of Toleration; and the Duty of the Magistrate about Religion* (1649), 8:203, original capitalisation and italics. In *A Peace-Offering*, 13:552, Owen affirms his complete agreement with "the first four general councils" of the early church: Nicæa, Constantinople, Ephesus and Chalcedon.

87. *Πνευματολογία*, 3:524.

CHAPTER FIFTEEN

A Surprising Catholicity?

The Church in Scottish Theology

Donald John MacLean

"Never did mariners use more speed to stop a leak in a ship, lest all should be drowned, than ministers especially, and all Christian men should haste to stop this beginning of the breaking in of these waters of strife, lest thereby the whole Church be overwhelmed."
James Durham[1]

"There is no danger from enemies without, like that from divisions within ... Division mars reformation in a church."
Thomas Boston[2]

---

1. James Durham, *The Dying Man's Testament to the Church of Scotland*, or, *A Treatise Concerning Scandal* (repr.; ed. Christopher Coldwell; Dallas: Naphtali Press, 1990), 260. See also, John MacPherson, *The Doctrine of the Church in Scottish Theology* (Edinburgh: Macniven & Wallace, 1903), 106-7.

2. Thomas Boston, *The Whole Works of the Late Reverend Thomas Boston, of Ettrick* (ed. Samuel M'Millan; 12 vols.; Aberdeen: George and Robert King, 1848), 7:611-2.

If Scottish Presbyterianism is known for anything, it is for its propensity to fracture into competing denominations. The old tale is of a Scottish Presbyterian stranded on a desert island. His rescuers, when they arrive, are bemused to find two church buildings on the island given he is the only inhabitant. He explains, that one building is the church he used to worship in, the other building is the church he worships in now. Scottish Presbyterians, apparently, can fall out even with themselves.

Given this reputation, it might seem strange to devote a chapter to the *catholicity* of the doctrine of the church in Scottish theology. Surely a study of the *sectarianism* of the Scottish doctrine of the church is more fitting? But this would be to mistake the sad current reality of the Scottish church for the doctrine and practice of her past leading theologians. Indeed, part of the rationale for considering the catholicity of the older Presbyterian doctrine of the church is to call the present divided and fractured Scottish Presbyterian church back to the doctrine of her fathers.[3] This older view is well expressed by James Walker, 'Separation from a true Church seemed to these good men ... to carry in it the destruction of the very idea of unity.'[4]

To outline this older view, two consequential theologians will be briefly considered—Samuel Rutherford (1600–61) and James Durham (1622–58). Each has contributed significantly to Scottish theology in general, and to the doctrine of the church in particular. As well as these figures, it is important to acknowledge that the reflections of John MacPherson in *The Doctrine of the Church in Scottish Theology* and James Walker in *The Theology*

---

3. This is fitting in a festschrift for Ian Hamilton who often quotes Calvin: "This other thing also is to be ranked among the chief evils of our time, viz., that the churches are so divided, that human fellowship is scarcely now in any repute among us, far less that Christian intercourse which all make a profession of, but few sincerely practice ... Thus it is that the members of the Church being severed, the body lies bleeding. So much does this concern me, that, could I be of any service, I would not grudge to cross even ten seas, if need were, on account of it." (John Calvin, *Tracts and Letters*, ed. Jules Bonnet [7 vols.; Repr.; Edinburgh: Banner of Truth, 2009], 5:347-348.)

4. James Walker, *The Theology and Theologians of Scotland: Chiefly of the Seventeenth and Eighteenth Centuries* (Edinburgh: T. & T. Clark, 1888), 98.

and Theologians of Scotland underpin much of the thought in this chapter.[5]

Samuel Rutherford (1600-61): Against Separatism

Rutherford is known as a man 'made of extremes.'[6] Usually this is taken as a reference to his marrying passionate heart religion with the refinements of scholastic theology. However, it could equally refer to his merging of polemic zeal for doctrinal orthodoxy with trenchant arguments for church unity despite serious theological and practical error. Rutherford spoke repeatedly of his own Church of Scotland as follows, 'Brother, we have cause to weep for our harlot-mother; her Husband is sending her to Rome's brothel-house, which is the gate she liketh well.'[7] Despite his extreme dissatisfaction with her sins, Rutherford would rather suffer within the Kirk, than contemplate separation from her. His reasons for this were profoundly theological: to separate from a true church, even one in grave error, was simply schism.

The Marks of the Church

Rutherford's refusal to separate over error, and therefore the failure of discipline in the life of the church, was consistent with identifying discipline as a mark of the church.[8] Early Scottish reformed theology had room for a church lacking discipline remaining a true church. John Craig's catechism, after stating that the marks of a true church are the Word, the sacraments, and discipline rightly used, considered the situation where there the mark of discipline is missing:

---

5. MacPherson, *The Doctrine of the Church in Scottish Theology*; Walker, *The Theology and Theologians of Scotland, 1560-1750*.

6. Samuel Rutherford, *Letters of Samuel Rutherford* (Andrew Bonar, ed.; Edinburgh: Oliphants, 1904), 315.

7. Rutherford, *Letters of Samuel Rutherford*, 410.

8. "The Scots Confession", Chapter 28 in James T. Dennison, ed., *Reformed Confessions of the Sixteenth and Seventeenth Centuries in English Translation, Volume 2 (1552-1566)* (Grand Rapids: Reformation Heritage Books, 2010), 198-9.

Q. What if no order of discipline be among them?
A. Then we should remain with the word and sacraments.

Q. But what if both the word and sacraments be corrupted?
A. Then we should not join ourselves with that company.⁹

The three marks were not equal in importance in early Scottish Reformed theology. Failure in discipline did not unchurch a church. Indeed, as MacPherson noted:

> Our covenanting forefathers ... made the preaching of the word the principal, and sometimes, it would seem, almost the only absolutely indispensable note of the true Church ... they refused to unchurch any communion in which the word was preached... though it might be accompanied with many additions of doctrine that have no scriptural warrant.[10]

What then would unchurch a church for Rutherford? What would give rightful grounds for division? He provides his answer as he works through the questions, 'Whither or no it be lawful to separate from a true Church visible, for the corruption of teachers, and the wickedness of Pastors and professors, where Faith is begotten by the preaching of professed truth?' and 'Whither or no separation from a true Church because of the sins of professors and manifest defence of scandalous persons can be proved from Gods word, to be lawful.'[11]

Separation Within and Out of a Church

Concerning separation, perhaps Rutherford's most important contention is that 'There is a separation in the visible Church,

---

9. John Craig, "Craig's Catechism" in Horatius Bonar, ed., *Catechisms of the Scottish Reformation* (London: J. Nisbet, 1866), 252.

10. MacPherson, *The Doctrine of the Church in Scottish Theology*, 107-8.

11. Samuel Rutherford, *A Peaceable and Temperate Plea for Paul's Presbyterie in Scotland, or A Modest and Brotherly Dispute of the Government of the Church of Scotland, Wherein, Our Discipline is demonstrated to be the true Apostolick way of divine Truth, and the Arguments on the contrary are friendly dissolved, the grounds of Separation and the Indepencie of particular Congregations, in defence of Ecclesiasticall Presbyteries, Synods and Assemblies, are examined and tried* (London: Printed for John Bartlet at the guilt-Cup neare St Austins-gate, 1642), 121-164. Spelling and punctuation have been conformed to current usage throughout this chapter.

and a Separation out of, and from the visible Church.'[12] This is what MacPherson notes as 'a way of distinguishing between separation in and separation from the Church.'[13] He explains that, for Rutherford, separation from sin 'may be done without separating from the Church. There may be a partial or negative separation ... that is to say, in regard to certain acts of public worship, in which we could not without sin take part.'[14] Indeed, separation was often an ineffectual way for dealing with sin, for separation is not 'the only way of testifying effectually against sins and errors; for if you have liberty, such a testimony can be far more effectually borne in union than in severance.'[15]

This separation within the church could even be to the extent of not being able to partake of the sacraments, 'yet are we not separated from the Church, for we professedly hear the word, and visibly allow truth of the [fundamental] doctrine maintained by that Church, which doe [yet] pollute the Sacraments.'[16] Sin must always be separated from, but the question for Rutherford is *how*? And the answer is, unless the foundation is destroyed, we are to separate *within* a church rather than *from* a church.

Division from Rome

Given this distinction, Rutherford had to justify separation *from* Rome, while arguing for only separation *within* protestant churches. His discussion of Rome is nuanced. For example, he held Rome's baptism and ordination remained valid.[17] Still, Rome was to be separated from. The grounds of separation

---

12. Rutherford, *A Peaceable and Temperate Plea for Paul's Presbyterie in Scotland*, 121.
13. MacPherson, *The Doctrine of the Church in Scottish Theology*, 91.
14. MacPherson, *The Doctrine of the Church in Scottish Theology*, 110. See also, Walker, *Theology and Theologians of Scotland, 1560-1750*, 100.
15. Walker, *Theology and Theologians of Scotland, 1560-1750*, 100.
16. Samuel Rutherford, *Due Right of Presbyteries, or, A peaceable Plea for the Government of the Church of Scotland* (London: E. Griffin, for Richard Whittaker and Andrew Crook, 1644), 254(2). (After p484 the numbering revers to 185 and continues from this. To indicate a reference to the second occurrence of a page number I include a (2) after the page.) For a later example of the same perspective, see Boston, *Works*, 7:603.
17. Rutherford, *A Peaceable and Temperate Plea for Paul's Presbyterie in Scotland*, 124.

included 'persecutions' so that 'we are patients and ejected rather than departers on foot and horse' and 'a necessity of professing fundamental errors, that subvert the foundation of faith.'[18] In essence Rutherford says, the Reformed were expelled by the Roman church, and if they had remained it would have required professing error in foundational truth.

He explained, 'some saving truths remain in the Church of Rome, and in that we keep yet a material and real union with Rome in as far as they profess one God; three persons, two natures in Christ,' nevertheless:

> We have separated from Rome. 1. Because their doctrine of professed and commanded Idolatry, and their other heresies everteth the foundation of Faith. 2. Because they lay another foundation above the foundation Christ, the Pope, and a multitude of idol-gods.[19]

Because of the serious nature of these errors it was necessary to separate: 'We may well hold that Ambrose saith well, that a Church wanting the foundation of the Apostles, is to be forsaken.'[20] However, even in this case, 'when we separate from a Church overturning the foundation of religion, as from Rome, we are to keep a desire of gaining them, howbeit not a brotherly fellowship with them.'[21]

Unity Within Reformed Churches

While Rome was to be separated from, Reformed churches were not.[22] To make the case, Rutherford turned to examples of churches in Scripture where there were substantial errors, but no separation. He adduced the example of Christ's treatment

---

18. Rutherford, *A Peaceable and Temperate Plea for Paul's Presbyterie in Scotland*, 124.
19. Rutherford, *A Peaceable and Temperate Plea for Paul's Presbyterie in Scotland*, 151-2. See also Rutherford, *Due Right of Presbyteries*, 229(2).
20. Rutherford, *Due Right of Presbyteries*, 254(2).
21. Rutherford, *A Peaceable and Temperate Plea for Paul's Presbyterie in Scotland*, 149.
22. Or, it would seem a Lutheran Church, for, "The learned Pareus sheweth that there be no difference betwixt us and Lutherans in heads absolutely necessary to salvation, the dissention is in one point onely anent the Lords Supper, not in the whole doctrine thereof, but in a part thereof, not necessary for salvation." Rutherford, *Due Right of Presbyteries*, 231(2).

of the Jewish church. The 'church in Christ's days was a most perverse church,' as church leaders 'denied that hatred and rash anger was a sin ... or heart adultery a sin ... polluted the worship with superstition ... devoured widows houses ... slew the Lord of glory ... killed and crucified the Prophets,'[23] and yet, 'Christ by practice and precept forbad to separate from this Church.'[24]

He also advances the example of many New Testament churches. He observes that Paul calls:

> The Galatians the Church of Christ, brethren ... receivers of the Spirit by the hearing of faith ... the children of God by faith in Christ ... and so esteemeth them a right constitute Church not to be separated from.[25]

This is despite them being:

> In part removed from Christ to another Gospel ... bewitched, foolish, joining circumcision and the works of the law with faith, and so fallen from Christ, Christ profiting them nothing, fallen from grace, running in vain, under the Law again, and not under Christ ... beginning in the Spirit, ending in the flesh.[26]

None of these errors, however, are grounds for separation: 'The proposition is clear... [Paul acknowledges] them [as] the body and spouse of Christ, and so it is not lawful to separate from them.'[27]

Corinth was no different, for 'Paul joined as a member with the Church of Corinth, and acknowledged them as a Church, and commanded to keep Church fellowship with them, 1 Cor. 5.4. even when this leavened lump was souring amongst them.'[28] This 'souring' notoriously includes division (e.g., 1 Cor. 1:12), immorality (1 Cor. 5:1), shocking defects in worship (1 Cor. 11:21) and questioning of fundamental truth (1 Cor. 15:12). And yet, the

---

23. Rutherford, *A Peaceable and Temperate Plea for Paul's Presbyterie in Scotland*, 133-4.
24. Rutherford, *A Peaceable and Temperate Plea for Paul's Presbyterie in Scotland*, 134. For a later restatement of this same perspective, see Boston, *Works*, 7:604-5.
25. Rutherford, *A Peaceable and Temperate Plea for Paul's Presbyterie in Scotland*, 144.
26. Rutherford, *A Peaceable and Temperate Plea for Paul's Presbyterie in Scotland*, 144.
27. Rutherford, *A Peaceable and Temperate Plea for Paul's Presbyterie in Scotland*, 144.
28. Rutherford, *A Peaceable and Temperate Plea for Paul's Presbyterie in Scotland*, 157-8.

command of Paul is to remain united. Specifically, the defective worship in Corinth did not warrant separation: 'There was much false worship in Corinth,' yet the New Testament 'never warneth the true and sound believers to separate and make a new Church' but only to separate within the church from 'act[s] of false worship.'[29]

The words of 2 Corinthians 6:17, 'Therefore go out from their midst, and be separate from them, says the Lord,' are not, for Rutherford, a call to separation from the church but from 'from the Idol-table of the Gentiles, at which some did eat at Corinth to the great offence of the weak.'[30] To draw a principle of separation from this verse would be to 'badly conclude separation out of the Church of Corinth, or any other true Church, where the Word and sacraments are in purity, suppose some errors be practised by some.'[31] It would also be 'contrary to' Paul's teaching in 1 Corinthians 5, 11, and 14, 'where he commandeth and alloweth their meeting and public church communion.'[32]

Rutherford makes the same argument from the letters to the seven churches in Revelation 2–3, observing that:

> The Church of Ephesus be a true Church, holding the candlestick of Christ and Christ's presence walking in ... yet had fallen from her first-love ... Pergamus held the doctrine of Balaam, and the Nicolaitans, and murdered the Saints, had Satan's throne amongst them ... Thyatira suffered the woman Jezebel to seduce the servants of Christ ... Sardis had a name to live, and was dead, and her works were not perfect before God ... Laodicea turned cold, indifferent and lukewarm in the matters of God, and was ready to be spewed out at Christs mouth.[33]

Despite their errors, all these were true churches. Therefore, a church may 'remain a true Church with a lawful, visible Ministry, having power of the word, seals and church discipline,' even with

---

29. Rutherford, *A Peaceable and Temperate Plea for Paul's Presbyterie in Scotland*, 161.
30. Rutherford, *A Peaceable and Temperate Plea for Paul's Presbyterie in Scotland*, 151.
31. Rutherford, *A Peaceable and Temperate Plea for Paul's Presbyterie in Scotland*, 151.
32. Rutherford, *A Peaceable and Temperate Plea for Paul's Presbyterie in Scotland*, 151.
33. Rutherford, *A Peaceable and Temperate Plea for Paul's Presbyterie in Scotland*, 145.

great sins, and so 'cannot be separated from, except we would leave the candlestick, and Christ walking in the midst of the golden candlesticks.'[34]

Nor were mixed churches to be left on the basis is would make those who remained in her communion guilty: 'It followeth not that they should separate from a Church that might infect, because that is not God's meane of eschewing infection to lowpe [leap] out of one true Church to another for one fault.'[35]

The standard needed to leave a church was that it is 'wholly leavened, and where the matter of the worship is leaven, and fundamental points corrupted and obtruded upon the conscience.'[36] Leaving for anything short of this was schism. Writing against Thomas Hooker, Rutherford noted this was simply the catholic doctrine:

> But *Augustine* citeth *Cyprian,* Because we see tares in the Church, yet let us not separate from the Church; for, saith *Augustine, When the godly and the wicked partake of the same Sacrament, neither the cause nor the person is hurt.*[37]

Thomas Boston would later say that 'the very foundation of the separation' is the teaching that 'mere joining in communion with a church, wherein there are many corruptions, be a sin.'[38] He regarded this as 'a gross untruth.'[39]

There, of course, were times where ungodliness reached a height and domination where separation was necessary. Paul was right to 'break off communion with the Church of the Jewes, whereof he was once a member, because after Christs death …

---

34. Rutherford, *A Peaceable and Temperate Plea for Paul's Presbyterie in Scotland*, 145.
35. Rutherford, *A Peaceable and Temperate Plea for Paul's Presbyterie in Scotland*, 157. See also, Samuel Rutherford, *Due Right of Presbyteries*, 72; Rutherford, *Due Right of Presbyteries*, 244(2).
36. Rutherford, *A Peaceable and Temperate Plea for Paul's Presbyterie in Scotland*, 157.
37. Samuel Rutherford, *A survey of the Survey of that summe of church-discipline penned by Mr. Thomas Hooker* (London: J.G. for Andr. Crook, at the Green Dragon in St Pauls Church-yard, 1658), 67.
38. Boston, *Works*, 7:604.
39. Boston, *Works*, 7:604.

which because the Jewes maliciously denied, they left off to be a Church.'⁴⁰ However, 'a scandalous life in many of the professors, is not for that any ground to separate from the visible Church, professing such fundamental points.'⁴¹

So Rutherford states, 'neither we, nor the reformed Churches, in words or by consequence overthrow the fundamental and necessary points of salvation, and if the Church of *Corinth* was not to be separated from, nor *Thyatira*, where the resurrection was denied, and false doctrine maintained, you have no reason to parallel us with *Papists, Atheists, Anabaptists*.'⁴² Rutherford, *jure divino* presbyterian that he was, included the Church of England of his day in this, stating that 'The godly in *England* who refused the *Popish ceremonies*, and *Antichristian Bishops*, did well not to separate from the visible Church in *England*.'⁴³

Final Reflection on Rutherford

Rutherford was no doctrinal minimalist. He laboured for a doctrinally robust church all his days. But he was also no separatist. The errors he would put up with in the church while maintaining unity fully justify James Walkers statement: 'Positions sufficiently startling were thus laid down by men whose whole life was nevertheless a battle for orthodoxy.'⁴⁴ And yet it was Rutherford's very commitment to an orthodox doctrine of the church that led him to his position. He was one of 'the divines of the seventeenth century' of whom it could be said 'In Augustine's views of the Catholic Church and of schism they seem to have heartily sympathised.'⁴⁵

James Durham (1622–58): For Union

Rutherford's younger contemporary James Durham wrote perhaps the classic work on church divisions in Scottish Theology, *The*

---

40. Rutherford, *Due Right of Presbyteries*, 246(2).
41. Rutherford, *Due Right of Presbyteries*, 246(2).
42. Rutherford, *Due Right of Presbyteries*, 242(2). For later reflections on Thyatira, see Boston, *Works*, 7:604
43. Rutherford, *Due Right of Presbyteries*, 254(2).
44. Walker, *Theology and Theologians of Scotland, 1560-1750*, 101.
45. Walker, *Theology and Theologians of Scotland, 1560-1750*, 101.

Dying Man's Testament to the Church of Scotland, or, A Treatise Concerning Scandal.[46] This work itself was borne out of a sad series of disputes in the Scottish church in the years following the Westminster Assembly, known as the Protestor/Resolutioner controversy.[47] The dispute saw men of the stature of Samuel Rutherford and David Dickson take opposite positions.

Durham took no side in the dispute and tried rather to heal divisions. As Robert Wodrow noted, 'He was a man greatly for the peace of the Church as his carriage at that time evidenced ... for he said either of the two Public Resolutions or Protestations was much better than the division they made about it.'[48] Sadly, his efforts proved futile.[49] Nevertheless, his *Treatise Concerning Scandal* was of lasting value for the church with, for example, both parties appealing to it in controversy that agitated the Free Church of Scotland in the nineteenth-century.[50]

To summarise this monumental work is impossible. Many aspects will have to be passed over, for example Durham's unsparing exposing of the causes of division,[51] his treatment of the psychology of division,[52] and his outlining of the evils of division.[53] Suffice to say that Durham believed that division was 'exceeding hurtful to the church and has been an inlet and nursery to the greatest errors. It is most pressingly condemned in the Scriptures.'[54]

What Division Implies?

For Durham, just like Rutherford, a division in the church implied the judgement that 'such a society ... be no church, or communion

---

46. Full bibliographical details in the first footnote of this chapter.

47. For further detail, see Kyle D. Holfelder, "Factionalism in the Kirk during the Cromwellian Invasion and Occupation of Scotland, 1650 to 1660: The Protester-Resolutioner Controversy" (Ph.D. diss., University of Edinburgh, 1998).

48. Robert Wodrow, *Analecta, or materials for a history of remarkable providences; mostly relating to Scotch Ministers and Christians* (4 vols.; Edinburgh: Maitland Club, 1842-1843), 3:106

49. See, e.g. Lachman, "Introduction" in Durham, *Scandal*, ix.

50. John MacLeod, *Some Favourite Books* (Edinburgh: Banner of Truth, 1988), 30.

51. Durham, *Scandal*, 234-240.

52. Durham, *Scandal*, 241-244.

53. Durham, *Scandal*, 258-9.

54. Durham, *Scandal*, 227.

with that church in other ordinances, to be unlawful because of such corruptions, or of such corrupt members.'[55] If the corruption was not that serious then it must follow that:

> Either the church of Christ in the earth is not one, (which truth of the unity of the catholick visible church, is the main ground of all church-union and communion), or, that that one church may be of such heterogeneous or dissimilar parts, as the one of them ought not to have communion with the other.[56]

Thus, Walker notes, 'true Churches of Christ, side by side with one another, forming separate organisations, with separate governments, seemed to them utterly inadmissible.'[57]

What Leads to Unity?

As well as depreciating division, Durham spent significant time encouraging union, particularly in his teaching on 'General Grounds Leading to Unity.'[58] There he began by laying down something he felt he could 'take for granted,' namely, 'that by way of precept there is an absolute necessity of uniting laid upon the Church ... union is both commanded as a duty, and ... as eminently tending to the edification of the church.'[59] It was obvious that division was wrong because 'Christ's church is but one body, and this [division] were deliberately to alter the nature thereof.'[60]

Taking this as a given, Durham was hopeful that 'there can be no division among orthodox divines or ministers, but it is possible also to compose it, and union is a thing attainable.'[61] He was only writing of union among those agreed on 'the fundamental things' and acknowledged that union would need to be achieved without

---

55. Durham, *Scandal*, 228.
56. Durham, *Scandal*, 228. See, Walker, *Theology and Theologians of Scotland, 1560-1750*, 99.
57. Walker, *Theology and Theologians of Scotland, 1560-1750*, 97.
58. Durham, *Scandal*, 261-277. There is a helpful summary in, MacPherson, *The Doctrine of the Church in Scottish Theology*, 116-8.
59. Durham *Scandal*, 262.
60. Durham *Scandal*, 262.
61. Durham *Scandal*, 263.

everyone being 'one in judgment in every point of truth.'⁶² Indeed, there would be:

> Many things defective that need forbearance in persons that are united [such as] difference of judgement in many things ... unworthy officers, or members ... many particular failings ... and defects in the exercise of government, as possibly the sparing of some corrupt officers and members ... yea, the censuring of some unjustly, or the admission of some that are unfit for the ministry, and such like [and] some defects in Worship, manner of Government, and rules that are necessary for good government in a Church.⁶³

Division was to be reckoned as worse than 'forbearance' on these failings. Durham was particularly insistent that failures in discipline were no grounds for continuing division. He used the example of the church of Thyatira and 'those church officers, their tolerating of Jezebel and the Nicolaitans to seduce the people, and to commit fornication,' noting 'yet neither is separation or division called for, or allowed either amongst Ministers or people.'⁶⁴ He also referred to the presence of believers in the Jewish church in the time of Christ, noting:

> There were such corrupt acts of all kinds amongst the Jews Church-officers; yet is it clear, that Nicodemus and Joseph of Arimathea did continue to govern jointly, notwithstanding thereof, who yet cannot be counted accessory to any of their deeds; Because ... men in such cases have access... to discountenance such corrupt acts, by not consenting thereto, and testifying against the same.⁶⁵

Neither were deficiencies in worship to be barriers to union. Durham notes worship was:

> Defective in the Church of Corinth, where the Sacrament was so disorderly administrated (as hath been marked) confusion in many things of Worship, and some things still to be set in order; yet doth the Apostle nowhere press union more than in these Epistles ... if

---

62. Durham *Scandal*, 263.
63. Durham *Scandal*, 264-5.
64. Durham *Scandal*, 264.
65. Durham *Scandal*, 264-5.

there be defects of that kind, it is union and not division that is to be looked upon as the commended mean for redressing of the same.'[66]

The coherence with Rutherford's teaching is evident.

What Errors are Consistent With Union?

Durham provided six rules for defects that were consistent with a union. First, he observed, 'what cannot warrant a breach where there is union, that cannot warrantably be the ground to keep up a division.'[67] The logic was simply, if the issue is not serious enough to warrant schism in the first place, it cannot be serious enough to justify the continuance of schism. Second, 'such defects as do not make communion in a church, and in its ordinances sinful, will not warrant a separation or division from the same.'[68] That is, if union would not positively require sin, then it is a duty. Third, where 'there is no physical or moral impediment barring him in the same. Others being defective in their duty, will not absolve him from his, which he owes by virtue of his station.'[69] That means the failures of some should not be a reason for others to neglect their duty of maintaining union, so long as it did not require sin. Fourth, 'while the general rules tending to edification in the main are acknowledged, union is to be kept, even though there be much failing in the application.'[70] That is, failure in practice, so long as they are not 'in the main' are not to prevent union. Fifth, 'there may and ought to be uniting when the evils that follow division or schism are greater and more hurtful to the church, than the evils that may be supposed to follow on union.'[71] Short of being required to sin, which was never to be done, Durham believed the evils of division, nearly always outweighed the cost of union. Union, in contrast to division, was 'commanded' as a means of

---

66. Durham, *Scandal*, 265.
67. Durham, *Scandal*, 265.
68. Durham *Scandal*, 266.
69. Durham *Scandal*, 266.
70. Durham *Scandal*, 266.
71. Durham *Scandal*, 266.

'edification.'[72] Schism, next to a fall into heresy, was 'one of the greatest hurts that can come to an orthodox Church.'[73] Further, the 'ills of division are most inevitable' while any perceived damage from union 'through God's blessing may be prevented.'[74] Finally, Durham held that 'when men may unite without personal guilt or accession to the defects or guilt of others, there may and ought to be union, even though there be failings and defects of several kinds in a Church.'[75] Durham relentlessly pursued the idea that unless union requires personal sin, or actively joining in the sin of others, whatever faults there are in the church, union is a duty.

Final Reflection on Durham

It is obvious that Durham is far from the prevailing caricature of a fractious Presbyterian. Much is to be given up for the sake of union; much error is to be tolerated for union. If its teachings were applied, there is perhaps no book that would transform the scene in the Reformed church for the better that Durham's *Dying Man's Testimony, Or A Treatise on Scandal*.

Conclusion

James Walker correctly notes of Rutherford, Durham and others, 'separatism was detested. Schism was a word of power.'[76] It was this atmosphere which produced the Westminster Confession of Faith which states: 'Saints by profession are bound to maintain a holy fellowship and communion in the worship of God' (WCF 26:2). To understand the historical meaning of these words, consider David Dickson's commentary on it:

> The apostle calls the Galatians, 'the church of Christ', 'brethren', and the 'children of God', who were yet in some measure removed from God to another Gospel ... (Gal. 3. 1). And yet since it was a

---

72. Durham *Scandal*, 268.
73. Durham *Scandal*, 268.
74. Durham *Scandal*, 268.
75. Durham *Scandal*, 268.
76. Walker, *Theology and Theologians of Scotland, 1560-1750*, 114.

constituted true church, it was his judgement, there should be no separation from it, notwithstanding of all the foresaid faults... the church of Ephesus was a true church, though they made defection from their first love. So was the church of Pergamus, though there were in it who held the doctrine of Balaam. So was the church of Thyatira, notwithstanding that they suffered Jezebel, that called herself a prophetess, and taught the servants of Christ to commit fornication, and to eat things sacrificed to idols.[77]

Dickson understood WCF 26:2 to teach the doctrine of Rutherford and Durham. Thomas Boston also referred to the Westminster Confession in this vein in his sermon against schism:

How doth their separating from this Church, lest they be involved in the guilt of the corruptions amongst us ... agree with Conf. chap. 26, § 2?[78]

In his sermon Boston self-consciously appealed to Rutherford and Durham: 'let them consult Rutherford's *Peaceable Plea for Presbytery*, and Durham *On Scandal*, and *On the Revelation*, both proving this point against the separatists of their time.'[79] This was the consistent Scottish understanding of the Confessional position.

The situation we face today is very different.[80] We are far from John MacLeod's description: 'The ideal of the Reformation and Puritan ages was that there should be one 'face of [the] kirk' in the nation.'[81] We are used to co-operating (to varying degrees) denominations with separate church governments, so that 'a state of matters which to Rutherford or Brown, or even Boston, would have been exceedingly perplexing' is said to 'seem all very natural to us.'[82] This disconnect between our confessional

---

77. David Dickson, *Truth's Victory Over Error* (repr.; Edinburgh: Banner of Truth, 2007), 206.

78. Boston, *Works*, 7:608.

79. Boston, *Works*, 7:605.

80. See, for example the discussion in Iain H. Murray, *A Scottish Christian Heritage* (Edinburgh: Banner of Truth, 2006), 289-96.

81. MacLeod, *Scottish Theology in Relation to Church History since the Reformation* (Rept.; Edinburgh: Banner of Truth, 2016), 48.

82. Walker, *Theology and Theologians of Scotland, 1560-1750*, 117-8.

standards and our current practice, Walker rightly said, 'seems to demand our earnest study.'[83] That study is more pressing now than it was when Walker wrote and needs to face the following challenging questions:

- How can the divided state of reformed churches be remedied? On any historic standard, the reasons for division between denominations which confess subscription to the Westminster Standards are insufficient. Indeed, meaningful subscription to WCF 26:2 impels us to be dissatisfied (at the very least) over our divisions.
- How can we recover the horror with which the old divines viewed division? In many respects division is one of the respectable sins of the church of our day. The old view of division was: 'Those who … separate from her [a true church], because of corruptions in her, while in the meantime they might keep communion with her without sin, are guilty of schism and sinful separation.'[84] If we held this view, then the urgency behind seeking union would be much greater.
- How can we combine a commitment to church unity without losing a zeal for orthodoxy? The older doctrine 'did not mean that the Church was to be lax. She was, on the contrary, to be the pillar and ground of the truth. She was to hunt out all scandals from her borders with a holy zeal. It is needless to say that Rutherford and Dickson were not latitudinarians.'[85] However, they understood that 'what ought to be borne from the Church, without breaking its visible unity, was an entirely different matter from what was the Church's duty in keeping purity of doctrine and life within her pale.'[86]

The answer, at least in part to these questions is that we need to listen to these older theologians as they instruct us on the importance on church unity. The last word here is given to

---

83. Walker, *Theology and Theologians of Scotland, 1560-1750*, 118.
84. Boston, *Works*, 7:603.
85. Walker, *Theology and Theologians of Scotland, 1560-1750*, 103.
86. Walker, *Theology and Theologians of Scotland, 1560-1750*, 103.

George Gillespie. If we listened to him (or Rutherford or Durham) there would be a sharp decrease in the number of reformed denominations, and the restoration of a reputation for catholicity:

> There is but one Christ, yea, the head and the body makes one Christ, so that you cannot divide the body without dividing Christ … O brethren, we shall be one in heaven, let us pack up differences in this place of our pilgrimage, the best way we can. Nay, we will not despair of unity in this world … Hath not the Mediator (whom the Father hears always) prayed that all his may be one? Brethren, it is not impossible, pray for it, endeavour it, press hard toward the mark of accommodation. How much better is it that you be one with the other Reformed Churches, though somewhat straitened and bound up, than to be divided though at full liberty and elbow room?[87]

---

87. George Gillespie, "Wholesome Severity reconciled with Christian Liberty" in *The Shorter Writings of George Gillespie, Volume* 1 (ed. Chris Coldwell; Dallas: Naphtali Press, 2021), 383-4. There is an example of a similar appeal in Boston, *Works*, 7:612-3.

Contributors' Biographical Information

Joel R. Beeke, PhD, was until 2023 President of Puritan Reformed Theological Seminary. He is currently the seminary's Chancellor and Professor of Systematic Theology and Homiletics, a pastor of Heritage Reformed Congregation in Grand Rapids, Board Chairman of Reformation Heritage Books, and author of *Reformed Systematic Theology*, 4 volumes (Crossway) and another 120 books. He is married to Mary, and they are blessed with three children and eleven grandchildren.

Benedict Bird, PhD, is Adjunct Professor of New Testament Greek at Westminster Seminary (UK). His doctoral dissertation was on John Owen's understanding of the doctrine of the perseverance of the saints. He is a trustee of London Seminary. He and his wife Caroline are members of Cambridge Presbyterian Church and have two adult children.

Chad Van Dixhoorn, PhD, is ordained in the Orthodox Presbyterian Church and serves as Professor of Church History and Theology at Reformed Theological Seminary, Charlotte. His latest publication is entitled, *John Lightfoot's Journals of the Westminster Assembly* (Oxford University Press, 2023). He and his wife Emily have five children and a wonderful son-in-law.

Sinclair Ferguson, PhD, was minister of two churches in Scotland, and in the USA at First Presbyterian Church, Columbia, South Carolina. Sinclair continues to have teaching commitments in the USA as Chancellor's Professor of Systematic Theology at Reformed Theological Seminary and as a Teaching Fellow of Ligonier Ministries. As a member of Trinity Church, Aberdeen, he serves as the Preaching Associate. He and Dorothy have four children and thirteen grandchildren.

Jonathan Gibson, PhD, is an ordained minister in the International Presbyterian Church (UK), and presently serves as Associate Professor of Old Testament, Westminster Theological Seminary, Philadelphia. He is married to Jackie, and together they have four children.

W. Robert Godfrey, PhD, is ordained in the United Reformed Churches in N. America and is President Emeritus and Professor Emeritus of Church History at Westminster Seminary California. He succeeded R. C. Sproul as chairman of the board at Ligonier Ministries. He is author of numerous books including *John Calvin: Pilgrim and Pastor* (Crossway).

Mark Johnston, has pastored churches in Ireland, London, Philadelphia and Cardiff. He is currently serving in N. Ireland and is a trustee of Banner of Truth and on the board of Ligonier Ministries, UK. Mark is editor of the Banner of Truth Magazine and has authored numbers of books including *This World is Not My Home* and *The Church* (Banner of Truth).

John MacArthur, MDiv, has been pastor of Grace Community Church, California since 1969. He is Chancellor Emeritus of The Master's University and The Master's Seminary. He has written or edited over 150 books including *Ashamed of the Gospel: When the Church Becomes like the World* (Crossway) and *Worship: The Ultimate Priority* (Moody Publishers).

CONTRIBUTORS

Donald John MacLean, PhD, is an elder in the Evangelical Presbyterian Church of England and Wales. He succeeded Ian Hamilton as President of Westminster Seminary (UK) and is Professor of Historical Theology at Westminster Seminary (UK). He is a trustee of the Banner of Truth. He is married to Ruth and has two children.

Jonathan Master, PhD, is President of Greenville Presbyterian Theological Seminary. He is the author and editor of a number of books and serves on the Executive Council of the Gospel Reformation Network as well the Board of Directors of the Alliance of Confessing Evangelicals.

Douglas McCallum, is ordained in the Evangelical Presbyterian Church of England and Wales. He is minister of Cambridge Presbyterian Church and with his wife, Rebecca, has two young children.

Peter Naylor, DPhil, is minister of Immanuel Presbyterian Church in Cardiff and Professor of Old Testament at Westminster Seminary (UK). He is married to Pam and the Lord has blessed them with three children and five grandchildren.

Jon D. Payne, MTh; D.Min, is pastor of Christ Church Presbyterian in Charleston, South Carolina. He serves as Executive Coordinator of the Gospel Reformation Network, and trustee of Westminster Seminary (UK). Payne is the series co-editor of the Lectio Continua Expository Commentary on the New Testament (Reformation Heritage Books), and is the author and editor of many books including *John Owen On The Lord's Supper* (Banner of Truth). He and his wife Marla have been married for over twenty-five years and have two adult children.

Dan Peters, BTh, MTh, is Assistant Professor of Practical Theology and Chair of Homiletics at Westminster Seminary (UK). He is minister of Newcastle Reformed Evangelical Church.

David Pfeiffer, MA, PGCE, is Adjunct Professor of Old Testament Hebrew at Westminster Seminary (UK). He is minister of Whaddon Road Evangelical Presbyterian Church, Cheltenham and ordained in the Evangelical Presbyterian Church of England and Wales. With his wife, Bethan, he has four children.

Joseph A. Pipa, Jr., M. Div, PhD, DD, is President Emeritus & Professor of Systematic & Applied Theology at Greenville Presbyterian Theological Seminary. He is Pastor of Antioch Presbyterian Church (Presbyterian Church of America). He is author of numerous books including *The Westminster Confession of Faith Study Book: A Study Guide for Churches* (Christian Focus). He and his wife, 'Sissy', have two adult children and ten grandchildren.

Peter Sanlon, MAOxon, PhD, is minister of Tunbridge Wells Presbyterian Church and Assistant Professor of Systematic Theology at Westminster Seminary (UK). He is author of *Simply God: Recovering the Classical Doctrine of the Trinity* (IVP) and *Augustine's Theology of Preaching* (Fortress). He is married to Susanna and they have two boys.

Andy Young is minister of Oxford Presbyterian Church and ordained in the Evangelical Presbyterian Church of England and Wales. With his wife, Davinia, he has four daughters.

Also available from Christian Focus Publications ...

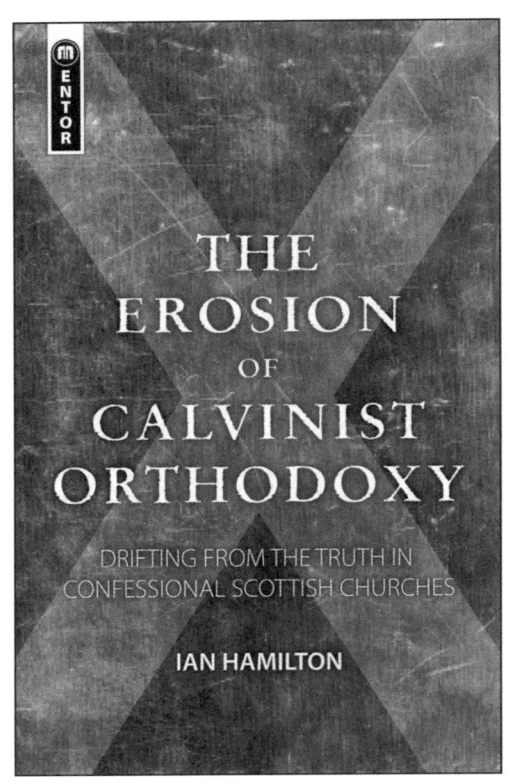

978-1-84550-514-1

The Erosion of Calvinist Orthodoxy
Drifting from the Truth in Confessional Scottish Churches

by Ian Hamilton

How do strong confessional churches that seem to be doing all the right things drift inexorably from the truth?. What is clear from Ian Hamilton's fascinating study is that it doesn't happen over night but it is a gradual erosion of theological and doctrinal standards.

Nineteenth century Scotland was seen as a Christian nation composed of church-going people. Among its churches, Presbyterianism was strongest, and within Presbyterianism there were several large denominations. The future looked bright and optimism marked many of the church leaders and congregations. Yet the sad fact is that most of them were blind to the presence of the warning signs that ultimately caused the decline and not the continued growth of the church in Scotland. This revealing read will give you an opportunity to learn from history.

The Erosion of Calvinist Orthodoxy is an invaluable historical case study of the fascinating and complex issues of Christian orthodoxy. In it Ian Hamilton carefully traces the arguments and positions which eventually fed into the theological liberalism of the nineteenth and twentieth centuries that has left the church moribund ... Ignorance of the past often leads to the repetition of its mistakes. Ian Hamilton here provides an important historical antidote for such theological amnesia.

SINCLAIR B. FERGUSON
Teaching Fellow, Ligonier Ministries

978-1-5271-0649-9

ALL THINGS ARE READY
Understanding the Gospel in its Fullness and Freeness

by Donald John MacLean

It is one of the glories of the gospel that it is universal in scope. There is nothing narrow or limited about the good news of salvation, but we often need to be reminded of this. When the world seems increasingly hostile the Church can be tempted to retreat in on itself. Donald John Maclean seeks to remind Christians of the fullness and freeness of the gospel, and to encourage them to share it with those who have not yet turned to Christ.

> The gospel of Jesus Christ is the greatest news the world has ever known. As Christians, we need to tell everyone about it. In this well-written book, Donald John Maclean expertly and concisely takes readers through the biblical, theological, and practical reasons why the gospel invitation is for all people.
> JOHN W. TWEEDDALE
> Vice President of Academics, Reformation Bible College
> Sanford, Florida

Christian Focus Publications

Our mission statement

Staying Faithful

In dependence upon God we seek to impact the world through literature faithful to His infallible Word, the Bible. Our aim is to ensure that the Lord Jesus Christ is presented as the only hope to obtain forgiveness of sin, live a useful life and look forward to heaven with Him.

Our Books are published in four imprints:

CHRISTIAN FOCUS

Popular works including biographies, commentaries, basic doctrine and Christian living.

MENTOR

Books written at a level suitable for Bible College and seminary students, pastors, and other serious readers. The imprint includes commentaries, doctrinal studies, examination of current issues and church history.

CHRISTIAN HERITAGE

Books representing some of the best material from the rich heritage of the church.

CF4KIDS

Children's books for quality Bible teaching and for all age groups: Sunday school curriculum, puzzle and activity books; personal and family devotional titles, biographies and inspirational stories – because you are never too young to know Jesus!

Christian Focus Publications Ltd,
Geanies House, Fearn, Ross-shire,
IV20 1TW, Scotland, United Kingdom.
www.christianfocus.com